FM 3-04.300

I0167869

Airfield and Flight Operations Procedures

AUGUST 2008

Headquarters, Department of the Army

Change 1

Airfield and Flight Operations Procedures

1. Change FM 3-04.300, 12 August 2008, as follows:

Remove old pages:	Insert new pages:
iii and iv	iii and iv
6-7 and 6-8	6-7 and 6-8
7-11 and 7-12	7-11 and 7-12
8-13 and 8-14	8-13 and 8-14

2. A star $\left(^{*}\right)$ marks new, changed, or location of deleted material.

3. File this transmittal sheet in front of the publication.

DISTRIBUTION RESTRICTION: Approved for public release; distribution is unlimited.

By Order of the Secretary of the Army:

GEORGE W. CASEY, JR.
General, United States Army
Chief of Staff

Official:

JOYCE E. MORROW
Administrative Assistant to the
Secretary of the Army
1009002

DISTRIBUTION: *Active Army, Army National Guard, and U.S. Army Reserve*: To be distributed per the initial distribution number (IDN) 110724, requirements for FM 3-04.300.

This page intentionally left blank.

Field Manual
No. 3-04.300

Headquarters
Department of the Army
Washington, D.C., 12 August 2008

Airfield and Flight Operations Procedures

Contents

---

*This publication supersedes FM 3-04.300, 26 April 2004.

PART TWO   AVIATION UNIT OPERATIONS

PART THREE AIRFIELD OPERATIONS

Figures

Tables

Preface

Field manual (FM) 3-04.300 is designed to serve as a doctrinal guide focusing on the primary aspects of airfield procedures in full spectrum operations. While it contains guidelines for aviation unit commanders and aviators, the manual is intended primarily for use by airfield operations battalions (AOBs) and installation flight operations personnel. It is applicable to division, corps, Theater Aviation Command (TAC), Theater and Area Sustainment Commands, and the Army aviation community, including members of allied, coalition, and civil support forces. This publication applies to the Active Army, the Army National Guard (ARNG)/Army National Guard of the United States (ARNGUS), and the United States Army Reserve (USAR) unless otherwise stated.

This manual outlines the organization and services of the theater airfield operations groups (TAOGs), AOBs, aviation unit plans and operations staff, and installation airfield management operations. It explains personnel qualifications, duties, and responsibilities; it provides information on airfield design and security and support requirements when planning and operating an airfield within a theater of operations (TO) or during homeland security operations. Installation airfield management structure, responsibilities, services, safety, and National Airspace System (NAS) requirements are presented in part III of this manual. Appendix A details the numerous checklists necessary for adequate airfield assessment and the duties required for airfield opening. Appendix B discusses the characteristics of military aircraft. Appendix C addresses Army and Air Force airfield planning. Appendix D discusses letters and facility memorandums. Appendix E discusses emergency plans and procedures.

The proponent for this publication is the United States Army Training and Doctrine Command (TRADOC). Send comments and recommendations on Department of the Army (DA) Form 2028 (Recommended Changes to publications and Blank Forms) to Commander, U.S. Army Aviation Center of Excellence, ATTN: ATZQ-TDD-D, Fort Rucker, Alabama 36362-5263 or complete the Directorate of Training and Doctrine (DOTD) electronic change request form at https://www.us.army.mil/suite/doc/7288766. Comments may be e-mailed to the DOTD at av.doctrine@us.army.mil. Other doctrinal information can be found on the Internet at the Aviation Doctrine Branch homepage (https://www.us.army.mil/suite/page/394729), Army Knowledge Online (AKO) or by calling defense switched network (DSN) 558-3551 or (334) 255-3551.

The publication has been reviewed for operations security considerations.

This page intentionally left blank.

PART ONE

Airfield Considerations for Full Spectrum Operations

Chapter 1

Fundamentals

Successful employment of Army aviation is contingent upon establishing and maintaining airfields that enable the positioning of aviation assets within the range of ground forces. This task becomes more complicated when airfields are host to a variety of allied military, nongovernmental organizations (NGOs), and commercial air activities. Army aviation transformation provides an airfield management structure for theater Army airfields through the deployment of theater airfield operations groups (TAOGs) and airfield operations battalions (AOBs). These organizations are designed to efficiently support Army and joint, interagency, intergovernmental, and multinational aviation operations.

SECTION I – OPERATIONAL ENVIRONMENT

1-1. The operational environment is described as a composite of conditions, circumstances, and influences that affect the employment of forces and decisions of commanders. Each of these areas impacts how Army forces combine, sequence, and conduct military operations.

Contents

ARMY AVIATION OPERATIONS

1-2. Army aviation combines reconnaissance, mobility, and firepower to provide battlefield leverage as an air maneuver and support force fully integrated into the combined arms team. Like ground combat systems, Army aviation requires airfields to conduct operations. How these airfields are managed enhances the speed, safety, sustainability, and survivability of aircraft and aircrews and ensures successful mission completion. Efficient management and thoughtful airfield design contributes to the timely response of Army aviation operations. Army aviation forward operating bases (FOBs) include, but are not limited to—

- Highway landing strips.
- Improved and unimproved austere airfields.
- Captured enemy airfields.
- Host and adjacent nation airfields.
- Airfields designated for homeland security operations.

1-3.   Expansion of the battlefield at each echelon may be dependent on forward operating airfields. These airfields enable the commander to seize the initiative and influence operations at critical points within the area of operations (AO). Aviation, augmented by armed and unarmed unmanned aircraft systems (UAS), expands the ground commander's battle area in both space and time. A forward airfield enhances—

- The range at which the commander can take advantage of intelligence collection and joint/coalition fires (direct and indirect) against either a conventional or an asymmetric threat.
- Economy of force and resources ensuring that Army aviation can range anywhere within the AO.
- Aviation's ability to provide close combat attack for engaged ground elements, conduct shaping operations, support sustainment, and provide aerial command and control (C2) platforms for supported tactical and operational commanders.
- The mobility, long-range fires, and sophisticated sensors of attack reconnaissance aircraft permitting enemy detection and engagement beyond the range of ground direct fire systems.
- Assault aviation's capability to transform light Soldiers into a mobile, flexible force.
- Conventional and asymmetric operations.
- Aviation maneuver (maneuver support and sustainment missions).

1-4.   Ground forces benefit from forward airfields through—

- Increased speed to support operations.
- Overwatch of moving forces.
- Insertion of light or dismounted forces to seize chokepoints and secure danger areas prior to heavy force linkup.
- Heavy helicopter movement of critical equipment and supplies forward.
- Information systems aircraft providing commanders mobility and communications links.

1-5.   Well-established and maintained airfields contribute to aviation tactical sustainment operations to include air movement and aerial sustainment in support of special operations, light, airborne, air assault, and heavy forces. It also supports high priority resupply and air movement throughout the theater of operations (TO).

1-6.   Airfield service elements must maintain the capability of continuous 24/7 operations with a capability to launch and recover aircraft in instrument flight rules (IFR) weather conditions. This requires—

- Battle rhythm management.
- Operational, sustainable, and certified navigational aids (NAVAIDs).
- Adequate airfield lighting.
- Advanced digitized communications systems providing increased situational awareness.

1-7.   Airfield planning principles and services are based on the types of aircraft utilizing the airfield and the assigned tasks associated with the airfield's mission. Depending on mission, enemy, terrain and weather, troops and support available, time available and civil considerations (METT-TC).

JOINT, INTERAGENCY, INTERGOVERNMENTAL, AND MULTINATIONAL AIRFIELD OPERATIONS

1-8.   AOBs with augmentation of weather support, firefighting capability, airfield lighting, cargo handling, and NAVAIDs can support the joint operations of inter and intra theater transport and movement. Such augmentation permits the number of airfields capable of these operations within lodgment areas, theater staging bases, and aerial ports of debarkation (APODs) to be increased.

1-9.   AOB support to maritime operations includes airfield operations in close proximity to seaports of debarkation (SPODs). These airfields increase the responsiveness and versatility of naval operations such as resupply and troop and equipment movement.

1-10. AOB support of special operations forces and interagency elements include all types of aviation missions launched and recovered from Army airfields. The AOB is challenged by compatible communications, synchronization and dissemination of airspace, and airfield procedures.

1-11. Multinational operations parallel joint and interagency support. Language and cultural challenges (the only exception) must be resolved by the AOB to effectively support these types of operations.

AIRLAND RESPONSIBILITIES

1-12. The Army and Air Force hold joint responsibility for selection of landing areas, with the objective of deploying and sustaining the force. They coordinate the landing zone (LZ) selection with the Air Force making the final decision. This decision is based on information gathered from a landing area study that highlights not only large, modern facilities, but also areas suitable only for takeoffs and landings and austere airfields similar to the one used by a C-17. Each identified site is classified based on suitability in terms of type and number of aircraft, and available and/or required support facilities. Any physical improvements necessary are the responsibility of the ranking Army engineer. Desirable characteristics of LZs are ease of identification from the air; a straight, unobstructed, secure approach for aircraft; and close proximity to ground objectives/units. LZs to be developed into theater airfields with more sophisticated facilities should possess the following additional characteristics:

- An area of sufficient size and trafficability to accommodate the number and type of aircraft to be landed.
- Parking and dispersal areas to accommodate the planned capacity of the facility.
- A road net to handle ground vehicular traffic.
- Minimum construction and maintenance requirements.
- Areas and facilities for air terminal operations.
- Facilities for holding patients awaiting evacuation.
- Sufficient aerial port capacity to handle incoming personnel and supplies.
- Facilities to support crash and rescue vehicles and equipment.

SECTION II – ORGANIZATIONAL DESIGN

1-13. TAOGs and AOBs were designed and implemented during Army transformation. Lessons learned identified the need for an airfield management capability to execute theater-level airfield missions. TAOGs provide the joint force commander (JFC) with the expertise to execute the theater airfield mission and coordinate all support requirements not organic to the AOB. These requirements include weather support, firefighting capabilities, airfield lighting, cargo handling, engineer and NAVAID support. The TAOG may be deployed in total or task organized by teams to provide the JFC with the coordination and C2 capability to operate a single airfield or conduct operations in multiple locations within the TO.

THEATER AIRFIELD OPERATIONS GROUP

1-14. The TAOG executes theater airfield operations and synchronizes air traffic in a joint environment. It establishes theater airfields in support of reception, staging, onward movement, and integration requirements, SPOD, and APOD operations. The TAOG coordinates and integrates terminal airspace use requirements with the Airspace Command and Control (AC2) element of controlling headquarters. The TAOG coordinates and schedules flight checks, reviews and processes terminal instrument procedures (TERPs), and provides quality assurance of the controller, air traffic control (ATC) maintenance, and flight operations training and certification programs. It also supports the Army Service Component Command regarding Title 10 air traffic services (ATS) issues, liaison responsibilities with host nation airspace authority, and other U.S. and combined services and agencies. The TAOG (figures 1-1, page 1-4) is organic to the theater aviation command. The TAOG consists of a headquarters and headquarters company and five AOBs.

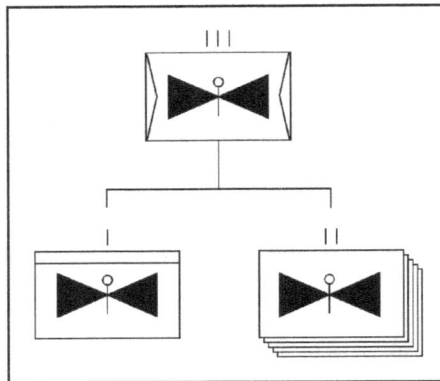

Figure 1-1. Theater airfield operations group organization

AIRFIELD OPERATIONS BATTALION

1-15. The AOB (figure 1-2) provides airfield management including airfield operations, flight dispatch services, and ATC. The AOB may provide battle command to other airfield support assets organized under its headquarters. Situational awareness (SA) on the digital battlefield requires the use of all systems utilized by AOBs to transmit and disseminate friendly, known, and suspected threat locations. This provides a common operating picture (COP) that enhances situational understanding (SU) for its flight operations section. Data from collection platforms, coupled with automated reports transmitted via digital communications, expands battlefield SU.

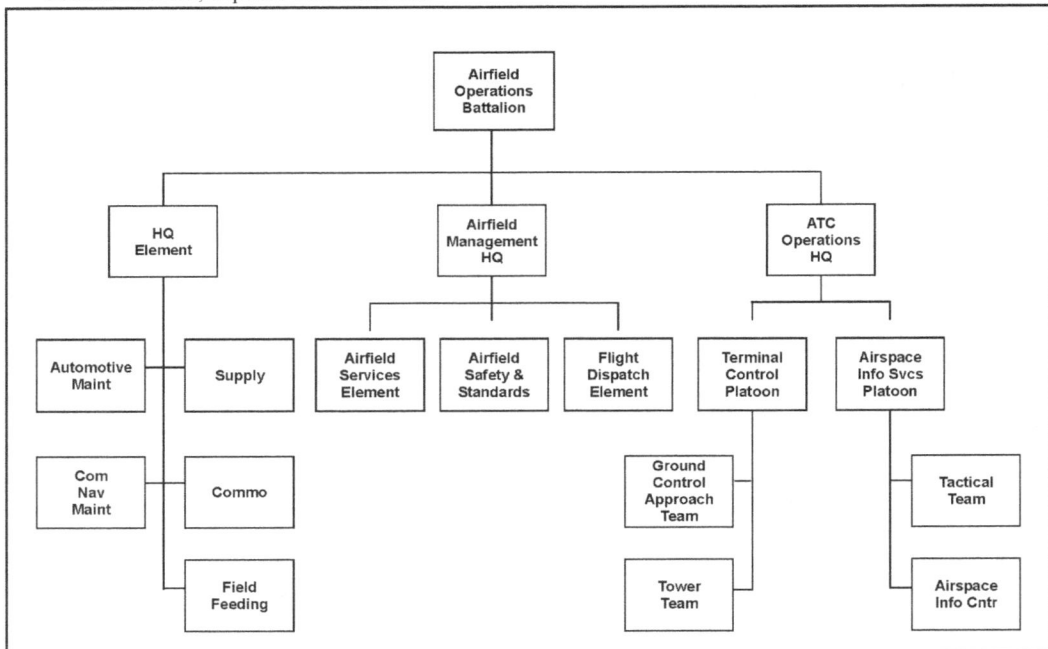

Figure 1-2. Airfield operations battalion organization

AIRFIELD HEADQUARTERS/ELEMENTS/SECTIONS

Airfield Management Headquarters

1-16. The airfield management headquarters is made up of a military occupational specialty (MOS) 15B ATC officer and a 15P50 ATC operations sergeant. This headquarters is responsible for—

- Development of local airfield standard operating procedures (SOPs) that govern areas such as:
    - Flight plan filing.
    - Use of airfield services.
    - Joint use of airspace.
    - Airfield facility use.
    - Night operation agreements.
    - Noise abatement.
    - Nap-of-the-earth (NOE) training area rules and other special interest areas.
    - Implementation of an airfield advisory council.
    - Expansion and acquisition efforts for the airfield.
    - Synchronization of aviation actions for the senior aviation commander.
- Training and performance of the flight operations branch and the airfield services/petroleum, oil, and lubricants (POL) services branch.
- Development and update of the local hazard map.
- Development of the preaccident plan.
- Development of operations letters (OLs) and letters of agreement (LOAs).
- Flight information publications (FLIPs) availability and currency.
- Coordinates for and acquires additional airfield services such as refuel, weather, engineer support, and firefighting.
- Interfaces with the AC2 system and the combined air operations center's crash rescue center.

Airfield Services Element

1-17. The airfield services element consists of a 15P20 aviation operations sergeant and a 15P10 aviation operations specialist. The airfield services element controls aircraft manifests and provides limited cargo transportation control. It also reports airfield status and coordinates notice to airman (NOTAM) advisories. The element maintains appropriate flight operation publications and disseminates appropriate airspace coordinating measures (ACMs) to aircrews. The airfield services element coordinates various flight activities in and around the airfield. Flight operations personnel coordinate directly with the airfield headquarters element, ATC, other airfield services organizations, and force protection elements. The airfield services element—

- Provides airspace and local airfield procedures briefings including air tasking order (ATO), airspace control order (ACO), and special instructions (SPINS) concerning local airspace to transient aviators and aviation units operating at the airfield.
- Develops SOPs for notification and dissemination of aircraft emergencies, severe weather warnings, and operations security (OPSEC) violations, and for the airfield services element.
- Initiates and maintains Department of the Army (DA) Form 1594 (Daily Staff Journal).

Airfield Safety/Standards Element

1-18. The airfield safety/standards element consists of a 153AB aviation safety officer (SO), 150A air traffic and airspace management officer, and a 15Q40 ATC senior sergeant. It develops and implements a comprehensive accident prevention program to minimize the risk of aviation operations. This element develops a preaccident plan and works collaboratively with airfield services elements and the aviation community. Airfield safety and standardization personnel coordinate aircraft accident investigations, review operational hazard reports, and publish flight procedures in theater-specific aviation procedure guides (APGs). Additional responsibilities include—

- Serving as a member of the airfield advisory council.
- Coordinating airspace usage agreements for training and airfield operations.
- Conducting initial and followup airfield safety inspections.
- Developing local airfield flight procedures and rules.
- Developing and ensuring currency of a local hazards map.
- Establishing the airfield crash system; coordinating and securing any additional assets needed.
- Reviewing and processing the TERPs data package for completeness and accuracy; requests flight inspections for NAVAIDs.

Flight Dispatch Element

1-19. The flight dispatch element consists of two aviation operation sergeants. The flight dispatch element processes flight plans through the combat airspace system or host nation system; it develops and maintains local checklists, logs, and other required documentation to support functional area responsibilities. The element also provides flight planning services to include current publications, maps and charts, NOTAM display, and weight and balance forms for Class 2 aircraft. Flight dispatch also—

- Develops local instructions for—
    - Inbound and outbound aircraft.
    - Distinguished visitors.
    - Aircraft requiring special handling (such as air evacuation and hazardous cargo).
    - Airfield restrictions (prior permission required [PPR]).
    - Crash alarm system.
    - FLIPs.
    - In-flight advisories.
    - Foreign object damage (FOD) checks of the airfield at least once per shift.
- Provides advisory service in the event of ATC facility closure.
- Develops a training program for newly assigned personnel.
- Ensures airfield advisory procedures are established when required.
- Ensures ground personnel operating near or on taxiways or runways are thoroughly briefed on two-way radio communication procedures and are familiar with the ATC light gun signals contained in the aeronautical information manual and the Federal Aviation Administration Handbook (FAAH) 7110.65.
- Establishes and maintains current flight information developed within the theater.

Air Traffic Control Operations Element

1-20. The ATC operations element is made up of a headquarters, a terminal platoon with a headquarters element, a tower team and ground controlled approach (GCA) team, and an airspace information services platoon. The airspace information services platoon consists of a headquarters, an airspace information center (AIC), and a tactical aviation control team (TACT). The AOB establishes an AIC that interfaces with airfield operations ensuring airspace information management and dissemination within its area of responsibility. The AIC receives airspace information changes and updates through communication links to the elements comprising the Army Air Ground System (AAGS) and the Theater Air Ground System (TAGS).

1-21. The AIC has responsibility for disseminating this information to aviation units operating within the airfield terminal area and throughout the theater. The TACT provides the AOB with the capability of terminal tower operations at a satellite heliport or airfield as required by the operational situation. The coordination of ATC procedures and establishment of air traffic services is the responsibility of the terminal and airspace information services platoons. These elements provide detailed planning for terminal and en route air traffic services in and out of the area of responsibility by developing aviation flight procedures and incorporating them into the theater airspace plan. ATC elements coordinate directly with the airfield management command group, other airfield services organizations, and force protection elements. The ATC operations element is responsible for—

- Assisting in the development of local airfield procedures.
- Developing a crash rescue plan with all associated procedures.
- Assisting in development and publication of the aviation procedures guide.
- Developing ATC facility training manuals and facility training programs .
- Initiating the TERPs data collection process if necessary or completing any portion of it to include an emergency recovery procedure in conjunction with the combat aviation brigade (CAB) standards officer.
- Securing and disseminating the ATO/ACO and associated SPINS.
- Providing terminal ATC and en route flight following.
- Establishing and maintaining current flight information developed within the theater.

AIRFIELD OPERATIONS BATTALION REQUIRED COMMUNICATIONS

1-22. The AOB requires a robust communication capability to execute its airfield management mission and send and receive critical information regarding current and future operations. These requirements (listed by section) are—

- Flight dispatch element.
    - Dedicated, secure, jam resistant very high frequency (VHF)-Frequency Modulation (FM), VHF-amplitude modulation (AM), and ultra high frequency (UHF)-AM radios.
    - Continuous monitoring VHF-AM and UHF-AM emergency (guard frequencies with guard transmit presets).
    - Secure jam resistant voice and data communications in the HF/single side band with automatic link establishment.
    - UHF-FM satellite communications-demand assigned multiple access for beyond line of sight communication.
    - Direct-voice landline communications to the control tower, airspace information center, Army and joint airspace control authorities, weather station, refueling point, and resident aviation units.
    - Mobile communication console integrating all radio and telephones landline communications providing centralized use.
    - Voice primary crash alarm system with circuit activation capability for five key agencies.
    - Handheld, short-range radio communications in the VHF-AM/FM frequency spectrum.
    - Aviation Mission Planning System (AMPS).
    - Telecommunications equipment to process flight data, flight movement messages.
    - Field telephones and switchboard for mission and routine use.
- Airfield services element.
    - Handheld, short-range radio communications in the VHF-AM/FM frequency spectrum.
    - Direct voice landline communications to the control tower, airspace information center, Army and joint airspace control authorities, weather station, refueling point, and resident aviation units.
    - Field telephones and switchboard for mission and routine use.

- Airfield safety/standards element.
  - Handheld, short-range radio communications in the VHF-AM/FM frequency spectrum.
  - Field telephones and switchboard for mission and routine use.

Communications Section

1-23. The communications section is made up of a 25U20 forward signal support sergeant and a 25U10 signal support systems specialist. The communications section installs, employs, maintains, troubleshoots, and assists users with battlefield signal support systems and terminal devices to include radio, wire, and battlefield automated systems. This section—

- Integrates signal systems and networks.
- Disseminates information service policies.
- Prepares maintenance and supply requests for signal support.

Communication/Navigational Aid Maintenance Section

1-24. The communication/navigational aid (COM/NAV) maintenance section consists of a 94D30 ATC systems maintenance supervisor, an E5 94D20 ATC equipment repairer, two 94D10 ATC equipment repairers, and a 94D ATC equipment repairer. This section is organic to the AOB and maintains equipment maintenance records, authorized spare parts, supply stock, tool lists, and technical manuals and instructional material for repair of ATC communication/navigation systems and equipment. The COM/NAV maintenance section also provides—

- Field-level maintenance to ATC systems.
- Component replacement and limited component repair.
- Installation and troubleshooting of ATC equipment, landing systems, and identification friend or foe/selective identification feature systems.
- Comparison checks on repaired equipment per test standards.
- Intermediate direct support maintenance and installation of ATC communications, NAVAIDs, and landing systems.
- Ground certification of NAVAIDs prior to flight checks.

Chapter 2

Combined Arms Operations

Combined arms operations in support of theater airfields unites military police forces, engineer support, fire support, air defense, and signal support to prevent or mitigate hostile actions against Army personnel, resources, facilities, and critical information. Combined arms operations enable AOBs to operate theater airfields while degrading opportunities for the enemy to disrupt the critical sustainment mission of theater airfields.

SECTION I – OVERVIEW

FORCE PROTECTION

2-1. Airfield physical security is integral to the protection of forces and equipment. Physical-security measures deter, detect, and defend against threats from terrorists, criminals, and unconventional forces. These measures include—

- Fencing and perimeter standoff space.
- Lighting and sensors.
- Vehicle barriers.
- Blast protection.
- Intrusion-detection systems and electronic surveillance.

<table>
<tr><td colspan="2" align="center">Contents</td></tr>
<tr><td>Section I – Overview</td><td>2-1</td></tr>
<tr><td>Section II – Military Police Operations</td><td>2-3</td></tr>
<tr><td>Section III – Defensive Operations</td><td>2-4</td></tr>
<tr><td>Section IV – Airfield Support</td><td>2-5</td></tr>
<tr><td>Section V – Movement Control</td><td>2-7</td></tr>
</table>

2-2. Procedural measures are designed to protect U.S. personnel and equipment regardless of mission or geographical location. Procedural measures include—

- Security checks.
- Training and awareness.
- Property accountability/inventory requirements.
- Physical security inspections of mission-essential or vulnerable areas (MEVAs).
- Physical security surveys of installations.

AIRFIELD DEFENSE

2-3. Base defense is the cornerstone of rear-area security. MPs are the AOB/base commander's link for detection, early warning, and employment against enemy attacks. Intelligence information gathered is dispersed throughout the sustainment area to apprise commanders of enemy activities occurring near bases. When the threat exceeds the capability of the base/airfield's quick reaction force (QRF) and assigned personnel, the AOB/base commander requests military police assistance through the base cluster operations cell (BCOC), area support group (ASG), or theater sustainment command (TSC) rear operations center (ROC). Airfield defense requires special military police coordination with the base defense operations cell (BDOC). MPs treat airfields like any other base or base cluster. The airfield may house the base-cluster commander, or it may be a cluster by itself. MPs are responsible for the airfield's external defense. Its internal defense is primarily the responsibility of the BDOC QRF and units assigned to the airfield. The quick reaction force provides in-depth defense for weapons, weapons systems, command centers, personnel, and other priority resources established by the BDOC commander.

BASE DEFENSE PLAN

2-4.   AOB commanders provide assistance as directed by the base commander in developing and implementing comprehensive defense plans to protect their airfields. The defense plan includes measures to detect, minimize, or defeat Level I and Level II threats. To maximize mutual support and prevent fratricide, the AOB, base, and base cluster commanders coordinate defense plans with adjacent base and base clusters and joint, multinational, and host nation (HN) forces. The TSC ROC ensures that all plans conform to the overall TSC and Army forces security plans. The AOB commander may never serve as a base cluster or base commander. The AOB commander responsibilities for base security and defense would mirror those of individual unit commanders. These responsibilities include—

- Developing and mentoring unit training as it relates to the base defense plan.
- Participating in base defense planning.
- Providing, staffing, and operating base defense facilities per base defense plans.
- Conducting individual and unit training to ensure force readiness in defense of the base.
- Providing appropriate facilities and essential personnel for the BDOC and base commander.
- Providing liaison personnel to advise the base commander on matters unique to the airfield.
- Providing communications systems, including common-user communications, within the command.

BASE AND BASE CLUSTERS

2-5.   Bases and base clusters form the basic building block for planning, coordinating, and executing base defense operations. A base may be a single-service or a joint-service base. A single service base is occupied by one service only. A joint-service base may consist of one service with a primary interest or two or more services having equal interests. ASGs and other subordinate support headquarters (such as an AOB) are responsible for coordinating base and base cluster defense in the TSC AO. This defense protects elements from Level I and II threats in their assigned areas. AOB commanders ensure their airfields train and prepare for their roles in base and base cluster defense. Cooperation and coordination between the support headquarters and tenants are critical.

2-6.   Units use observation posts, listening posts, or unattended sensors on likely avenues of approach to collect intelligence on threat activity. In areas where the populace is friendly, local law enforcement or government agencies can provide information on threats in the area.

2-7.   Within the base cluster, the three types of commanders are—

- The base cluster commander.
- The base commander.
- The individual unit commander.

2-8.   The TSC G-3, as the overall TSC terrain manager, and the TSC ROC, organize units and appoint base cluster commanders from units located in the cluster. The base cluster commander, usually the senior commander in the base cluster, forms a BCOC from his staff and available base assets. The BDOC assists with planning, directing, coordinating, integrating, and controlling base defense efforts. The base cluster commander also appoints base commanders, who then form their own BDOCs.

2-9.   The base cluster commander is responsible for securing his base, coordinating the defense of bases within his base cluster, and integrating base defense plans into a base cluster defense plan. His specific responsibilities include—

- Establishing a BCOC from his staff and available base or base cluster assets controlling base cluster defense activities. BCOCs implement an integrated warning plan within their cluster and with adjacent bases or base clusters.

- Providing appropriate facilities, housing, and services for necessary liaison personnel from within the cluster.

2-10. The base commander is responsible for base security and defense. All forces assigned for base defense purposes are operational control (OPCON) to the base commander. Base defense responsibilities include—

- Establishing a BDOC from available base assets to serve as the base's focal point for security and defense.
- Establishing an alternate BDOC from base resources or, if base assets are not available, designating a headquarters element from units dedicated to the base for its local defense.
- Planning for transient units by ensuring that base defense plans include provisions for augmenting regularly assigned base defense forces with units present during periods of threat.

SECTION II – MILITARY POLICE OPERATIONS

2-11. The military police corps supports shaping and sustainment operations. These units are able to provide the commander with an array of support operations across the entire spectrum of military operations.

2-12. Their assets are limited; specific functions are determined by—

- The needs of the supported commander.
- The intensity of the conflict.
- The availability of police resources.

2-13. The AOB commander, through the area support command's provost marshal (PM), sets priorities for military police operations in support of airfields. The PM continuously evaluates the tradeoff between the support requested by the AOB commander and the support that can be provided. The AOB commander, in conjunction with the airfield management headquarters, develops a tactical plan that sets priorities for the PM. This assists the PM in the allocation and employment of these assets for—

- Police maneuvers.
- Combat support.
- Sustainment operations.

2-14. They also support the AOB commander's security of forces and means programs by—

- Controlling or monitoring installation, airfield, or base-cluster access or entrance points.
- Monitoring intrusion-detection systems and providing a response force.
- Conducting physical-security inspections.
- Conducting perimeter security or site surveillance.
- Recommending placement of walls, berms, gates, or barriers around designated MEVAs, high-value areas, or perimeters.
- Supporting the commander's risk-analysis effort.
- Conducting roving patrols, checkpoints, and roadblocks.
- Performing other physical-security measures as required by the commander.

2-15. Military police are the airfield and base-cluster commander's response force against enemy attacks. They gather enemy information and provide it to commanders while performing missions throughout the AO. They also provide a mobile response force by consolidating into platoons and responding as quickly as possible to conduct combat operations. Military police forces performing as a response force are capable of conducting the following operations:

- Movement to contact.
- Hasty ambush and/or attack.
- Delay.
- Call for fire.

- Repel attack against critical sites.
- Defense of critical sites.
- Battle handover to the tactical combat force.

2-16. To conduct these missions, military police consolidate into squads or platoons to delay, defeat, or defend against the threat.

SECTION III – DEFENSIVE OPERATIONS

DEFENSE METHODS

2-17. Early engagement and defense in depth are methods used for airfield air defense. Early engagement is achieved by positioning weapons to engage the threat before ordnance release; ideally, weapons should engage and destroy the enemy before it can fire on the airfield or defended asset. Defense in depth is the method most associated with base defense zones. This method is achieved by positioning weapons so the air threat will come under an increasing volume of fire as it approaches the airfield or protected asset. Defense in depth lowers the probability that threat aircraft will reach the defended asset.

RESPONSE FORCE OPERATIONS

2-18. The airfield QRF should be trained and equipped to detect, delay, and deny Level I threats. If a Level II or III threat is present, the QRF along with assigned airfield units are tasked with delaying actions; however, other support must be employed to defeat these threats.

2-19. Attack helicopters and slower fixed-wing (FW) close air support (CAS) should be used in airfield defense due to their ability to observe the target thus avoiding nearby friendly elements. Attack helicopters may be the most responsive and efficient means of providing fires to an airfield.

AIR AND MISSILE DEFENSE IN FORCE PROTECTION

2-20. Air and missile defense operations are important active force protection measures. These measures are addressed in the AOB's base defense plan and coordinated with the ASG ensuring offensive counterair and theater missile defense (TMD) operations are sufficient to defeat or suppress threat capabilities. Defensive counterair and TMD operations destroy enemy aircraft and missiles threatening airfields.

2-21. The air defense artillery (ADA) commander considers METT-TC, intelligence preparation of the battlefield (IPB), and the supported commander's intent and concept of operations to develop air and missile defense priorities. Priorities are based on the factors of criticality, vulnerability, recuperability, and the threat. The ADA commander recommends these priorities to the TSC ROC for approval.

COUNTERFIRE OPERATIONS

2-22. The principles of fires planning and coordination for airfields do not differ significantly from those in the forward areas and apply to both the offense and defense. There is, however, a difference in the facilities available. Counterfire radar systems such as the counter-rocket, artillery, and mortar may be employed to support critical assets such as airfields. These systems have an automated counterfire delivery capability. The use of these systems in support of an AOB will require an LOA outlining procedures for use in defense of the airfield and friendly aircraft.

2-23. With few exceptions, indirect fire assets should not be employed against a Level I threat or against those Level II threat forces that can be defeated by airfield, base cluster units, and military police reaction forces. Level III threats have the size and combat power that could require the use of indirect fire assets.

2-24. The applicable fire support coordination measures (FSCMs) for airfields will be restrictive measures (for example, no fire areas, restrictive fire areas, and restrictive fire lines). The airfield base defense operations cell should establish them as part of the overall airfield defense plan. The procedures for establishing FSCMs in the sustainment area must become part of the overall planning process. Forces employed to deal with a Level III force are given an AO. The establishment of a boundary within the rear and the possible addition of a task force fire support officer (FSO) require close coordination with the airfield BDOC. These measures should be reviewed routinely by higher headquarters; posted on operations maps; entered into the Advanced Field Artillery Tactical Data System; and given to any supporting component forces, reaction forces, and BDOCs.

2-25. The supporting field artillery must be positioned to support airfields. Since the AOB does not have a maneuver unit with an FSO normally assigned to it, the headquarters and headquarters battery commander (from the direct support [DS] battalion) often serves as an ad hoc FSO. He will coordinate fires positioning with the airfield BDOC to avoid fratricide and destruction of critical assets during counterfire operations. This action also facilitates the ability of the airfield BDOC to coordinate terrain management, movement control, and sustainment.

SECTION IV – AIRFIELD SUPPORT

ENGINEER SUPPORT

2-26. Engineers plan, design, construct, and repair airfields and heliports in the TO. To ensure these facilities meet proposed requirements, the responsible area support group or theater support command engineer officer will coordinate closely with the AOB and aviation commanders. The airfield commander will set work priorities for the engineer support. Engineers depend on the appropriate commanders for information on the weight and traffic frequency of using aircraft, facility life support, protection requirements, and the geographic boundaries of the airfield. The time available for repair and construction is dictated by the operation plan. Planning, reconnaissance, and site investigations are often limited by lack of time or the tactical situation. If ground reconnaissance and on-site investigations are not possible, the engineer should obtain photographs of the area.

2-27. Extensive field surveys coordinated through the TSC provide aeronautical and other information in support of contingency airfields, providing the basic required information for the formulation of terminal instrument procedures and the safe operation of aircraft using the airfield. These surveys provide source information on—

- Position.
- Azimuth.
- Elevation.
- Runways and stopways.
- NAVAIDs.
- Federal Aviation Regulation (FAR), Part 77 obstructions.
- Aircraft movement and apron areas.
- Prominent airport buildings.
- Selected roads and other traverse ways.
- Cultural and natural features of landmark value.
- Miscellaneous and special request items.

2-28. Positioning and orientation information for NAVAIDs is required to certify airfield instrument-landing approaches. Airfield obstruction charts establish geodetic control in the airport vicinity, consisting of permanent survey marks accurately connected to the National Spatial Reference System (NSRS). The NSRS connection ensures accuracy between surveyed points on the airfield and other surveyed points in the theater airspace, including navigation satellites.

2-29. The support provided to airfields by engineers takes many forms, including—

- Commercial power requirements.
- Repair of existing facilities.

- Construction of new facilities.
- Life support requirements.

2-30. Construction of defensive measures includes—
- Berms for—
    - Aircraft.
    - Power generation units
    - Fuel supplies.
- Bunkers for—
    - Ammunition.
    - Fighting positions.
    - Protection of the force.

2-31. Engineers provide the following troop construction support to the ground and air commanders:
- Development of engineering designs, standard plans, and materiel to meet requirements.
- Reconnaissance, survey, design, construction, repair and improvement of airfields, roads, utilities, and structures.
- Rehabilitation of air bases and facilities beyond the immediate emergency recovery requirements of the air commander.
- Supply of materials and equipment to perform engineering missions.
- Construction of temporary standard air base facilities.
- Repair management of war damage and base development, including supervision of engineer personnel.

2-32. The amount of work in the theater and the limited engineer resources available make it imperative that existing host nation or captured enemy facilities be used whenever possible. The use of captured enemy airfields requires extensive planning and review of possible sites to ensure needed requirements are met.

2-33. Engineer brigades and groups usually conduct site reconnaissance, make location recommendations, and complete detailed design work. Engineer battalions usually construct the airfield and adapt the design to local conditions.

2-34. Engineer construction units, under the appropriate Army command, are responsible for construction on a general and direct support basis. The execution of large construction projects is usually based on the general support of missions as defined by project directives. Units assigned in general support of a specific Army element may be assigned in direct support of that element for restoration of an airfield.

SIGNAL SUPPORT

2-35. The communication section of the AOB will request signal support through their ASG to the TSC. This section should establish a liaison capability with theater signal units to ensure their requirements are understood and met. See FM 3-04.120 for more information on AOB communications means and methods.

2-36. Theater signal units support airfields as they have greater technical capabilities then the small communication section organic to the AOBs. Theater signal support has the capability to deploy, interface, and interoperate with equipment from other services, allies, commercial, and host-nation infrastructures. Theater signal support provides a communications architecture for all AOB requirements.

SECTION V – MOVEMENT CONTROL

2-37. Movement control is the planning, routing, scheduling, controlling, coordination, and in-transit visibility of personnel, units, equipment, and supplies moving over lines of communication (LOCs) and the commitment of allocated transportation assets according to command planning directives. It is a continuum that involves synchronizing and integrating logistics efforts with other programs that span the spectrum of military operations. Movement control is a tool used to help allocate resources based on the combatant commander's priorities, and to balance requirements against capabilities.

AERIAL DELIVERY

2-38. Aerial delivery includes airdrop, airland, and sling-load operations. Airdrop and airland distribution are joint (Army and United States Air Force [USAF]) operations requiring large FW aircraft; sling-load operations are usually unilateral using rotary-wing aircraft. Historically, U.S. military forces have been called on to execute aerial delivery operations in support of unilateral and allied force combat operations or humanitarian relief efforts throughout the world. Future operations will require a smaller, continental United States (CONUS)-based, force projection Army, capable of conducting full spectrum combat operations. Therefore, forward deployed airfields will continue to play an increasingly vital role in the supporting distribution system necessary to meet the requirements of the force.

2-39. Current battlefields have large AOs; however, future battlefields' AOs will be even greater. Combat organizations will operate within a box as large as 1,000 kilometers by 1,000 kilometers or in a noncontiguous AO with large unsecured areas. Units will have increasingly smaller logistics footprints. Aerial delivery and airfields will be required to have more responsive and efficient delivery. LOCs will be longer with a large proportion of the support provided by intermediate staging bases (ISBs) that could be hundreds of miles away. In this environment, aerial delivery plays an ever-increasing role in the total distribution system; to be effective, friendly forces must control airspace and operate airfields throughout the AO.

2-40. Aerial delivery is no longer the last resort, but rather, through necessity, is becoming a viable mode of distribution in support of the fight against a very flexible, fluid, and ever-changing threat environment. Army transformation has given the Army an airfield management capability, and with augmentation, the ability to manage large airfields capable of aerial delivery and distribution throughout the TO. The goal is to give combat units a previously unknown freedom of movement by drastically reducing their dependence on logistical support. A primary objective of this transformation is to reduce the logistics footprint by substituting large, redundant supply bases with a distribution-based logistics system. In this system, the "pipeline" becomes the supply base. To achieve this objective, the speed of supplies moving through the pipeline must be increased. Aerial delivery provides necessary acceleration and sustainment capabilities. This delivery method provides support without hampering maneuvers. Army distribution is discussed in detail in FM 100-10-1 and FM 10-1.

AERIAL DELIVERY ORGANIZATIONS

2-41. There are major Army and Air Force organizations common to both airland and airdrop operations. AOB commanders coordinate these assets through the ASG to the TSC ensuring required assets are available for cargo handling and management. The following organizations are designated by the TSC to assist the AOBs with their cargo handling needs.

Arrival/Departure Airfield Control Group

2-42. The departure airfield control group (DACG) is a provisional Army organization established by the supported land component commander from personnel not currently deploying. Its mission is to coordinate with the Air Force, and control loading of Army supplies and personnel onto Air Force aircraft. In airland operations, the supported unit commander will also establish an arrival airfield control group. It will have the same mission as the DACG, but will concentrate on the unloading rather than the loading mission. In large operations, airfield control groups will have both the departure and arrival missions; these groups are referred to as arrival/departure airfield control groups (A/DACGs).

Movement Control Team

2-43. The movement control team is an Army provisional unit. It works with the A/DACG but is under the control of the TSC's materiel management center (MMC). This team documents and directs loading/unloading of Army equipment onto aircraft.

Terminal Transfer Units

2-44. Army corps or theater-level transportation assets provide terminal transfer units. They load and unload aircraft, move supplies to and from a marshalling area, and provide onward movement of cargo. They unload and reconfigure cargo from one of several modes that could involve wheel, FW and/or rotary-wing assets and reload the reconfigured cargo on the appropriate mode of transportation.

Chapter 3

Airfield Construction and Design

Ideally, theater airfields are developed through many hours, days, and weeks of advanced planning to gather needed information, translate it into specific requirements that meet mission needs, and establish a base development plan. The airfield development plan determines and ensures that required manpower, equipment, and materials are available at the appropriate place and time. It takes the combined talents of the planner, designer, constructor, operator, supplier, transporter, and maintainer to ensure the best and most effective plan of action to meet mission requirements.

SECTION I – AIRFIELD SURVEYS

3-1. Airfield obstruction chart surveys are used to determine any combination of the following:

- Location of obstacles within 10 nautical miles of an airfield center.
- Dimensions of runways and taxiways, height of control towers, and NAVAIDs.
- Safe approach angles to runways and minimum, safe glide angle.
- Elevation of the barometer on an airfield.
- Positions and azimuths of points designated for Inertial Navigation System checkpoints.

Contents

- Information used to assist military aircraft crash or disaster incident investigation.
- Development of instrument approach and departure procedures.
- Maximum takeoff weights.
- Airport certification for certain types of operations.
- Updating of official aeronautical publications.
- Geodetic control for engineering projects related to runway/taxiway construction, NAVAID positioning, obstruction clearing, and other airport improvements.
- Assistance in airport planning and land-use studies.

ROTARY-WING OPERATIONS

3-2. AOBs utilized at airfields where rotary-wing operations are conducted may not be required to conduct all aspects of the airfield survey listed above. The four levels of heliport development in the TO each meet certain requirements based on the following:

- Mission.
- Length of operations.
- Type and number of aircraft.
- Location.

AIRFIELD/HELIPORT CLASSES

3-3.   Army deployment objectives require strategic responsiveness wherever needed. This operational concept depends on flexible combinations of Army and joint capabilities across the entire spectrum of operations. The Army establishes airfields and FOBs to increase responsiveness and reduce battlefield distances. The following factors are considered when planning airfields and FOBs:

- Occupy host nation airfields if available and tactically acceptable.
- Using abandoned or captured airfields to reduce construction and support requirements.
- Use roads, highways, or parking lots if airfields are not available in sufficient quantity or unsuitably located.
- Construct an airfield or FOB.

3-4.   These planning factors broadly establish the environment for which aviation operations are expected to operate. Campaign planning at joint level establishes airfield requirements early on with consideration of service-specific objectives. Army, Air Force, Navy, and Marine engineers all have the capability to design, plan, construct, upgrade, and maintain airfields and heliports. Airfields and heliports are classified by their degree of permanence and the type of aircraft they are designed to support. Army airfields and heliports are divided into six classes (table 3-1).

Table 3-1. Army airfield and heliport classes

Class	Definition (controlling aircraft weights reflect operational weight)
I	Heliports/pads with aircraft 25,000 lb (11,340 kg) or less. Controlling aircraft (UH-60)-16,300 lb (7,395 kg).
II	Heliports/pads with aircraft over 25,000 lb (11,340 kg). Controlling aircraft (CH-47)-50,000 lb (22,680 kg).
III	Airfield with class A runways. Controlling aircraft (combination of C-23 aircraft-24,600 lb (11,200 kg) & a CH-47 aircraft at a 50,000 lb (22,680 kg). Class A runways are primarily used for small aircraft (C-12 and C-23).
IV	Airfields w/class B runways. The controlling aircraft is a C-130 aircraft at a 155,000 lb (70,310 kg) operational weight or a C-17 aircraft at a 580,000 lb (263,100 kg) operational weight. Class B runways are primarily used for high performance and large heavy aircraft (C-130, C-17, and C-141).
V	Heliports/pads supporting Army assault training missions. Controlling aircraft (CH-47)-50,000 lb (22,680 kg).
VI	Assault LZs for operations supporting Army training missions that have semi-prepared or paved landing surfaces. Controlling aircraft (C-130-155,000 lb [70,310 kg] or C-17-580,000 lb [263,100 kg]).

3-5.   An airfield is also described on the basis of its location within the AO. FOB/support area heliports are intended to provide focused logistics support or to support combat missions of short-range aircraft such as attack helicopters and UASs. These airfields are designed for initial or temporary operational standards, depending on mission requirements, and may be paved or semi-prepared. Support area airfields provide general logistics support and support of combat missions of longer-range aircraft. These airfields are designed to temporary or semipermanent standards, depending on mission and operational requirements. Normally, these airfields are paved and provide a link between FOBs/support area heliports and sustainment area heliports/airfields. Sustainment area heliports/airfields provide logistics support from fixed, secure bases, and support combat operations of long-range aircraft and are designed to be semipermanent or permanent facilities. (See figures 3-1 and 3-2, page 3-3, for notional heliport/airfield layouts.)

3-6.   After seizing an FOB or available airfield from which sustained main base or base camp operations can be conducted, the CAB may be able to request joint fixed-wing (FW) refuel/resupply support.

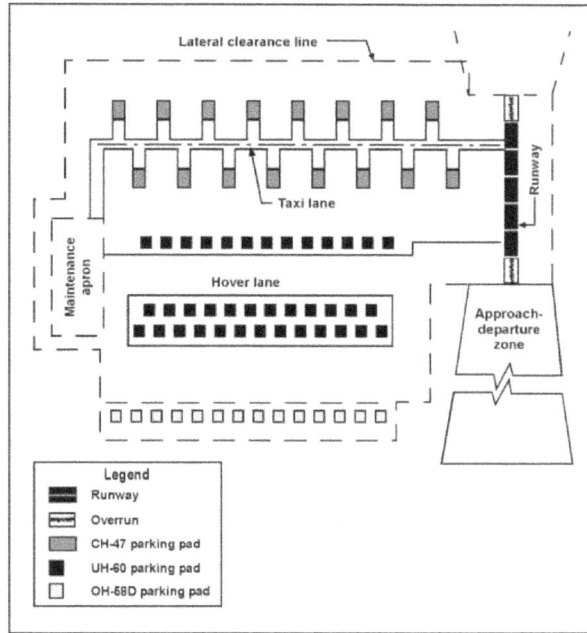

Figure 3-1. Notional combat aviation brigade support area heliport layout

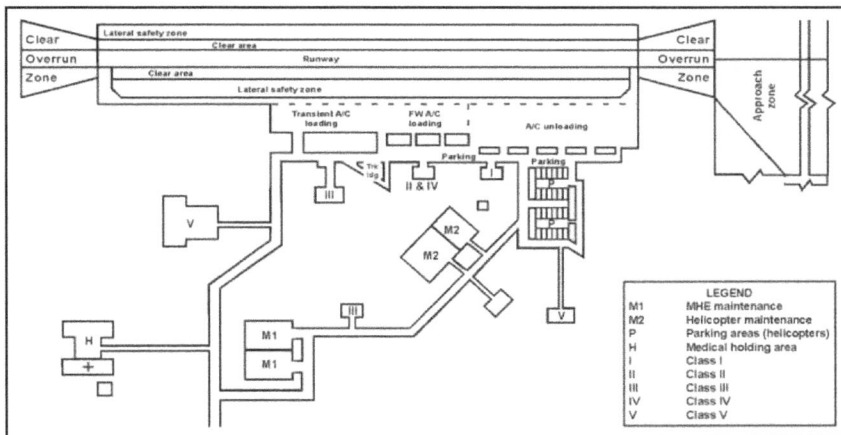

Figure 3-2. Notional sustainment area heliport/airfield

3-7.   Army H-60 and CH-47 aircraft can establish refuel points from the aircraft (Fat Hawk operations for H-60s and Fat Cow for CH-47s), while the Marine Corps CH-53s have a unique refueling capability that can support supply points, operations in noncontiguous areas, and other specialized mission applications.

3-8.   The KC-130 or C-17 can operate from small airfields with limited supporting infrastructure. The airfield runway must be 3,000 to 5,000 feet (914 – 1,524 meters) long and 90 feet (27.4 meters) wide with graded and compacted gravel or clay. If KC-130 or C-17 is used as a primary means of resupply, runway repair requirements will increase dictating engineer augmentation. CH-53 tactical bladder fuel distribution system and CH-47 Fat Cow refueling does not require a runway, but does require a large relatively flat area similar in size.

Helipads

3-9.   Helipads are constructed for aircraft that do not require a runway to become airborne. They are most advantageous where a limited number of helicopters are to be located, or at heliports that handle a large volume of traffic where separate landing and takeoff operations are desired. Helipad layouts have been developed for the various helicopters. Refer to FM 5-430-00-2 for detailed information on various helipad construction standards.

AIRFIELD OPERATIONS BATTALION RESPONSIBILITIES

3-10.   The AOB commander requests an airfield survey be conducted by engineers at the outset of operations. The information obtained from this survey is used to develop the airfield plan. This information provides insight into construction and repair requirements of the airfield based on the expected type and amount of air traffic utilizing the landing surface. The airfield survey determines the length of time the landing surface can be used without extensive construction or repair.

3-11.   AOBs have certain responsibilities during the conduct of an airfield survey. AOBs inspect airfields for obstacles that violate airfield imaginary surface criteria, such as—

● Construction activities (for example, cranes).
● Tree growth.
● Dirt/snow piles.
● Sandbag bunkers.

3-12.   This information is then compiled along with engineer survey data and forwarded to the theater to assist in the development of the airfield plan.

APPLICATION OF CRITERIA

Existing Facilities

3-13.   Criteria in unified facilities criteria (UFC) 3-260-01 is not intended to apply to existing facilities located or constructed under previous standards. This includes cases where runways may lack paved shoulders or other physical features as they were not previously required or authorized. These facilities can remain in use without impairing operational efficiency and safety. If used by the USAF, AOBs must identify such facilities on airfield obstruction maps using a building restriction line (BRL) to encompass exempt areas or an annotation on or near the feature noting its exempt status. Refer to attachment 19 of UFC 3-260-01 for guidelines used to establish the BRL.

3-14.   Existing airfield facilities need not be modified or upgraded to conform to UFC 3-260-01 criteria. If a change in mission results in a facility category code reclassification, an upgrade to current standards is required. Upgraded facilities must be maintained at a level that will sustain compliance with current standards. When existing airfield facilities are modified, construction must conform to UFC 3-260-01 criteria, unless waived per paragraph 1.8 of UFC 3-260-01. Modified portions of facilities must be maintained at a level that will sustain compliance with current standards. Standards for TO facilities are contained in Army FM 5-430-00-2/Air Force Joint Pamphlet 32-8013, volume 2.

Note: The JFC will determine the minimum acceptable airfield criteria to be used in the theater.

AIRFIELD INSPECTION AREAS

3-15. Lateral clearance areas (runways [RWYs], taxiways [TWYs], and aprons) are inspected for violations (fixed or mobile) per Army Regulation (AR) 95-2/Air Force Instruction (AFI) 13-213. Table 3-2 describes inspected areas.

Table 3-2. Airfield inspection areas

1. Obstacle clearance criteria (tree growth vegetation, dirt/snow piles, ponding, construction, depressions, mobile/fixed obstacles)
a.   RWY clear zones 304.8 m X 914.4 m/1,000 x 3,000 ft (first 304.8 m/1,000 ft must be cleared)
b.   RWY lateral clearance 152.4 m/500 ft centerline
c.   TWY lateral clearance 45.72 m/150 ft centerline
d.   Apron lateral clearance 30.48 m/100 ft Class A, 38.1 m/125 ft Class B
e.   Construction areas
f.   Perimeter/access roads
g.   Transition slope (7:1)
2. Foreign object damage (FOD) control
a.   RWYs/overruns, TWYs/shoulders
b.   Parking aprons
c.   Infield areas between RWYs/TWYs
d.   Perimeter/access roads (controls points)
3. Signs/markings (faded/broken)
a.   Visual flight rules (VFR) holding positions
b.   Instrument holding positions
c.   Elevation signs
d.   NAVAID ground receiver checkpoints
e.   Closed areas
4. RWYs/TWYs/aprons/shoulders widths
a.   RWY 15.24 m/50 ft Class A, 60.96 m/200 ft Class B
b.   TWY 7.62 m/25 ft Class A, 15.24 m/50 ft Class B
c.   Apron 7.62 m/25 ft Class A, 15.24 m/50 ft Class B
5. Construction
a.   Parking
b.   Rules compliance
c.   Work site (lighting/marking)
d.   Storage
e.   Vehicles lighted/marked
f.   FOD
6. Pavement conditions (rubber deposits, cracks, spalling, marking, FOD, paint buildup/chipping)
a.   RWY/overruns
b.   TWYs
c.   Parking aprons
d.   Access roads

Lighting Check

3-16. The following lighting areas are inspected per AR 95-2, UFC 3-535-01, and Federal Aviation Administration (FAA) Advisory Circular (AC) 150/5340-26:

- RWY edge lights.
- Visual glide slope indicator.
- Threshold.
- Approach Light System.
- Runway end identifier lights.
- TWY.
- Obstruction lights.
- Rotating beacon.
- Wind cones.
- NAVAID checkpoints.
- Apron lights.

Daily Airfield Inspections

3-17. Daily airfield inspections are conducted using established airfield criteria by the AOB's airfield service element. Each operational day the airfield service element inspects—

- Airfield for obstacles that violate airfield imaginary surface criteria.
- RWYs, TWYs, aprons, and lateral clearance areas for violations (fixed or mobile).
- Construction areas, ensuring a high level of safety is maintained. Check barricades, construction lights, equipment parking, stockpiled materiels, and debris and foreign objects.
- Airfield markings for peeling, chipping, fading, and obscurity due to rubber buildup. Markings must be correct, properly sited, and reflective during hours of darkness.
- Airfield signs to ensure correct background and legend colors, legibility, clearance of vegetation, dirt, and snow, frangible mounting, and proper illumination, if required for night operations.
- Airfield lighting systems to ensure they are frangible mounted and foundations do not extend three inches above the finished surface of surrounding area and not obscured.
- Pavement areas for conditions that could cause ponding, obscure markings, attract wildlife or otherwise impair safe aircraft operations. For example, scaling, spalling, cracks, holes, or surface variations such as—
    - Bumps/low spots.
    - Rubber deposits.
    - Vegetation growth.
- Pavement areas for loose aggregate or other foreign objects and contaminants. Foreign objects and contaminants must be promptly removed.

3-18. An airfield /heliport self-inspection checklist can be found in AR 95-2, appendix E.

SECTION II – AIRFIELD MARKING AND LIGHTING

3-19. The airfield marking system is a visual aid in landing aircraft. It requires illumination from either an aircraft lighting system or daylight. Standards for airfield marking have been adopted by the Army and Air Force. Determination of an airfield marking system is a theater-level responsibility. The methods and configurations described here are those most commonly applicable to theater-level airfields. For a more detailed discussion of airfield marking, refer to UFC 3-260-5A, Army Facilities Component System (AFCS) facility drawings, and AFI 32-1044.

RUNWAY MARKINGS

3-20. The marking elements that apply to runways in general are described in the following paragraphs.

CENTERLINE MARKING

3-21. Centerline marking is a broken line with 30.48 meters (100 foot) dashes and 18.288 meters (60 foot) blank spaces. The minimum width for a basic runway centerline marking is 18 inches. For precision and nonprecision instrument runways, the minimum width is 0.9144 meters (3 feet).

RUNWAY DESIGNATION NUMBERS

3-22. Runway designation numbers are required on all runways (basic, precision, and nonprecision instrument). They are not required on a minimum operating strip or short-field assault strip. The numbers designate the runway direction and accent the end limits of the runway environment. Runway designation numbers are normally 9.144 meters (30 feet) high and 3.048 meters (10 feet) wide, excluding the number one that is 9.144 meters (30 feet) high and 0.762 meters (2.5 feet) wide. For specific information on runway designation numbers refer to FM 5-430-00-2 or UFC 3-260-01. The number assigned to the runway is the whole number closest to one-tenth the magnetic azimuth of the centerline of the runway, measured clockwise from magnetic north. Single digits are preceded by a zero.

THRESHOLD MARKING

3-23. Threshold marking is required on all precision and nonprecision instrument runways (refer to table 3-2). Threshold markings for runways must be at least 45.72 meters (150 feet) wide. On runways less than 45.72 meters (150 feet) wide, start threshold markings 3.048 meters (10 feet) from each edge of the runway. Reduce all other widths in proportion to the threshold marking overall width. Table 3-3 depicts threshold marking dimensions.

Table 3-3. Threshold marking dimensions

Stripe dimensions	Meters	Feet
Length	30.500	100.0
Width	1.830	6.0
Distance from runway edge	1.520	5.0
Distance between stripes	1.830	6.0
Center line distance between stripes	3.660	12.0

TOUCHDOWN-ZONE MARKINGS AND EDGE STRIPES

3-24. Touchdown zone markings and edge strips are required on runways served by a precision instrument approach. Their use in the TO should be kept to a minimum due to the time and effort required to obliterate them if the tactical situation requires it. For marking dimensions, refer to FM 5-430-00-2 and UFC 3-260-01.

FIXED-DISTANCE MARKINGS

3-25. Fixed-distance markings are rectangular painted blocks 9.144 meters (30 feet) wide by 45.72 meters (150 feet) long, beginning 304.8 meters (1,000 feet) from the threshold. They are placed equidistant from the centerline and 21.9456 meters (72 feet) apart at the inner edges. They are required on all runways 45.72 meters (150 feet) wide or wider and 1,219.2 meters (4,000 feet) long or longer and used by jet aircraft.

EXPEDIENT RUNWAY MARKING

3-26. For expedient construction, surfacing is normally soil-stabilized pavement, membrane, or airfield landing mat. An inverted T is placed at the end of the runway combined with a centerline stripe, edge markings and a transverse stripe mark at the threshold (152.4 meters [500 feet] and at the runway midpoint). Runway direction numbers are not provided on landing mat surfaces.

3-27. Figure 3-3 and figure 3-4 (page 3-9) depict typical airfield marking and lighting layout for both day and instrument/nighttime operations.

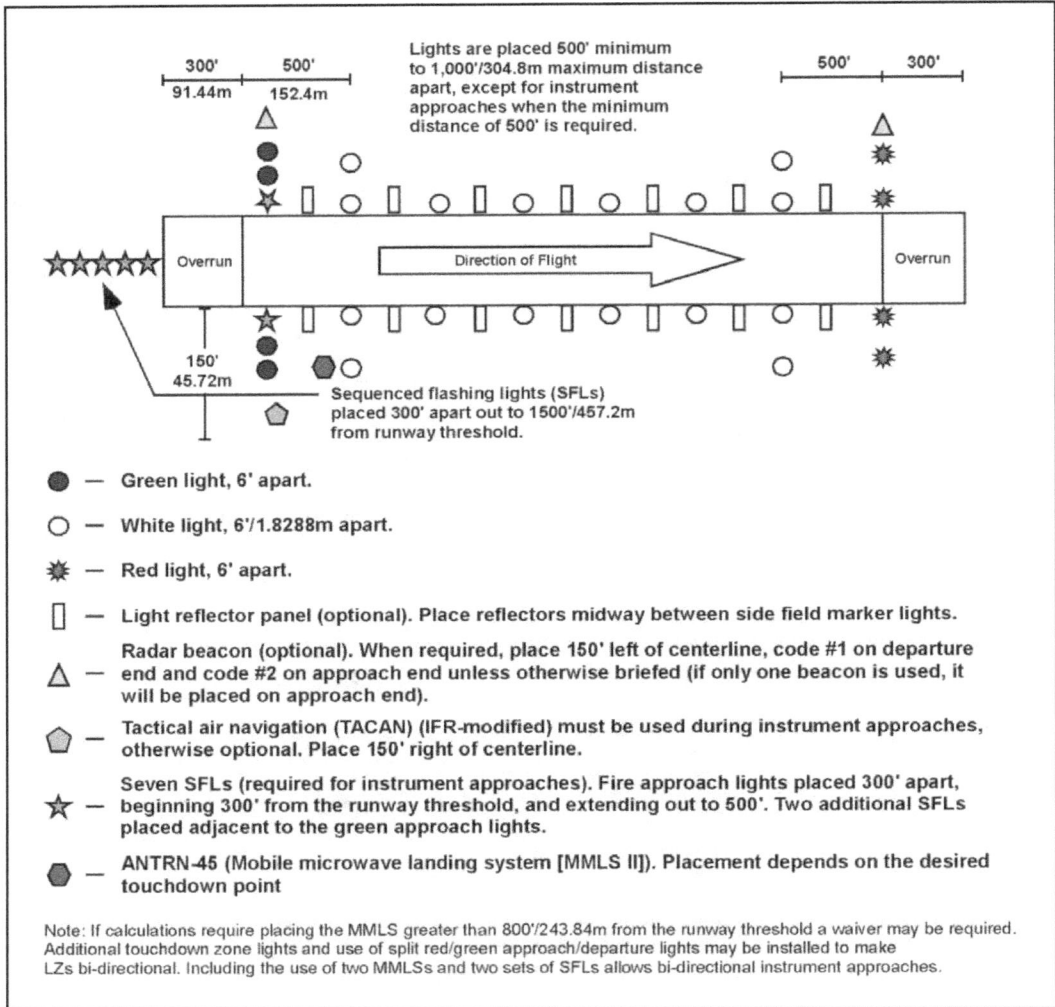

Figure 3-3. Expedient airfield marking pattern (night/instrument)

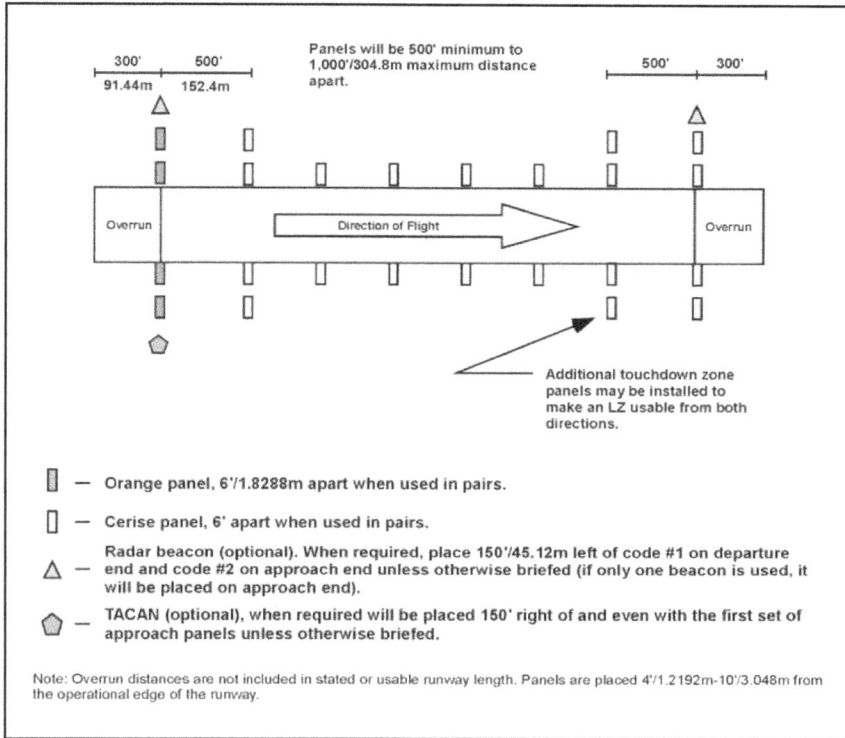

Figure 3-4. Expedient airfield marking pattern (day)

TAXIWAY MARKING

3-28. Taxiways should be marked to conform to the following requirements.

Centerline Stripes

3-29. Mark each taxiway with a single, continuous stripe along the centerline. These stripes should have a minimum width of 15.24 centimeters (6 inches). At taxiway intersections with runway ends, taxiway stripes should end in line with the nearest runway edge. At taxiway intersections, the taxiway centerline markings should intersect.

Holding Line Marking

3-30. Place a taxiway holding line marking not less than 30.48 meters (100 feet) and not more than 60.96 meters (200 feet) from the nearest edge of the runway or taxiway the taxiway intersects. This distance is measured on a line perpendicular to the runway or taxiway centerline intersected. Increase the distance from the minimum 30.48 meters (100 feet) to one that provides adequate clearance between large aircraft operating on the runway or taxiway and holding aircraft.

MARKING MATERIELS AND METHODS

3-31. Materiels and methods used in airfield marking must provide visual contrast with the airfield surface. They vary primarily with the surface type and less directly with the construction type or stage. Fewer permanent materials require constant maintenance. Use the following guides to select marking materials:

- Paint is used only on permanent surfaces.
- Lime is used primarily for marking unsurfaced areas such as earth, membranes, or similar surfaces.
- Oil or similar liquids are used for marking unsurfaced areas.
- Panels made of materials such as cloth or canvas, properly fastened to the pavement, may be used for many marking requirements.
- Use yellow flags to show temporary obstructions caused by flying accidents or enemy action. As temporary expedients, sandwich-board markers or stake mounted signs may be used to define the runway width. These markers are 0.6096 meters (2 feet) by 0.6096 meters (2 feet) in size, have black and white triangles on each side, and are spaced 200 feet apart longitudinally on the outer runway shoulder edge.
- For taxiways, sandwich-board markers or flat pieces of wood or metal painted with black and white triangles may serve as expedient markers. Fasten these 30.48 centimeter (12 inch) by 30.48 centimeter (12 inch) markers to stakes and place them 30.48 meters (100 feet) apart along the outer taxiway shoulder edge.

Note: All expedient markers should be lightweight and constructed to break readily if struck by an aircraft; they should never be hazardous to the aircraft.

3-32. Markers for snow covered runways should be conspicuous. Upright spruce trees, about 1.524 meters (5 feet) high, or light, wooden tripods may be used. Place the markers along the sides of the snow-covered runway. Space them not more than 100.548 meters (330 feet) apart and locate them symmetrically about the axis of the runway. Place enough markings across the end of the runway to show the threshold. Aluminum powder and dyes can effectively mark snow in the runway area.

OBSTRUCTION MARKING

3-33. Obstructions are marked either by color, markers, flags, or red lights. Mark objects by color according to the requirements described below.

SOLID

3-34. A solid is an object whose projection on any vertical plane in a clear zone is less than 1.524 meters (5 feet) in both dimensions and colored aviation-surface orange.

BANDS

3-35. A band is an object with unbroken surfaces whose projection on any vertical plane is 1.524 meters (5 feet) or more in one dimension and less than 4.572 meters (15 feet) in the other dimension. It is colored to show alternate bands of aviation-surface orange and white. It is also any skeleton (broken surface) structure or smokestack-type structure having both dimensions greater than 1.524 meters (5 feet) and colored in alternate bands of aviation-surface orange and white. Widths of the aviation-surface orange and white bands should be equal and approximately one-seventh of the object's major axis length if the band has a width of not more than 12.192 meters (40 feet) or less than 0.4572 meters (1.5 feet). The bands are placed perpendicular to the major axis of construction. Bands at the extremities of the object should be aviation-surface orange.

CHECKERBOARD PATTERN

3-36. Checkerboard patterns are objects with unbroken surfaces whose projection on any vertical plane is 4.572 meters (15 feet) or more in both dimensions. They are colored to show a checkerboard pattern of alternate rectangles of aviation-surface orange and white. The rectangles are not less than 1.524 meters (5 feet) and not more than 6.096 meters (20 feet) on a side and the corner rectangles are aviation-surface orange. If part or all of the objects with spherical shapes do not permit exact application of the checkerboard pattern, modify the shape of the alternate aviation-surface orange and white rectangles, covering the spherical shape to fit the structural surface. Ensure the dimensions of the modified rectangles remain within the specified limits.

MARKERS

3-37. Use markers when it is impractical to mark the surface of objects with color. Markers are used in addition to color providing protection for air navigation. Obstruction markers should be distinctive so they are not mistaken for markers employed to convey other information; color them as specified earlier. Markers should be recognizable in clear air from a distance of at least 304.8 meters (1,000 feet) in all the directions an aircraft is likely to approach. Position markers so the hazard presented by the object they mark is not increased. Locate markers displayed on or adjacent to obstructions in conspicuous positions to retain the general definition of the obstructions. Markers displayed on overhead wires are usually placed not more than 45.72 meters (150 feet) apart, with the top of each marker not below the level of the highest wire at the point marked. However, when overhead wires are more than 4,572 meters (15,000 feet) from the center of the landing area, the distance between markers may be increased to not more than 182.88 meters (600 feet).

MARKING BY FLAGS

3-38. Use flags to mark temporary obstructions or obstructions impractical to mark by coloring or markers. The flags should be rectangular and have stiffeners to keep them from drooping in calm or light wind. Use one of the following patterns on flags marking obstructions:
- Solid color, aviation-surface orange, not less than 0.6096 meters (2 feet) on a side.
- Two triangular sections–one aviation-surface orange and one aviation-surface white–combined to form a rectangle not less than 0.6096 meters (2 feet) on a side.
- A checkerboard of aviation-surface orange and white squares, each 0.3048 meters (1 foot) plus or minus 10 percent on a side, combined to form a rectangle not less than 0.9144 meters (3 feet) on a side.
- Position flags so the hazard they mark is not increased. Display flags on top of or around the perimeter of the object's highest edge. Flags used to mark extensive objects or groups of closely spaced objects should be displayed at approximately 15.24 meters (50-foot) intervals.

AIRFIELD LIGHTING

3-39. The Army does not have a standard tactical airfield lighting system. The Precision Approach Lighting System will be a component of the Mobile Tower System, scheduled to be fielded beginning fiscal year 2010.

3-40. Airfield lighting systems are illuminated visual signals that help pilots operate aircraft safely and efficiently at night and during periods of restricted visibility (IFR conditions). In general, airfield lighting is comprised of runway, approach, taxiway, obstruction, and hazard lighting.

3-41. The colors and configuration used in airfield lighting are generally standardized on an international scale, and there is no difference between permanent and TO installations. The basic color code are—
- **Blue.** Taxiway lighting.
- **Clear (white).** Sides of a usable landing area.
- **Green.** Ends of a usable landing area (threshold lights). When used with a beacon, green indicates a lighted and attended airfield.
- **Red.** Hazard, obstruction, or area unsuitable for landing.
- **Yellow.** Caution. When used with a beacon, yellow indicates a water airport.

RUNWAY LIGHTING

3-42. Runway lighting, the principal element of airfield lighting, provides the standard pattern of lights to outline the runway and show side and end limits. Side limits are marked by two parallel rows of white lights, one row on each side and equidistant from the runway centerline. Lights within the rows are uniformly spaced, and the rows extend the entire runway length. End limits are outlined by green runway threshold lights.

3-43. Space runway threshold lights along the threshold line, which is 0 to 3.048 meters (10 feet) from the end of the runway and perpendicular to the centerline extended off the runway. Runway lighting is divided into two classes–high intensity, to support aircraft operations under IFR conditions, and medium intensity, to support aircraft operations under VFR conditions.

APPROACH LIGHTING

3-44. This light system is used to guide aircraft safely to the runway on airfields intended for instrument flying and all weather operations. The system is installed in the primary approach to the Stage II runway. Its use is generally confined to airfields provided with precision, electronic, and low-approach facilities. Never use approach lighting with a medium-intensity runway lighting system.

TAXIWAY LIGHTING

3-45. When an airfield becomes fully operational, lights and reflectors are used to increase safety in aircraft ground movements. Taxiway lighting is standardized. In general, blue taxiway lights mark the lateral limits, turns, and terminals of taxiway sections.

3-46. Reflectors are also used to delineate taxiways. Standard taxiway reflectors are panels approximately 30.48 centimeters (12 inches) high by 22.86 centimeters (9 inches) wide. Both sides of the panels consist of a retro reflective material that reflects incident light back to the light source (aircraft landing or taxiing lights). Mounting wickets can be manufactured locally from galvanized steel wire, size number six or larger. The wire, cut into 106.68 centimeters (42-inch) pieces, is bent into a U-shape making the parallel sides 19.05 centimeters (7.5 inches) apart. Install reflectors along straight sections and long-radius curves at 30.48 meters (100 feet) intervals. At intersections and on short-radius curves, set the reflectors 6.096 meters (20 feet) apart and perpendicular to one another. Embed wickets 30.48 to 38.1 centimeters (12 to 15 inches) in the ground and set them firmly. When reflectors are set where grass or other vegetation grows 5.08 centimeters (2 inches) or more in height, treat the ground surface with engine oil or salt to prevent this growth.

BEACONS

3-47. Airport-type beacons are not commonly used in a combat area. They may be used in sustainment areas of the TO. Beacons are considered organizational equipment and not part of the construction program.

EXPEDIENT LIGHTING

3-48. Expedients may be used for lighting if issue equipment is not available. Lanterns, smudge pots, vehicle headlights, or reflectors may be used to distinguish runway edges. Reflectors are also useful when placed along taxiways and at hardstands to guide pilots in dark or limited visibility. An electrical circuit may be laid around the runway with light globes spaced at regular intervals and covered by improvised hoods made from cans. A searchlight, pointed straight in the air, is sometimes used as a substitute for beacon lights. The searchlight is placed beyond the downwind end of the runway. Portable airfield lighting is used when permanent lighting has been damaged or is not available.

OBSTRUCTION LIGHTING

3-49. Obstruction lights reveal the existence of obstructions. These lights are aviation red, with an intensity of not less than 10 candlepower. The number and arrangement of lights at each level should be such that the obstruction is visible from every angle.

Vertical Arrangement

3-50. Locate a minimum of two lamps at the top of the obstruction, operating either simultaneously or circuited so if one fails the other operates. An exception is made for chimneys of similar structures. The top lights on such structures are placed between 1.524 to 3.048 meters (5 to 10 feet) below the top. Where the top of the obstruction is more than 45.72 meters (150 feet) above ground level, provide an intermediate light or lights for each additional 45.72 meters (150 feet) or fraction thereof. Space the intermediate lights equally between the top light or lights and ground level.

Horizontal Arrangement

3-51. Built-up and tree-covered areas have extensive obstructions. Where an extensive obstruction or group of closely spaced obstructions is marked with obstruction lights, display the top lights on the point or edge of the highest obstruction. Space the lights at intervals of not more than 45.72 meters (150 feet) so they will reflect the general definition and extent of the obstruction. If two or more edges of an obstruction located near an airfield are at the same height, light the edges nearest the airfield.

Lighting of Overhead Wires

3-52. When obstruction lighting of overhead wires is needed, place the lights not more than 45.72 meters (150 feet) apart at a level not below the highest wire at each point lighted. When the overhead wires are more than 4572 meters (15,000 feet) from the center of the landing area, the distance between the lights may be increased to no more than 182.88 meters (600 feet).

SECTION III – AIRFIELD PARKING

AIRCRAFT PARKING APRONS

3-53. Aircraft parking aprons are paved areas for aircraft parking, loading, unloading, and servicing. They include the necessary maneuvering area for access and exit to parking positions. Aprons are designed to permit safe and controlled movement of aircraft under their own power. Aircraft apron types are described as follows:

- Aircraft parking apron.
- Transient parking apron.
- Mobilization apron.
- Aircraft maintenance apron.
- Hangar access apron.
- Warm-up pad (holding apron).
- Unsuppressed power check pads.
- Arm/disarm pad.
- Compass calibration pad.
- Hazardous cargo pad.
- Alert pad.
- Aircraft wash rack.

ARMY PARKING APRONS

3-54. Army aircraft parking aprons are divided into the following three categories:

- **Unit Parking Apron.** The unit parking apron supports fixed- and rotary-wing aircraft assigned to the facility.
- **General Purpose Apron.** When no tenant units are assigned to an aviation facility and transient aircraft parking is anticipated, a personnel loading apron or aircraft general purpose apron should be provided in lieu of a mass parking apron.
- **Special Purpose Apron.** Special purpose aprons are provided for specific operations such as safe areas for arming/disarming aircraft and other specific mission requirements that demand separation or distinct handling procedures for aircraft.

PARKING APRONS FOR FIXED-WING AIRCRAFT

3-55. FW parking at an aviation facility may consist of separate aprons for parking operational, transient, and transport aircraft, or an apron for consolidated parking. Parking aprons should be located near and contiguous to maintenance and hangar facilities. Do not locate within runway and taxiway lateral clearance distances. Figure 3-5 (page 3-15) depicts FW apron criteria.

Fixed-Wing Apron Size

3-56. As a general rule, there is no standard size for aircraft aprons. Aprons are individually designed to support aircraft and missions at specific facilities. Actual apron dimensions are based on the number of authorized aircraft, maneuvering space, and type of activity the apron serves. Parking apron dimensions for Air Force facilities are based on the specific aircraft assigned to the facility and criteria presented in AFH 32-1084. Navy and Marine Corps criteria can be found in naval facility (NAVFAC) P-80 and MIL–HDBK–1021/1. A typical mass parking apron should be arranged in rows. The ideal apron size affords maximum parking capacity with a minimum amount of paving. Generally, this is achieved by reducing the area dedicated for use as taxi lanes by parking aircraft perpendicular to the long axis of the apron.

Army Parking Apron Layout

3-57. Where there is a large variety of FW aircraft, mass parking apron dimensions are based on the C-23. The C-23 parking space is 22.86 meters (75 feet) wide and is 22.5552 meters (74 feet) long. If assigned aircraft are predominantly one type, the mass parking apron is based on specific dimensions of that aircraft.

Layout for Combined Army and Air Force Parking Aprons

3-58. Parking apron dimensions for combined Army and Air Force facilities are based on the largest aircraft assigned to the facility. Figure 3-6 (page 3-16) depicts Army and Air Force parking plan.

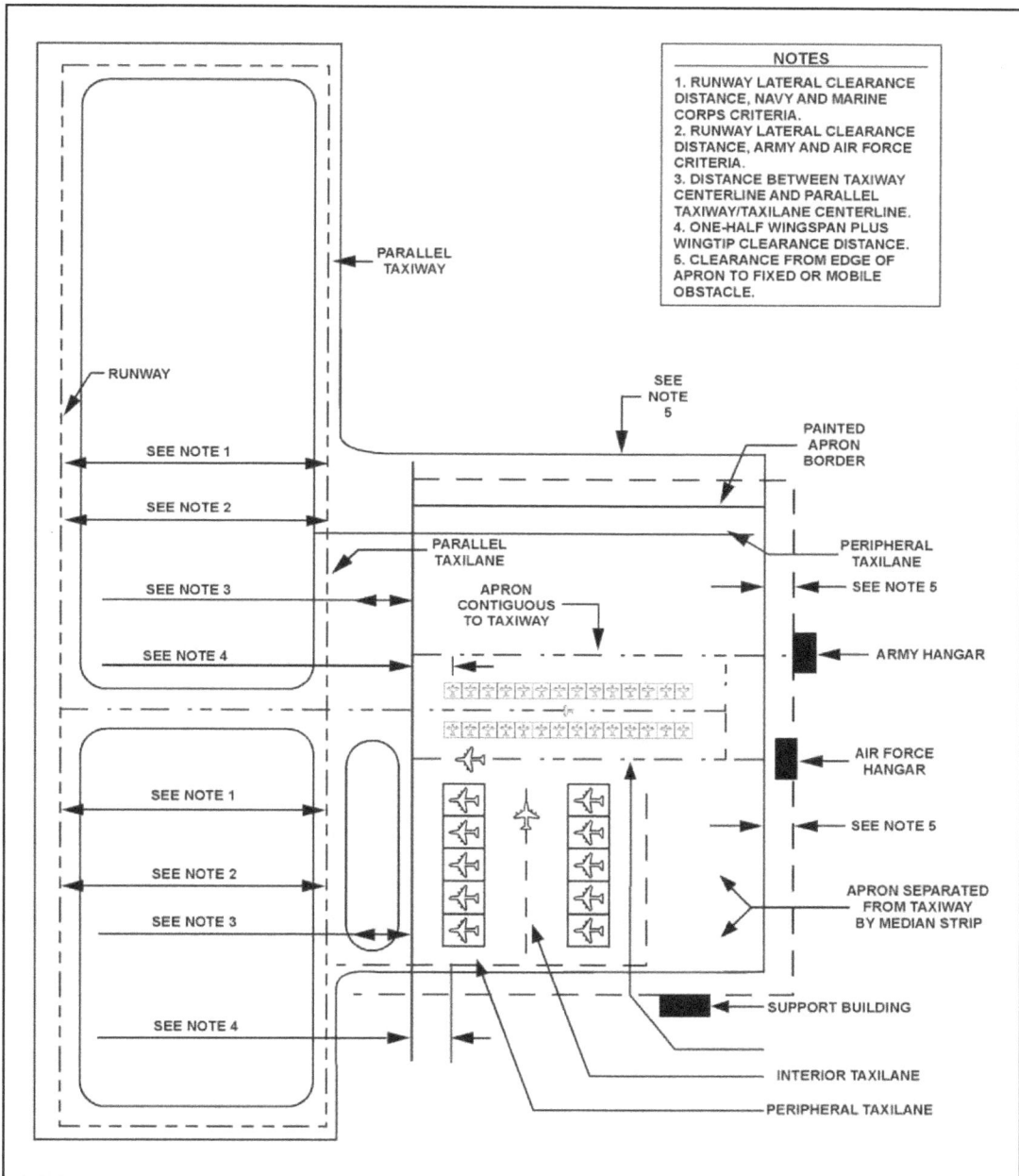

NOTES

1. RUNWAY LATERAL CLEARANCE DISTANCE, NAVY AND MARINE CORPS CRITERIA.
2. RUNWAY LATERAL CLEARANCE DISTANCE, ARMY AND AIR FORCE CRITERIA.
3. DISTANCE BETWEEN TAXIWAY CENTERLINE AND PARALLEL TAXIWAY/TAXILANE CENTERLINE.
4. ONE-HALF WINGSPAN PLUS WINGTIP CLEARANCE DISTANCE.
5. CLEARANCE FROM EDGE OF APRON TO FIXED OR MOBILE OBSTACLE.

Figure 3-5. Fixed-wing apron criteria

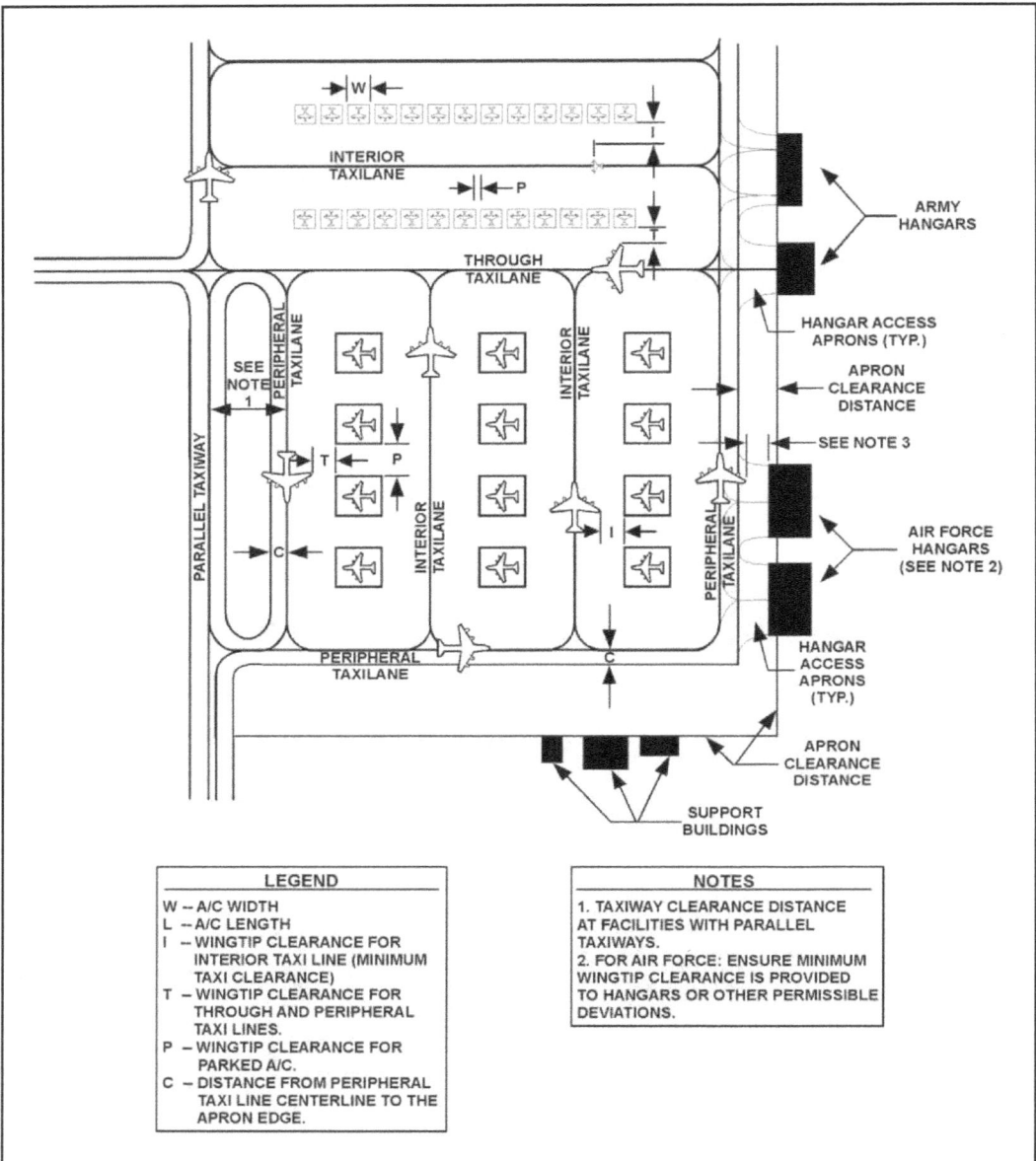

Figure 3-6. Army and Air Force parking plan

Parking Dimensions

3-59. When designing new aprons for Air Mobility Command (AMC) bases hosting C-5, C-17, KC-10, and KC-135 aircraft, provide 15.3 meter (50 foot) wingtip separation. **EXCEPTION:** When rehabilitating an existing apron, provide the maximum wingtip separation the existing apron size will allow (up to 15.3 meters [50 feet], but not less than 7.7 meters [25 feet]). This additional separation is both desirable and permitted. At non-AMC bases, the maximum separation that can reasonably be provided for these aircraft is desirable. Table 3-3 describes cargo apron areas needed for current Air Force transport aircraft.

Table 3-2. Cargo apron areas

Aircraft Type	Area per Aircraft (square meters/yards)
C-130	3,913.632 square meters (4,280 square yards)
C-5A	11,384.28 square meters (12,450 square yards)
C-17	10,287 square meters (11,250 square yards)

Jet Blast Considerations

3-60. The effects of jet blast are far more serious than those of prop wash and must be considered when designing aircraft parking configurations for all military and civil aircraft. These high velocities are capable of causing bodily injury to personnel or damage to airport equipment, certain pavements, and other erodible surfaces.

3-61. High temperatures are also a by-product of jet exhaust. The area exposed to hazardous high temperatures is typically smaller than the area subjected to hazardous blast velocities.

3-62. Blast velocities greater than 48 kilometers (30 miles) per hour can cause loose objects on the pavement to become airborne and cause injury and damage to personnel and equipment that may be a considerable distance behind the aircraft. The layout of aviation facilities must protect personnel and equipment from projectiles.

3-63. The minimum clearance from the rear of a jet operating at military power needed to dissipate the temperature and velocity to levels that will not endanger aircraft personnel and damage other aircraft is referred to as the safe distance.

Protection from Jet Blast Effects

3-64. Equipment such as blast deflectors may be required at locations where continued jet engine run-up interferes with aircraft parking or taxiing, vehicle movement, and activities of maintenance or aircraft personnel. Jet blast deflectors can substantially reduce the damaging effects of jet blast on structures, equipment, and personnel. Jet blast deflectors can also reduce the effects of noise and fumes associated with jet engine operation. Erosion of shoulders not protected by asphalt-concrete surfacing can be mitigated by blast deflectors. Blast deflectors consist of a concave corrugated sheet metal surface, with or without baffles, fastened and braced to a concrete base to withstand the force of the jet blast and deflect it upward. The deflector is usually located 20 to 40 meters (66 to 120 feet) aft of the jet engine nozzle, but not less than 15 meters (50 feet) from the aircraft tail. Size and configuration of jet blast deflectors are based on jet blast velocity, and location and elevation of nozzles. Commercially available jet blast deflectors should be considered when designing jet blast protection.

3-65. When blast deflectors are placed off the edge of a paved apron, a shoulder is required between them. Airfield unprotected areas that receive continued exposure to jet blast can erode and cause release of soil, stones, and other debris that can be ingested into jet engines and cause engine damage.

3-66. Protection against noise exposure is required whenever the sound level exceeds 85 dB(A) continuous, or 140 dB(A) impulse, regardless of the duration of exposure.

Jet Blast Requirements

3-67. AFH 32-1084 criteria states that a minimum clearance is needed to the rear of an engine to dissipate jet blast to less than 56 kilometers per hour (35 miles per hour) and not endanger personnel. Velocities of 48 to 56 kilometers (30 to 35 miles) per hour can occur over 490 meters (1,600 feet) to the rear of certain aircraft with their engines operating at takeoff thrust. These velocities decrease rapidly with distance behind the jet engine.

Parking Apron for Rotary-Wing Aircraft

3-68. Mass parking of rotary-wing aircraft requires an apron designated for rotary-wing aircraft. Parking for transient rotary-wing aircraft, and at aviation facilities where only a few rotary-wing aircraft are assigned, may be located on aprons for FW aircraft or taxiways and sod areas. At aviation facilities with assigned rotary-wing aircraft, a transport apron for FW aircraft is desirable.

Location

3-69. Parking aprons for rotary-wing aircraft should be located similar to those for FW aircraft. Generally, company units should be parked together in rows for organizational integrity in locations adjacent to their assigned hangars. Parking aprons for small helicopters (OH, UH, and AH) should be separate from parking areas used by cargo helicopters due to the critical operating characteristics of larger aircraft.

Apron Size

3-70. There is no standard size for rotary-wing aircraft aprons. The actual dimensions are based on the number of authorized aircraft, maneuvering space, and type of activity the apron serves. The layout of rotary-wing parking should allow aircraft maneuverability to airfield locations. For additional information on rotary-wing aircraft parking refer to UFC 3-260-1.

3-71. Rotary-wing aircraft are parked in one of two configurations referred to as Type 1 or Type 2.

- **Type 1.** In this configuration, rotary-wing aircraft are parked in a single lane perpendicular to the taxi lane. This arrangement resembles FW aircraft parking and is preferred for wheeled aircraft. Parking space dimensions for all rotary-wing aircraft (except the CH-47) measure 25 meters (80 feet) in width and 30 meters (100 feet) in length. Parking space dimensions for the CH-47 measure 30 meters (100 feet) in width and 46 meters (150 feet) in length. Figures 3-7 (page 3-19) and figure 3-8 (page 3-20) depict Type 1 rotary-wing parking.
- **Type 2.** Rotary-wing aircraft are parked in a double lane parallel to the taxi lane. This arrangement is preferred for skid-gear aircraft. Parking space dimensions for skid-gear rotary-wing aircraft measure 25 meters in width (80 feet) and 30 meters (100 feet) in length. Parking space dimensions for all wheeled rotary-wing aircraft measure 30 meters (100 feet) in width and 50 meters (160 feet) in length. Figure 3-9 (page 3-21) and figure 3-10 (page 3-22) depict type 2 rotary wing parking.

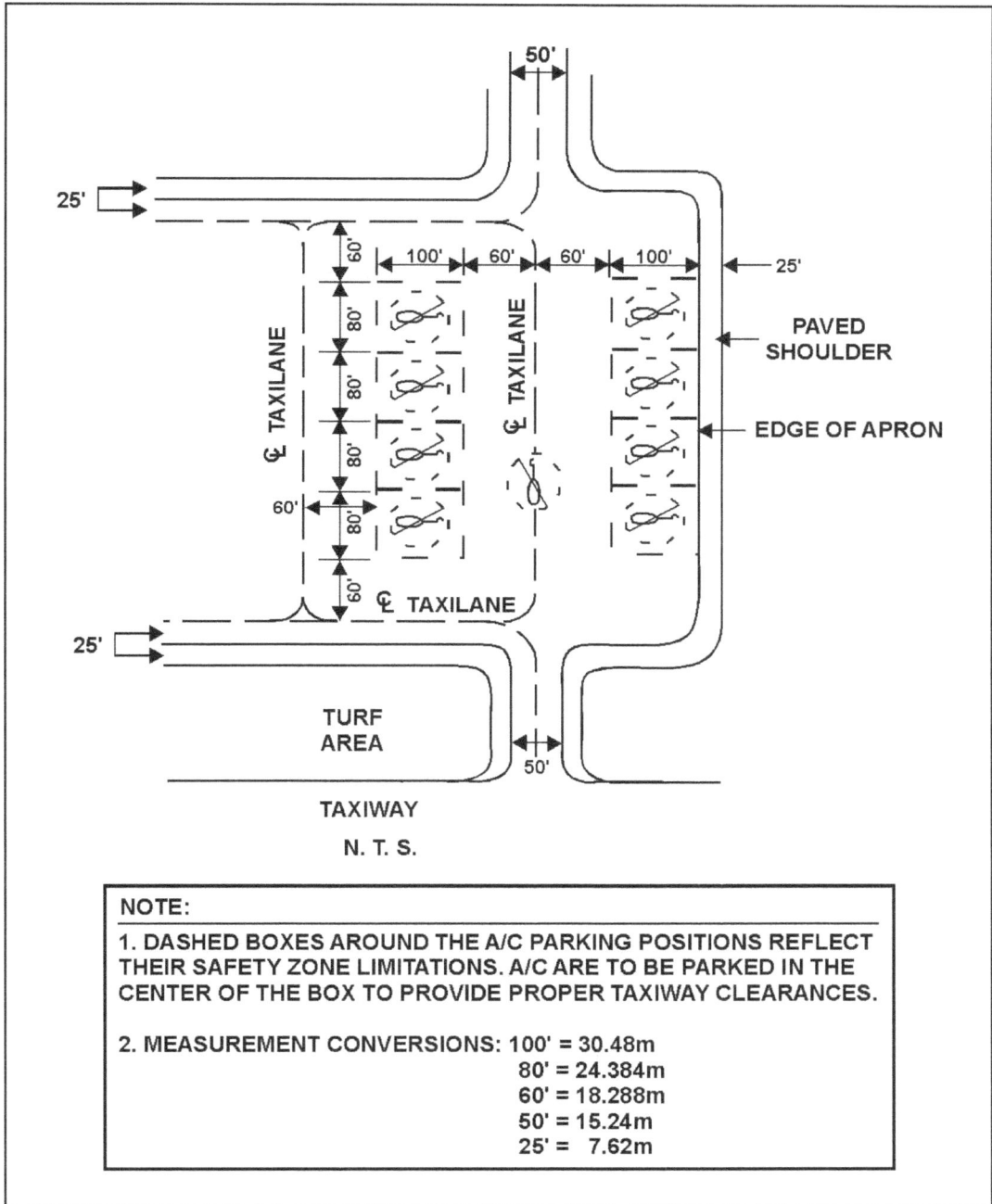

Figure 3-7. Type I parking for all rotary-wing aircraft (except CH-47)

NOTE:

1. DASHED BOXES AROUND THE A/C PARKING POSITIONS REFLECT THEIR SAFETY ZONE LIMITATIONS. A/C ARE TO BE PARKED IN THE CENTER OF THE BOX TO PROVIDE PROPER TAXIWAY CLEARANCES.

2. MEASUREMENT CONVERSIONS: 100' = 30.48m
                            80' = 24.384m
                            60' = 18.288m
                            50' = 15.24m
                            25' = 7.62m

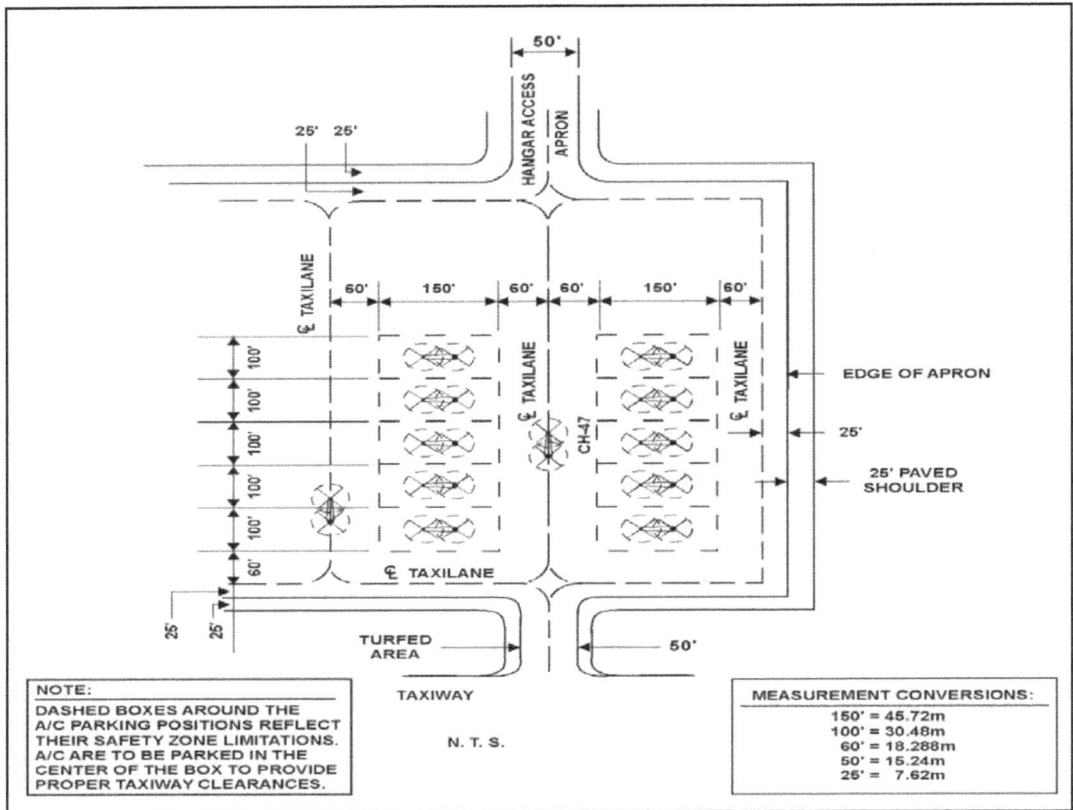

Figure 3-8. Type I parking for CH-47

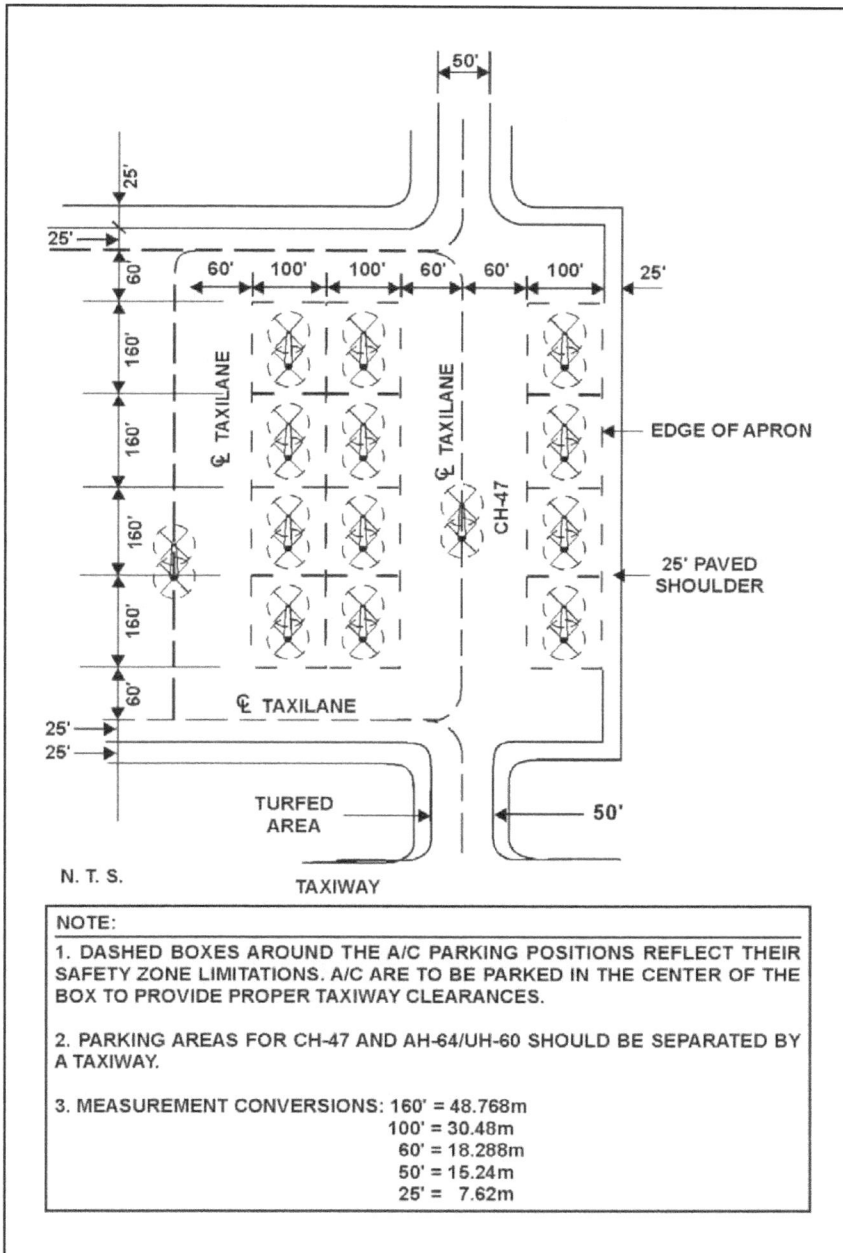

Figure 3-9. Type 2 parking for wheeled rotary-wing aircraft

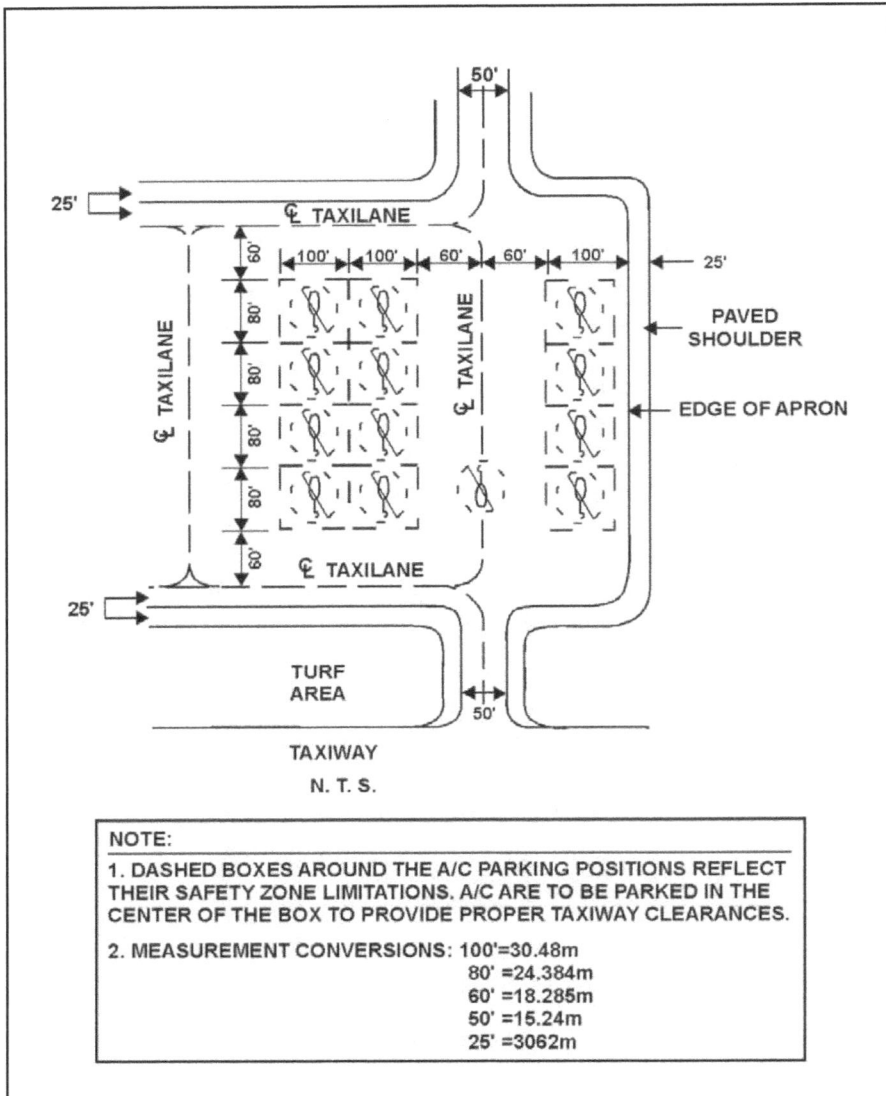

Figure 3-10. Type 2 parking for skid rotary-wing aircraft

SECTION IV – REFUEL, ARMAMENT, AND HAZARDOUS CARGO

REFUELING CONSIDERATIONS

3-72. Layout of aircraft parking locations and taxi lanes should consider aircraft taxiing routes when an aircraft is refueled. Refueling operations should not prevent an aircraft from leaving the parking apron. Two routes in and out of the apron may be required.

FIXED-WING AIRCRAFT

3-73. During refueling, active ignition sources such as sparks from ground support equipment or jet engines (aircraft) are prohibited from a zone around the aircraft. The Army and Air Force refer to this zone as the fuel servicing safety zone. The Navy and Marine Corps refer to this zone as the Refueling Safety Zone. The safety zone is the area within 15 meters (50 feet) of a pressurized fuel carrying servicing component (servicing hose, fuel nozzle, single-point receptacle, hydrant hose car, and ramp hydrant connection point) and 7.6 meters (25 feet) around aircraft fuel vent outlets. The fuel servicing safety zone is established and maintained during pressurization and movement of fuel. For additional information refer to Air Force T.O. 00-25-172. For Navy, also refer to MIL-HDBK-274.

ROTARY-WING AIRCRAFT

3-74. The safety zone for rotary-wing aircraft is the area 3 meters (10 feet) greater than the area bounded by the blades and tail of the aircraft. For additional information, refer to Air Force T.O. 00-25-172.

ARMAMENT PADS

3-75. Arm/disarm pads are used for arming aircraft immediately before takeoff and disarming (safing) weapons retained or not expended on their return.

LOCATION

3-76. Arm/disarm pads should be located adjacent to runway thresholds and sited such that armed aircraft are oriented in the direction of least populated areas or towards revetments. Barricades should be built around the ready ammunition supply area (RASA), basic load storage area, and rearm pads. Barricades should be at least 3 feet (0.9144 meters) thick to effectively reduce hazards from a fire or explosion.

3-77. Table 3-4 shows the minimum distances permitted between rearm points, RASAs, and nonammunition related activities that require safety distances. These distances are based on rotor clearances.

Table 3-3. Minimum safe distances (in meters/feet)

			Barricaded	*Unbarricaded*
From	**Rearm pad**			
	To	Rearm pad	30.48 – 54.864/100-180	30.48 – 54.864/100-180
		Buildings and aircraft	121.92/400	243.83/800
		Public highways	73.152/240	146.304/480
		POL storage or refuel facilities	137.16/450	243.83/800
From	**Ammunition storage area**			
	To	Rearm pad	22.86/75/	42.672/140
		Building and aircraft	153.924/505	307.848/1010
		Public highways	92.964/305	185.928/610
		POL storage or refuel facilities	15.24/50	307.848/1010

ARMAMENT PAD SETUP

3-78. Armament pad setup affects overall aircraft turnaround times. During combat missions, enough ammunition for at least one arming sequence should be placed on the armament pad before aircraft arrive and laid out in the order it will be loaded. A full load of ammunition must be ready to load in the event the aircraft has expended its entire initial load. Figure 3-11 shows two typical layouts for helicopter rearm points, and figure 3-12 shows a three-dimensional view of one plan.

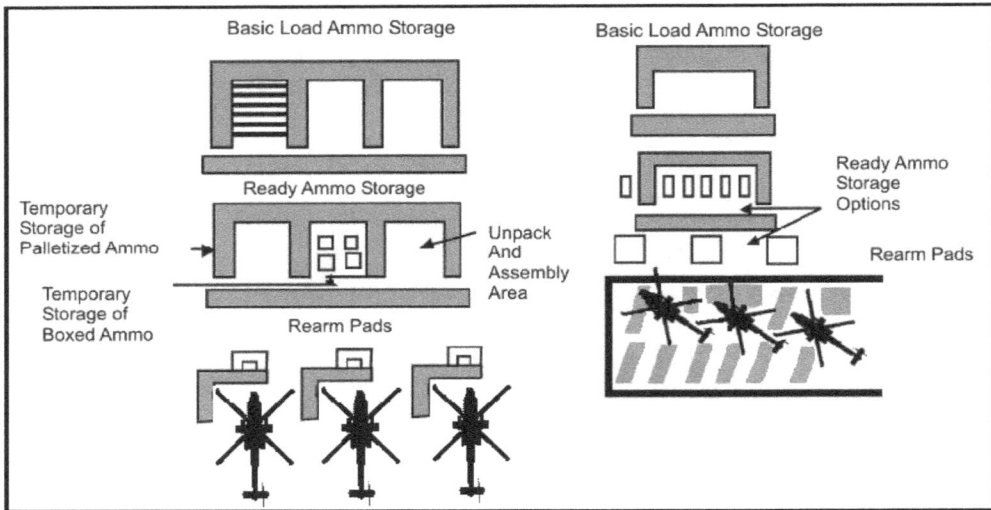

Figure 3-11.Two typical layouts for helicopter rearm points

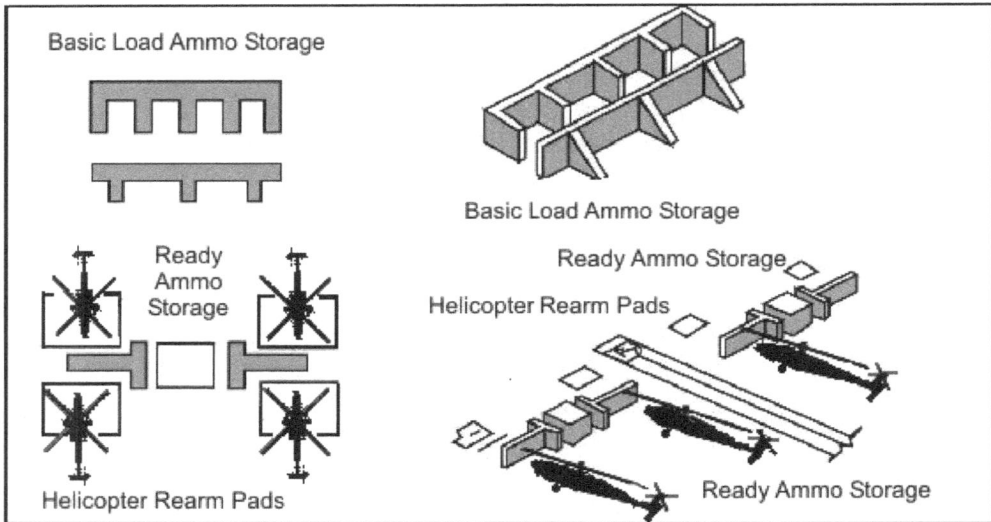

Figure 3-12. Three-dimensional view of a helicopter rearm point plan

HAZARDOUS CARGO/MATERIELS PADS

3-79. Hazardous cargo pads are paved areas for loading and unloading explosives and other hazardous cargo from aircraft. Hazardous cargo pads are required at facilities where existing aprons cannot be used for loading and unloading hazardous cargo.

HAZARDOUS CARGO PAD SETUP

3-80. Hazardous cargo pad setup is as follows:

- **Circular Pad.** At aviation facilities used by small cargo aircraft a circular pad shown in figure 3-13 is used.
- **Semi-Circular Pad.** At aviation facilities used by large cargo aircraft, aerial ports of embarkation, and APOD, a semi-circular pad as shown in figure 3-14 is used. This pad is adequate for aircraft up to and including a C-5.
- **Other Pad Size.** The geometric dimensions shown in figure 3-13 and figure 3-14 (page 3-25) are minimum requirements. Hazardous cargo pads may be larger in design if aircraft cannot maneuver on the pad.

3-81. An access taxiway is provided from the primary taxiway to the hazardous cargo pad. The taxiway should be designed for aircraft to taxi into the hazardous cargo pad under its own power.

3-82. All explosives locations, including locations where aircraft loaded with explosives are parked, must be sited per Department of Defense (DOD) Standard 6055.9 and applicable service explosives safety regulations.

3-83. Explosives site plans, approved through command channels to DOD, ensure minimal acceptable risk exists between explosives and other airfield resources. To prevent inadvertent ignition of electro-explosive devices (EEDs), separation between sources of electromagnetic radiation is required.

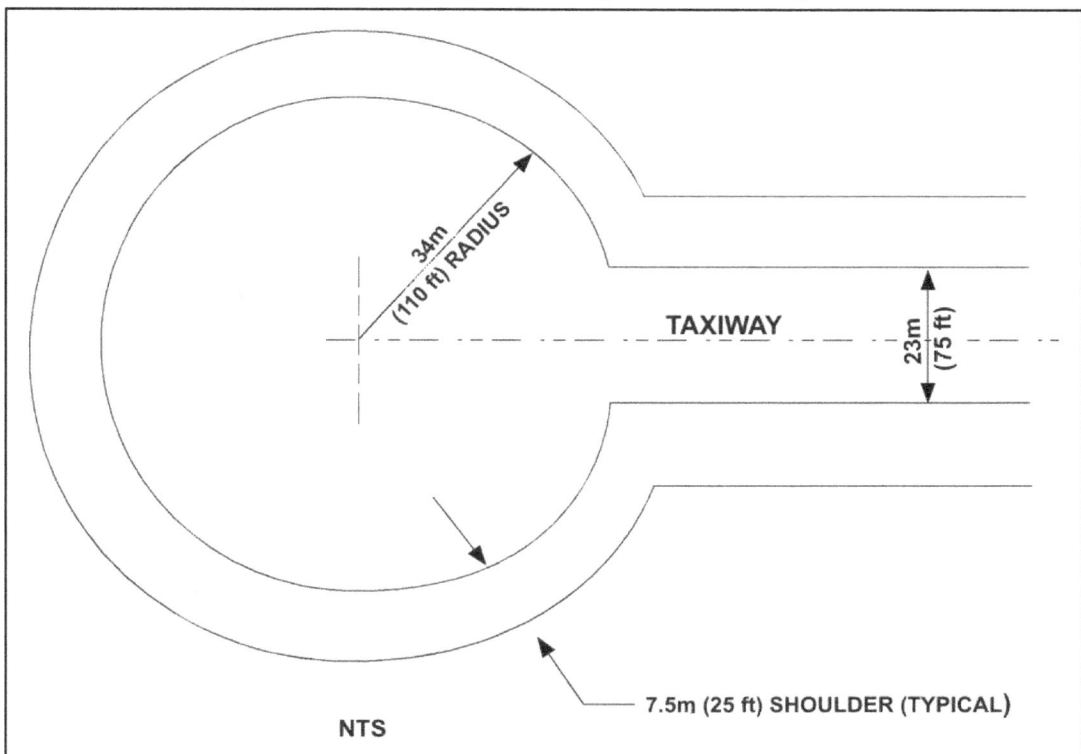

Figure 3-13. Sample of a circular pad for small cargo aircraft

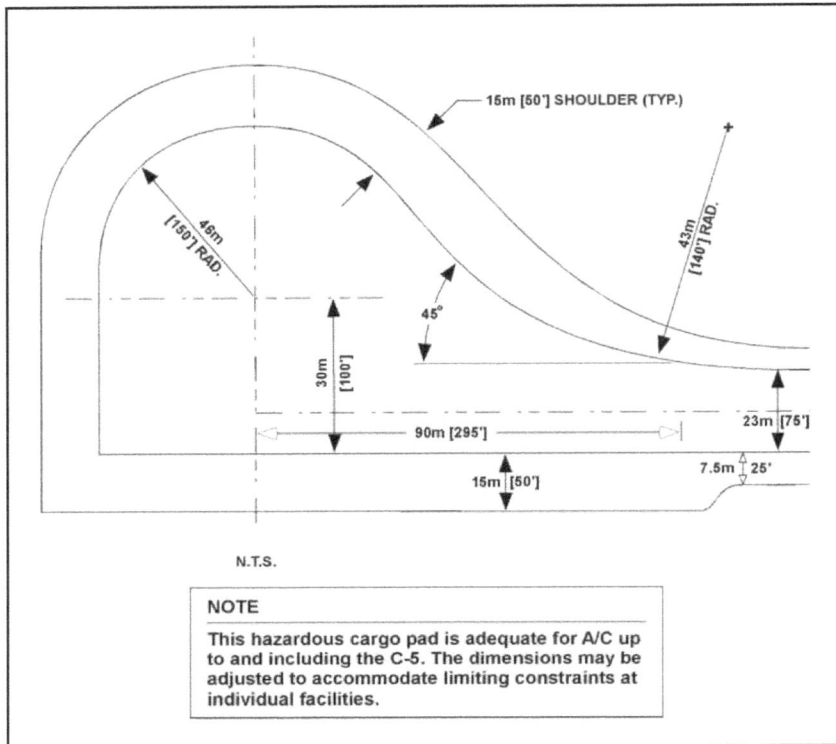

Figure 3-14. Sample of a semicircular pad for large cargo aircraft

Separation Distance Requirements

3-84. Minimum standards for separating explosives (explosion separation distances and quantity-distance [Q-D] relationships) loaded aircraft from runways, taxiways, inhabited buildings, and other loaded aircraft are established in AR 385-10, chapter 5 (Army), and Air Force manual (AFMAN) 91-201 (Air Force). These documents also establish Q-D relationships for separating related and unrelated potential explosion sites and explosive and nonexplosive exposed sites.

Prohibited Zones

3-85. Explosives, explosive facilities, and parked explosives-loaded aircraft (or those loading or unloading) are prohibited from being located in Accident Potential Zones I and II and clear zones as set forth in AR 385-10, chapter 6 and AFMAN 91-201.

Hazards of Electromagnetic Radiation to Electro-Explosive Devices

3-86. EED on aircraft are initiated electrically. Accidental firing of EED carried on aircraft initiated by stray electromagnetic energy is a possible hazard on an airfield. A large number of these devices are initiated by low levels of electrical energy and susceptible to unintentional ignition by many forms of direct or induced stray electrical energy, such as radio frequency energy from ground and airborne emitters (transmitters). Additional sources of stray electrical energy are—

- Lightning discharges.
- Static electricity.
- Triboelectric (friction-generated) effects.
- Operation of electrical and electronic subsystem onboard weapon systems.

Lightning Protection

3-87. Lightning protection must be installed on open pads used for manufacturing, processing, handling, or storing explosives and ammunition. Lightning protection systems must comply with DOD Standard 6055.9, AFMAN 88-9/technical manual (TM) 5-811-3, chapter 3, AFI 32-1065, and National Fire Protection Association (NFPA) 780. Aircraft loaded with explosives must be grounded at all times. Aircraft grounding is per applicable weapons systems technical orders.

SECTION V – NAVIGATIONAL AIDS AND FLIGHT INSPECTION

3-88. The potential for a major military contingency or natural disaster underlines the need to respond quickly to a military emergency. This necessitates advanced planning and the definition of operational requirements. In such circumstances, military flight inspection resources become critical in restoration of NAVAIDs. The ability to provide sustained flight inspection support for numerous and diverse requirements that may exist is predicated on the use of abbreviated flight inspection procedures. Flight inspections for restoration and commissioning of NAVAIDs depend greatly on the AOB's airfield management, air traffic, and COM/NAV maintenance support and preparations prior to the flight inspection.

EMERGENCY FLIGHT INSPECTIONS

3-89. The guidance, procedures, and tolerances contained in this section describe minimum facility performance standards for emergency military situations requiring deviation from normal standards. Basic flight inspection requirements and methods of taking measurements apply to the emergencies unless specific guidance or tolerances are given. Operational facilities using these procedures shall be reinspected to normal standards when circumstances permit.

AUTHORITY FOR ABBREVIATED FLIGHT INSPECTION PROCEDURES

3-90. Authority to implement these provisions may be exercised by either the military or FAA. When military authority determines an operational situation dictates application of these procedures and tolerances, the appropriate flight inspection activity and FAA Aviation System Standards Office (AVN) Manager, Flight Inspection Operations Division, AVN-200, shall be notified. Application to civil facilities is determined by appropriate FAA authority, who shall notify both AVN-200 and appropriate military authority. The Flight Inspection Operations Division, AVN-200, is responsible for issuing a General Notice and initiating a NOTAM regarding implementation of abbreviated procedures to provide facilities for emergency use.

TYPES AND PRIORITIES OF EMERGENCY FLIGHT INSPECTION

3-91. Only special and commissioning type flight inspections will be conducted under emergency conditions using the procedures in TM 95-225, section 104. After-accident flight inspections may also be conducted under emergency conditions; however, normal procedures shall be followed. Priorities shall be established by the component commander or his designated representative.

Preinspection Requirements

3-92. Prior to arriving on location, the AOB's airfield management element and COM/NAV section coordinate the following items for the flight inspector:
- Arrival time.
- Emergency operational requirements as defined by the terminal platoon leader.
- Airspace requirements for conducting the flight inspection profile.
- Anticipated support such as refueling and ground transportation for a theodolite operator.

3-93. The terminal platoon leader accomplishes the following actions prior to arrival of the flight inspection aircraft:

- Makes final determination regarding emergency operational requirements for the facilities and special instrument approach procedures (SIAPs) requiring flight inspection; is prepared to brief changes on initial contact.
- Coordinates airspace requirements and obtains necessary clearances from appropriate airspace control authorities for conducting the inspection.
- If required, designates and briefs the air traffic controller to work the flight inspection aircraft.
- If available, provides current facility data (FAA Form 8240-22 [Facility Data Sheet] in FAA Order 8240.52) for each facility to be inspected.

3-94. The ATC systems maintenance supervisor—

- Ensures adequate radio communications are available and operational.
- Assigns qualified maintenance personnel to support flight inspection of the equipment being inspected.
- Assists terminal platoon leader in completing FAA Form 8240-22 for each facility inspected.
- Arranges ground transportation for the theodolite operator if necessary.

Approach Procedures

3-95. The minimum flight inspection required to certify published SIAPs is inspection of the final and missed approach segments.

3-96. If an approach must be established, the flight inspector may be responsible for establishing final and missed approach procedures. Both segments of the procedure are flown and recorded to establish and document flyability, accuracy, reliability, and obstacle clearance. The flight inspector records the emergency SIAP procedures on the flight inspection report and provides the ATC supervisor with adequate detail for issuance of the NOTAM by the airfield management element.

3-97. The flight inspector determines, through visual evaluation, that the final and missed approach segments provide adequate terrain and obstacle clearance.

Facility Status and Notices to Airmen

3-98. The flight inspector ascertains from ATC the intended operational use of the facility. After completing the inspection, the flight inspector determines the facility status for emergency use and advises the ATC supervisor prior to departing the area.

3-99. The ATC supervisor ensures issuance of a NOTAM by the airfield management element. Unusable SIAPs, or portions thereof, are included in the NOTAM. The NOTAM for a civil facility must be issued as a NOTAM D to ensure information is made available using the most expeditious method.

3-100. NOTAMs that are lengthy and describe emergency-use NAVAIDs in great detail will not be issued. The flight inspector subsequently records the NOTAM text in the remarks section of the applicable flight inspection report.

3-101. The flight inspector has the authority and responsibility for determining whether a NAVAID can safely and adequately support operations intended under emergency conditions. However, the AOB commander has final authority and responsibility for operation of military facilities not part of an existing common system, and may elect to use those facilities for military missions. Additionally, the military may elect to use a military or civil NAVAID, which is part of a common system, even though that NAVAID is considered unusable by the flight inspector. In all such cases, the AOB commander is responsible for issuance of an appropriate NOTAM advising that the NAVAID is in operation "For Military Emergency Use Only" to support emergency operations.

Flight Inspection Documentation and Reports

3-102. Flight inspection recordings are retained until the facility is inspected using normal procedures and tolerances. In the event flight inspection equipment is inoperative or not available, flight inspections continue to meet emergency operational requirements until replacement or repair is practical. Under these circumstances, the flight inspection pilot and airborne electronic technician are jointly responsible for documenting all applicable data displayed by instrumentation at their crew duty positions. All such manually acquired data are identified in the remarks section of the flight inspection report. The facility/SIAP is reflown with operational flight inspection equipment when conditions permit.

3-103. Completion and distribution of flight inspection reports are secondary to the accomplishment of emergency flight inspection. After completing the inspection, the flight inspector passes the facility status to the ATC supervisor on an air traffic frequency. This suffices as the official report until the written report is completed and distributed.

3-104. The flight inspector ensures flight inspection reports are completed and submitted for processing. Each parameter specified in the emergency flight inspection procedures checklists contained herein is reported. Recordings and reports reflect the inspection was accomplished using **"MILITARY EMERGENCY AND NATURAL DISASTER FLIGHT INSPECTION PROCEDURES"**.

This page intentionally left blank.

Chapter 4
Joint Considerations

The formation of a major airfield requires a joint effort from its seizure or construction to its opening and daily operations. Each service possesses unique assets and capabilities contributing to the establishment and operation of theater airfields. AOBs normally are used to support theater Army airfield operations and may be tasked to provide support for joint and multinational operations at an austere landing site. Cooperation and coordination ensures that service-specific requirements are met, and joint air operations are safe, efficient, and provide the required support necessary to ensure overall success of the campaign plan.

SECTION I – AIRFIELD ASSESSMENT

4-1. Tentative enemy airfield sites are selected using maps and aerial photography, supplementing data from reports of aerial observers or intelligence sources. These sites may be undeveloped areas or operating enemy installations. For an undeveloped site, the object of reconnaissance is to verify or amend tentative selections and layouts, and to estimate the material, equipment, and troop requirements for the planned construction. If the area is a captured airfield, estimates of the engineering necessary to restore the airfield may be required.

Contents

PLANNING FACTORS

4-2. As a key theater asset, threats to the airfield are of prime concern. The types of survivability and vulnerability reduction measures required are determined early by planners. In any environment, aircraft on the ground must be protected, airfield systems must be kept operational, and logistics support must survive to ensure continual air operations. The threat will determine—

- How individual facilities and facility groups should be configured, dispersed, or concentrated.
- Whether utility plants can be centralized or dispersed.
- How much and what kind of protection will be required for parked aircraft.
- Whether vulnerability reduction measures (such as facility protection, camouflage, or concealment) are needed.

4-3. Surface area requirement estimations should include space for immediate development and contemplated expansion. Area requirements include—

- Mission.
- Number and type of aircraft.
- Length of stay.
- Size of airfield.
- Maintenance.
- Housing.

- Administration.
- Supply.
- Transportation.
- Security.

SECTION II – AIRFIELD SEIZURE/OPENING

4-4. An airfield seizure is executed to clear and control a designated airstrip. The purpose may be to allow follow-on airfield and air traffic management forces to conduct sustainment operations or to establish a lodgment to continue combat operations from that location. Airfields can be seized and occupied by friendly forces for a definite or indefinite period.

4-5. Requirements for seizure and subsequent securing of the airfield, and the introduction of follow-on forces depend heavily on the factors of METT-TC and the commander's concept of the operation.

PLANNING FACTORS

4-6. Certain factors must be considered when conducting the estimate for an airfield seizure.

- The key element of airfield seizure is surprise. Assault of the airfield should be conducted at night to maximize surprise, security, and protection of the force. Timing is critical; the assault should be executed so that the follow-on assault echelon (airdrop or airland) can also be delivered under the cloak of darkness.
- Enemy air defenses near the airfield and along aircraft approach and departure routes must be suppressed.
- The size of the airfield must be sufficient for landing and takeoff of aircraft to be used there. Minimum operating length determines how much of the airfield must be cleared.
- The configuration and condition of the airfield, including taxiways and parking, determines the maximum-on-ground capacity for aircraft at one time. This combined with offload/transload time estimates impacts directly on scheduling follow-on airflow into the airfield. Surface composition and condition and predicted weather conditions must permit the airfield to accept the required number of sorties without deteriorating the surface below minimum acceptable safety standards.
- The airfield location must facilitate follow-on operations. If transload operations must occur, the follow-on target must be within the range of the aircraft to be used. If the target is not in range, then forward area rearm/refuel assets must be available and positioned to support the follow-on operation.
- The airfield must be defensible initially with assault forces against any immediate threat and with planned follow-on forces against larger, coordinated counterattacks.

4-7. USAF combat control teams (CCTs) may be required to provide airspace management assistance as well as control of aircraft after landing (for example, parking locations and taxiing control). The CCT can be inserted ahead of the force as part of a joint airborne advance party; it can jump with the airborne assault or land with the first assault aircraft.

4-8. Engineer units should also accompany the assault force. Their task is to clear runways of obstacles. Special consideration is given to the type and quantity of obstacles on the runway. These obstacles have a major impact on engineer assets required by the task force, the time for clearance, and the planned time of arrival of airland sorties. To assist engineers, bulldozers and mine detectors (metallic and nonmetallic) can be dropped in the initial assault. Selected personnel can be tasked to jump-start disabled or airfield support vehicles required to assist the offload. Once the assault echelon has seized initial objectives, runway clearance teams (engineers, infantry, and other designated personnel) begin clearing or repairing the runway(s).

4-9. Certain objectives near the airfield and key terrain surrounding it (control towers, communications nodes, terminal guidance facilities) should be secured at the same time units are clearing the runways. This requirement increases the number of personnel designated to participate in the initial assault.

REHABILITATION OF CAPTURED AIRFIELDS

4-10. The decision to rehabilitate a captured enemy airfield and the decision as to type and construction standard of the rehabilitated field are Air Force and Army responsibilities. The work is ordinarily accomplished by a combat-heavy engineer battalion.

4-11. The engineer mission is to convert existing facilities, which are usually damaged, to the standard decided on by the Air Force and Army, with a minimum outlay of labor, equipment, and materials. Considerable discretion must be exercised in applying standard specifications to captured airfields. No large-scale relocation of facilities should be undertaken merely to conform to standard patterns if existing patterns serve the same purpose in a satisfactory manner. Sensible, existing substitutions and deviations from specified agreements must be recognized and accepted.

4-12. An appraisal of the damage to a captured field precedes the decision to rehabilitate it. Occasionally, it is necessary to expend more effort to restore a badly damaged airfield than to construct a new one. Installation damage includes war damage by our forces securing the airfield. Complete destruction of an airfield is a major undertaking; therefore, the enemy will likely resort to one or more of the following less destructive measures:

- Placing delayed-action bombs, mines, and booby traps.
- Demolishing drainage systems and pavements.
- Placing obstacles and debris in the runway.
- Plowing turfed areas.
- Flooding surfaced areas.
- Blowing craters in runways, taxiways, and hardstands.
- Demolishing buildings, utilities, and similar installations.

4-13. Commanders should plan for worst case scenarios and assume these damages were inflicted when conducting an assessment of the airfield. Use the following criteria to prioritize rehabilitation operations:

- Establish minimum facilities and utilities to include the establishment of an operating strip for immediate use by friendly aircraft. This includes removing unexploded ordinance (UXO), delayed-action bombs, mines, and booby traps from the traffic areas; clearing debris from those areas and repairing craters on the runway and taxiway surfaces. Promptly repair the drainage system. Concentrate runway work first on a minimum operating strip; second, on an access route; and finally, on other traffic areas. Give early attention to the provision of suitable sanitary and water facilities. Training Circular (TC) 5-340, chapter 7 provides detailed information regarding these areas.
- The second priority is improvements to the minimum operational facilities. Restore remaining runways, taxiways, hardstands, parking aprons, access and service roads, and fuel and bomb storage areas before rehabilitating other less vital facilities.
- The third priority is the repair of buildings such as the control tower, operational buildings, crew shelters, communication centers, and other maintenance facilities.
- The fourth priority is the camouflage of installations; the restoration of utilities (making use of any utility map and any available citizen labor familiar with the installation's utilities); and the repair or establishment of bathing, dining, and recreational facilities. A complete cleanup of the grounds, including the removal of debris and seeding and sodding, is the last phase of a rehabilitation project.

DAMAGE REPAIR RESPONSIBILITIES FOR AIRFIELDS

4-14. The immediate, emergency-damage recovery of an airfield is considered to be the minimum work required to permit aircraft to land and take off. The Air Force is primarily responsible for the emergency runway repair. This includes the emergency repair of paved surfaces or rapid runway repair. This is accomplished through the employment of Air Force base civil engineering troop assets; prime base engineer emergency forces (Prime BEEF) and rapid engineering deployable heavy operational repair squadrons engineering (RED HORSE) units. The Army is responsible for semipermanent construction beyond emergency repair of the air base and, upon request, emergency repairs that exceed Air Force capabilities. Joint service regulation AR 4 15-30/Air Force Regulation (AFR) 93-10 specifies repair responsibilities for each service.

Army Responsibilities

4-15. The Army provides engineer support to the Air Force overseas. It ensures units are equipped, manned, and trained to support Air Force needs. This support includes—

- Assisting in emergency repair of war damaged air bases where requirements exceed the Air Force's organic repair capability.
- Repairing and restoring damaged air bases with beyond-emergency repairs.
- Developing engineer designs, plans and materials to meet Air Force needs as agreed upon by the Air Force. Where practicable, designs are based on the AFCS.
- Supplying construction materials and equipment, except for that provided by the Air Force.
- Upon request, assisting within their capabilities in the removal of UXO declared safe by explosive ordnance disposal personnel and limited damage assessment operations.
- Managing and supervising the repair and restoration of war damage performed by Army personnel.

4-16. The Air Force base commander sets the priorities for air base repair.

Air Force Responsibilities

4-17. The Air Force provides military troop engineering support from its resources and ensures that units are equipped, manned, and trained adequately to support its needs. This support includes—

- Emergency repair of war damage to airfields.
- Organizing host-nation support (overseas).
- Force beddown of units and weapon systems, excluding Army base development responsibilities.
- Operation and maintenance of facilities and installations.
- Crash rescue and fire suppression.
- Managing force beddown and the emergency repair of war damage.
- Supplying material and equipment to perform its engineering mission.
- Providing logistical support to the Army for all classes of supply except Classes II, V, VII, and IX.
- Conducting damage assessment and removal of UXO.
- Providing chemical, biological, radiological, and nuclear (CBRN) collective shelters and establishing and operating personnel and equipment decontamination sites for the air base and the Army. There are shortages of these assets on air bases, and support to Army units may be limited.

4-18. Airfield support agreements may be established in some theaters between the Air Force and the host nation where airfield damage repair (ADR) support capability exists. These host nation support agreements may include equipment, materials, and manpower assets.

4-19. For a detailed description of personnel, equipment, and material requirements and critical path schedules for repair of runways cratered by high-explosive bombs, refer to AFR 93-2. For a detailed discussion of general ADR, refer to TC 5-340.

SECTION III – AIRFIELD OPERATIONS BATTALION AUGMENTATION REQUIREMENTS

4-20. AOB's operating theater airfields can provide services such as airfield management, safety and standards, flight operations, flight dispatch, and ATC. However, these services under one command are a new capability for the Army. To provide a full range of airfield services, AOBs rely on TSC support for—

- Weather support.
- Refuel.
- Airfield crash rescue and firefighting.
- Aircraft maintenance.
- Cargo handling.

UNITED STATES AIR FORCE WEATHER SUPPORT

4-21. The global mission of the United States Armed Forces requires an extensive network of weather observers, analysts, and forecasters. The network consists of the national weather services of each friendly country, our own National Oceanographic and Atmospheric Administration, and weather or environmental units within the U.S. Army, Navy, Air Force, and Marine Corps.

4-22. Meteorological services of each country provide the basic observation network and related weather facilities in the country. Current and future global weather conditions can be forecast by exchanging data among nations. Peacetime cooperation among nations for weather services provides global and hemispheric analyses in support of military operations anywhere in the world. During wartime, meteorological control and other security restrictions may drastically limit the availability of other national and indigenous weather information. U.S. military weather services and units are specialized organizations with worldwide capabilities structured to satisfy unique military requirements. They exchange weather data with national weather services and have access to national and international weather databases. Characteristics of the military weather services are—

- Mobility.
- Responsiveness to command.
- Combat readiness.

4-23. Weather support is most effective when weather personnel know the mission, organization, capabilities, plans, and procedures of the Army units they support. The demands placed on weather support organizations are more realistic when Army personnel understand the basic principles of weather forecasting and recognize the capabilities, limitations, and support requirements of the weather team (WETM).

4-24. Weather support for Army tactical operations is based on the following principles:

- Tactical units must consider weather effects during all planning and operational phases, including deployment and employment.
- Commanders must consider favorable and unfavorable weather conditions to determine the best course of action to accomplish the mission.
- Accuracy of weather forecasts depends on the density and timeliness of weather observations. All weather observations, particularly those taken by Army personnel forward of the division TOC, must have high priority and be rapidly transmitted to a USAF WETM.
- Timely, reliable primary and alternate communications must be provided.
- Because of continually changing atmospheric conditions, weather information is highly perishable. Weather observations and forecasts must be monitored and updated continually.

AIR FORCE RESPONSIBILITIES

4-25. The Air Force provides the bulk of weather support required by the Army. AR 115-10/AFR 105-3 specifies each service's functions and responsibilities associated with that support. The USAF Chief of Staff, through the AMC Air Weather Service (AWS), provides—

- Weather personnel with the technical training and skills necessary to support the Army.
- Direct weather support for theater, divisions, separate brigades, aviation brigades, regiments, and groups according to jointly agreed upon tactical doctrine and operational support concepts.
- Weather training for Army personnel assigned to take limited surface weather observations in support of Air Force forecasting operations or Army ATC operations.
- Possible effects of weather on systems, tactics, and operations based on critical threshold values identified by the Army.
- Weather observations, forecasts, staff support, and timely warnings of expected weather that may adversely affect operations or that could be a hazard to personnel or materiel.
- Weather support products for use in soil trafficability and hydrographical prediction.
- Unique and specialized meteorological observations and forecasts of data elements not included in standard surface weather observations or critical values on request.
- Climatological support for tactical missions, IPB, and tactical decision aids.

ARMY RESPONSIBILITIES

4-26. WETMs supporting Army tactical organizations depend on the supported Army unit totally for sustainment. This support includes—

- Food service.
- Maintenance.
- Supply.
  - Class I – Rations.
  - Class II – Clothing.
  - Class III – POL.
  - Class IV – Construction.
  - Class V – Ammunition.
  - Class VI – Personal demand items.
  - Class VII – Major end items.
  - Class VIII – Medical.
- Other sustainment functions required by WETMs.
- Administrative support.

4-27. AR 115-10/AFR 105-3 establishes support responsibilities. The Air Force provides specialized meteorological equipment, and the maintenance and supplies required to support it.

REFUEL SERVICES

4-28. The petroleum group is the principal organization responsible for bulk fuel distribution. It is assigned to the TSC and may have a petroleum supply battalion attached to an ASG. AOBs receive their bulk supply of jet propulsion fuel type 8 through the area support command. The AOB relies on the TSC to provide aircraft refuel capability. These services may come through internal assets if available or from the following:

- Contractor support.
- Local nationals.
- Host nation capabilities.

CRASH/RESCUE AND FIREFIGHTING OPERATIONS

4-29. Aircraft rescue firefighting operations include aircraft incidents and accidents, medical evacuation (MEDEVAC), search and rescue, refuel/defuel, and maintenance standby operations.

FIREFIGHTING PERSONNEL

4-30. Personnel provide fire-prevention and fire-protection services for deployed forces in stability and support operations. The teams are used when HN fire-protection support cannot provide adequate protection. The teams protect internal and external (HN and other U.S. services) Army assets. They maintain fire-protection equipment, advise higher commanders of fire-defense plans, and train auxiliary firefighters as required. There are three types of firefighting teams: engineer firefighting headquarters (LA) team, engineer firefighting firetruck (LB) team, and engineer firefighting water truck (LC) team. They are designed to provide task-oriented support, depending on the tactical and logistical considerations involved.

Firefighting Headquarters Team

4-31. An LA team provides C2 and administrative support for three to seven firefighting teams and coordinates engineer firefighting activities within a TO. When an LA team is not deployed, the senior firefighter of an LB or LC team provides C2. Firefighting teams depend on the unit to which they are assigned or attached for supply, food, health, religious, finance, communication-equipment-repair, legal, and administrative services.

4-32. The LA team is assigned to theater Army, corps, or division and exercises operational command over all firefighting teams assigned to its AO. LA team capabilities include—

- Planning firefighting programs for a TO.
- Supervising rescue and firefighting operations during aircraft crash incidents, structural fires, vehicle emergencies, natural-cover fires, and emergency response during hazardous material (HAZMAT) incidents.
- Planning and conducting fire-prevention operations, HAZMAT emergencies, and initial fire ground investigations.
- Coordinating resupply of firefighting assets, agents, self-contained breathing apparatus, and fuel.
- Coordinating mutual aid with other services and HN fire-protection assets.
- Providing maintenance support for technical firefighting equipment (military adaptation of commercial items [MACI] firetruck).

Firefighting Teams

4-33. These teams perform the operational task of firefighting within their AO. Senior firefighting personnel assigned to an LB or LC team that deploys without a headquarters team are responsible for that team. If several teams are assigned together, the senior firefighter takes charge of the teams and performs the functions of the headquarters team.

4-34. LB and LC teams depend on the headquarters firefighting team for C2 and maintenance of the MACI firetruck. When that support is not available, the senior firefighter assumes C2 responsibility. Assigned to theater Army, corps, or divisions, LB and LC teams are allocated as follows: one per air traffic services company and one per headquarters and headquarters company of the corps support group; two per petroleum supply company and two per petroleum-pipeline and terminal-operating company. The teams—

- Provide 24 hours of fire protection and personnel rescue, and administer first aid.
- Implement a fire-protection program for the logistics-storage area, intermediate staging base, FOB, and airfields and major facilities. Such facilities include but are not limited to petroleum tank farms, petroleum-distribution sites, open and closed warehouse facilities or general warehouses, and enemy prisoner of war and civilian internee camps.
- Fight aviation fires and extricate personnel and equipment from crashed aircraft.

- Provide firefighting protection against grass or brush fires within their assigned area of responsibility when augmented with combat or construction engineer Soldiers.
- Provide 6,000 gallons of water per trip to support the MACI firetruck.

4-35. An LC team identifies all bodies of water that may be used to combat a fire or resupply empty firefighting vehicles. It then develops a plan identifying the locations and equipment needed to use these water sources. The sources should be within a camp's perimeter or within a 2-mile radius. Sources will be plotted on an AO map located in the airspace information center (AIC).

AIRCRAFT CRASH OPERATIONS

4-36. An aircraft crash/rescue team provides support to Army aviation, and Air Force, Navy, Marine, allied, and civil aviation assets, in support of Army operations. The types of support include crash/rescue, emergency evacuation, and basic life support.

4-37. The standard requirement for crash/rescue operations will be a minimum of one LB team and one LC team. Aircraft that are over 10,000 pounds have a normal fuel load over 400 gallons, or an average load of 12 or more persons will require two LB teams and one LC team, as a minimum. Additional LB teams can be assigned, if available.

AIRCRAFT PREFIRE PLANS

4-38. Firefighters encounter many different types of aircraft in a TO. The armament and hazards of these aircraft can be varied, extensive, and quite lethal. Firefighters must acquire and maintain knowledge of the aircraft particular to their AO. A copy of TO 00-105E-9 should be available to Code of Federal Regulations crews. This manual contains information on most FW and rotary-wing aircraft, crash/rescue data, and aircraft specifications for all services.

4-39. Prefire plans for aircraft crash/rescue operations require more flexibility than prefire plans for structural fires. Because the exact crash location is unknown, units should only make general plans as to likely crash sites. When developing prefire plans, consider the following factors relating to your airfield:

- Location.
- Mission.
- Climate.
- Terrain.

4-40. Prefire plans should include information on the different types of aircraft handled at an installation. The control tower can obtain specific information (number of personnel, amount of fuel, amount and type of ordnance onboard, nature of an emergency) at the time of the emergency.

4-41. Weather, terrain, runway conditions, amount of available equipment and remaining fuel, and crash location are some factors that govern placing equipment at an aircraft's crash operation. Prefire plans can only cover general placement procedures and should allow for flexibility, based on the situation. Other factors to consider include—

- Aircraft's landing speed.
- Wind direction and speed.
- Aircraft's stopping distance.

4-42. Prefire plans should also include provisions for acquiring additional equipment.

SECTION IV – AIRFIELD DEVELOPMENT

ENGINEER RESPONSIBILITIES

4-43. When executing emergency restoration plans, engineer units receive detailed operational requirements from the supported commander. The engineer commander is concerned with site reconnaissance, location, alignment recommendations, airfield design and construction, and the support facilities available. The engineer is usually furnished standard designs for the type and capacity of the airfield required. However, these designs must often be altered to meet time and material limitations or limitations imposed by local topography, area, or obstructions. The engineer in charge of construction may alter designs within the limits prescribed by the headquarters directing construction; however, major changes must be approved by the headquarters before work begins. The following are standard design requirements for most airfield construction or restoration missions:

- Design of drainage system structures.
- Geometric design of runway, taxiways, and hardstands (including overruns, blast areas, and turnarounds).
- Selection of soils found in cuts and use of soil to improve subgrade.
- Compaction or stabilization requirements of the subgrade.
- Determination of type and thickness of the base and surface courses.
- Selection of grade to minimize earthwork while still meeting specifications.
- Design of access and service roads.
- Design of ammunition and POL storage areas; NAVAIDs; hardstands; maintenance and warm up aprons; corrosion control facilities; control towers; airfield lighting; and other facilities.

BARE BASE AIRFIELDS (AIR FORCE)

4-44. A bare base airfield is a site with a usable runway, a taxiway, parking areas, and a source of water that can be made potable. It must be capable of supporting assigned aircraft and providing other mission-essential resources, such as a logistical support and services infrastructure composed of people, facilities, equipment, and supplies. This concept requires mobile facilities, utilities, and support equipment that can be rapidly deployed and installed.

4-45. Undeveloped real estate must be transformed into an operational air base virtually overnight. In today's world, the concept of the bare base is more important than ever before.

4-46. While many foreign countries resist development of major fixed installations on their soil, these underdeveloped nations may have runways, taxiways, and air terminal facilities that could be offered to our forces during contingency situations.

4-47. There are roughly 1,200 in the free world that could support air operations, although many bare bases are limited and inadequate. Since most of these underdeveloped nations are subject to aggression, the military must be able to deploy and operate from their facilities.

4-48. During contingency operations, efficient and effective use of limited airfield capacity and resources is often critical to a successful military response. The task is complicated when foreign airfields are host to a variety of allied military, nongovernmental organizations (NGOs), and commercial air activities. To achieve a unity of effort of airfield operations, there should always be a senior airfield authority (SAA) appointed for each airfield. The SAA is an individual designated by the joint force commander to be responsible for the control, operation, and maintenance of an airfield to include runways, associated taxiways, parking ramps, land, and facilities whose proximity affect airfield operations. This has traditionally been an Air Force mission; however, with the airfield management and operations capability now in AOBs, the joint force commander may designate them as the senior airfield authority based on airfield mission and the assets available.

ORGANIZATIONS

Contingency Response Group

4-49. Today's mobility concept is to rapidly deploy a force, complete with shelters and support facilities, capable of independently supporting and launching sustained combat operations with the same independence as fixed theater installations. The organization at the heart of the Air Force response is the contingency response group (CRG). Their mission is to assess, open, and initially operate airfields. The group consists of a standardized force module dedicated to the airfield opening task. This module includes a tailored selection of all forces needed after seizure, or handoff from seizure forces, to assess an airfield, establish initial air mobility C2, and operate the flow of air mobility into and out of that airfield. CRGs may open an airfield for the Air Force, another service, or a coalition partner. To ensure continuity of operations, CRGs should coordinate planning and agreements with the theater commander Air Force/joint force air component commander staff.

Contingency Response Element

4-50. The contingency response element (CRE) is a mobile organization responsible for providing continuous onsite air mobility operations management. Commanded by a commissioned officer, CREs deploy to provide air mobility mission support when C2, mission reporting, and/or other support functions at the destination do not meet operational requirements. CREs also provide aerial port, logistics, maintenance, weather, medical, and intelligence services, as necessary. CRE size is based on projected operations flow and local conditions.

Airfield Survey Team

4-51. Each CRG possesses an airfield survey team as part of their capability. These personnel are trained and equipped to assess the capabilities of the airfield and its supporting facilities. They relay that information to the appropriate authorities who deploy any needed augmentation or engineer forces.

REQUIREMENTS

4-52. The assumption is that joint tactical forces will continue to have a bare-base requirement to conduct sustained air operations on a worldwide basis. This requires the use of joint assets in the management and operation of theater-level airfields as determined by the joint force commander and coordinated between the service organizations charged with the operation of theater airfields. Written agreements such as joint manning documents or support requirements may be necessary to effect coordination between the services.

4-53. It is important in the preliminary planning stage to know the location of existing facilities and utilities. As a result, any layouts, drawings, or aerial photographs are vitally needed. As equally important are the lengths and widths of the runway, taxiways, ramps, and aprons. Commanders must answer the following questions:

- Does runway lighting exist? If so, is it adequate?
- Is there a requirement for aircraft arresting barriers?
- What kinds of water sources are available?
- Does the water come from a well, river, lake, or ocean? What is the water temperature?
- How far away is the water source?
- Is the site being developed using hard or soft-wall shelters? (If the answer is soft wall shelters, latrines will be field expedient.)

PART TWO

Aviation Unit Operations

Chapter 5

Fundamentals

The specific organization of an aviation battalion depends on several factors including the unit's primary mission and official table of organization and equipment (TOE). The plans and operations section is the nerve center of the aviation battalion. Operations personnel coordinate activities and work directly with all other staff sections. Aviation unit operations control unit missions, daily operations, flight operations, and training. This chapter discusses fundamentals of the basic operations organization, principal mission focus, and capabilities of operations personnel.

SECTION I – ORGANIZATION AND STAFF

5-1. The deployment of theater level airfield management forces may not always reside at all airfields within the TO. The CAB or its aviation battalions may be required to conduct limited airfield management tasks in areas where primacy of effort is weighted for Army aviation operations. In this capacity, a member of the aviation brigade or battalion staff may be designated as the senior airfield authority with the task of integrating tenant units such as military intelligence operating

Contents

unmanned aerial systems or other aviation forces operating from the same airfield. Airfield management functions may be limited in scope and could include—

- Use and coordination of airfield services/facilities.
- Development of airfield procedures and terminal airspace.
- Coordination of construction and expansion efforts for the airfield.
- Establishment of airfield preaccident plan.
- Integration of aviation support into base defensive measures.
- Dissemination of airfield NOTAMs.

5-2. The flight battalions as directed by the CAB commander may share these responsibilities. Figure 5-1 (page 5-1) depicts a typical battalion aviation unit operations organization. The aviation unit operations approved structure will be determined by the modified table of organization and equipment (MTOE).

Personal Staff

Commander
CSM
Chaplain
XO

Special Staff

Chemical Officer
Flight Surgeon
Safety Officer
Standardization Officer

Coordinating Staff

S-1
S-2
S-3
S-4
S-6

S-3 Section
Avn LNO Element
S-4 Section

TACOPS
TAC CP
AMO

MOC

AMO - aviation materiel officer
CSM - command sergeant major
LNO - liaison officer
MOC - medical operations cell
S-1 - personnel staff officer
S-2 - intelligence staff officer
S-3 - operations staff officer

S-4 - logistics staff officer
S-6 - command, control, communications, and
　　　and computer operations (C4 OPS) staff officer
TAC CP - tactical command post
TACOPS - tactical operations
XO - executive officer

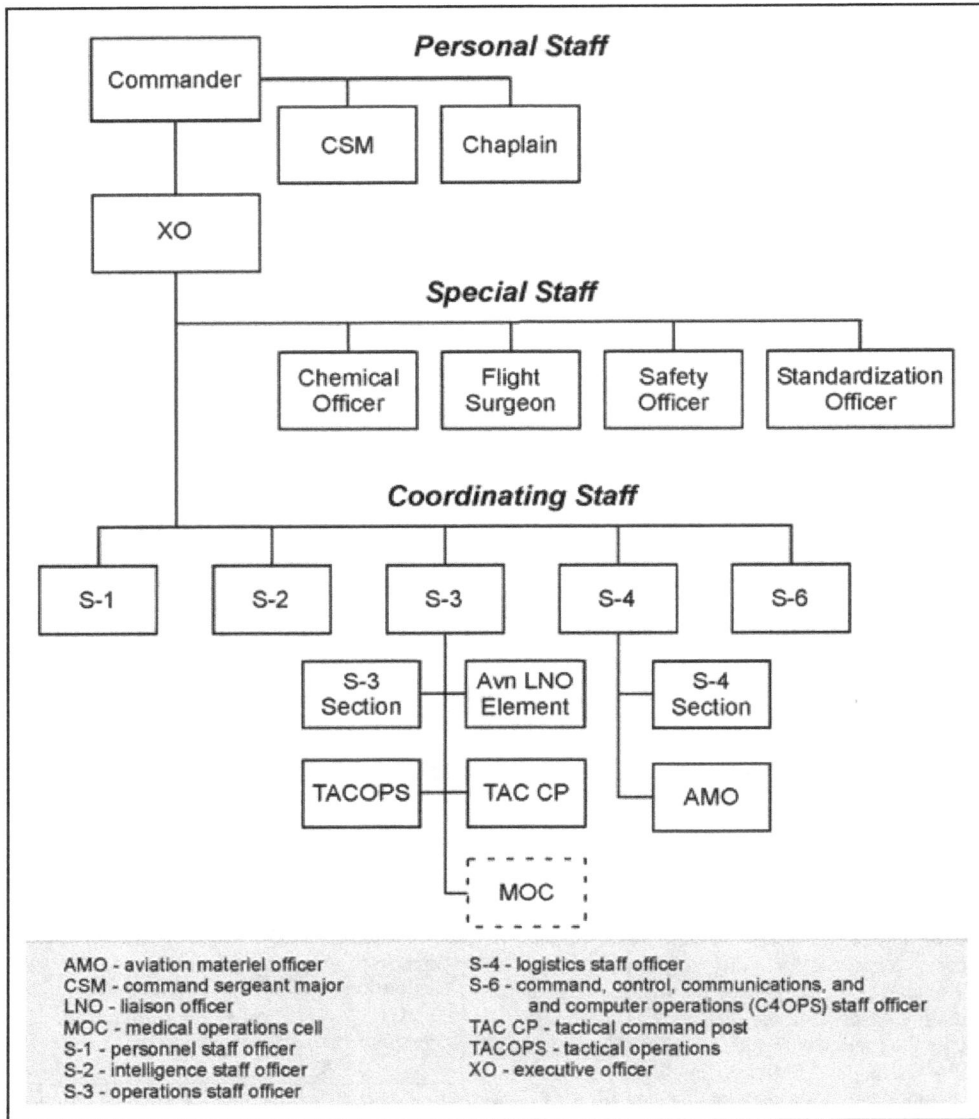

Figure 5-1. Battalion aviation unit operations organization

OPERATIONS STAFF OFFICER

5-3.　The operations staff officer (S-3) is responsible for matters pertaining to operational employment, training, and mission execution of battalion and supporting elements. The S-3 monitors the battle; ensures necessary assets are in place when and where required; develops the intelligence, surveillance, and reconnaissance plan; and anticipates developing situations. The S-3 maintains close coordination with the logistics staff officer (S-4) and personnel staff officer (S-1) for logistics and personnel statuses.

SENIOR AVIATION OPERATIONS SERGEANT

5-4. The operations noncommissioned officer in charge (NCOIC) obtains training information, coordinates taskings and training, supervises enlisted personnel, and compiles reports. He should be a graduate of the battle staff noncommissioned officer (NCO) and Joint Firepower Control courses. The operations NCOIC is responsible for—

- Establishing the main command post (CP) or tactical command post, (TAC CP), serving as the key enlisted member of the quartering party to establish CPs.
- Planning, coordinating, and supervising the emplacement of Army Battle Command System and communication systems throughout the CP.
- Establishing CP manning, shift schedules, and CP operational guidelines/SOPs.
- Conducting or directing enlisted training of all operations personnel.
- Providing tactical and technical expertise regarding aviation operations.
- Assisting with the preparation of operation orders and plans.
- Maintaining daily staff journals.
- Monitoring current operations and assisting the battle captain as appropriate.

OPERATIONS SECTION

5-5. The S-3 section maintains routine reporting, coordinates activities of liaison personnel, and plans ahead. The S-3 section produces orders for battalion operations (including recovery of personnel) and ensures procedures are in place to resolve complexities posed by different communications systems, Army Tactical Command and Control Systems (ATCCS), and connectivity with aircraft.

FLIGHT OPERATIONS OFFICER

5-6. The commander may designate a battalion flight operations officer. NCOs and flight operations specialists assist the flight operations officer. His responsibilities include—

- Monitoring and briefing applicable portions of SPINS and the ATO relevant to operations.
- Providing relevant ACMs to mission aircrews.
- Maintaining airspace overlay.
- Establishing and maintaining flight following net for unit aircraft, when required.
- Coordinating ATS requirements.
- Maintaining the aircrew information reading file.
- Maintaining the flying-hour program and individual flight record folders.

TACTICAL OPERATIONS OFFICER

5-7. The tactical operations (TACOPS) officer advises the battalion commander and staff on appropriate aircraft survivability equipment (ASE) techniques and procedures for each mission. He should be included in all aviation mission planning. The TACOPS officer can serve as the other crewmember for the battalion commander or S-3. Other responsibilities include, but are not limited to—

- Conducting the ASE/early warning portion of the risk management process.
- Integrating the unit's operational plan into the theater airspace structure.
- Assisting with development of unit tactics, techniques, and procedures.
- Managing the organization's personnel program.
- Assisting in the military decisionmaking process (MDMP), CAS, and fire support (FS) planning.
- Operating the battalion AMPS.

AVIATION MASTER GUNNER

5-8. The battalion master gunner manages helicopter gunnery training and sustainment while deployed in theater. He also assists the TACOPS in selection of weapons and employment techniques during the mission planning process. In addition, the battalion master gunner is a primary advisor to the commander for the gunnery training program. He assists the S-3 in forecasting and allocating ammunition and monitors gunnery training device usage. He also develops gunnery training to include realistic target arrays and coordinates scheduling with local range-control officials. During training events, the master gunner serves as the primary scorer/evaluator on unit live-fire ranges. The master gunner works with the armament officer ensuring the readiness of the unit's helicopter armament.

CHEMICAL OFFICER

5-9. The chemical officer advises the commander on CBRN operations, decontamination, smoke, obscurants, and flame. The chemical officer works directly for the S-3 and is responsible for integrating CBRN into all aspects of operations. The chemical officer may have other S-3 section responsibilities, and can act as an assistant S-3 or battle captain when directed.

AVIATION OPERATIONS SERGEANT

5-10. The aviation operations sergeant is concerned with the technical aspects of flight operations. He also acts as the operations platoon sergeant. The duties of the flight operations sergeant are to—
- Assist the flight operations officer.
- Coordinate mission requirements.
- Requisition FLIPs.
- Assist aircrews in processing flight plans and manifests.
- Ensure the availability of current flight and weather information.
- Supervise the maintenance of individual flight logs and records and operations maps and charts. (Printed maps are required for display even though digital systems may depict flight area information).
- Ensure that personnel observe OPSEC procedures when using communications equipment.
- Supervise the work of subordinates in installing, operating, and/or maintaining platoon and/or section vehicles and equipment.
- Ensure that the support provided is timely.
- Assist flight operations officer on flying-hour reports.

AVIATION OPERATIONS SPECIALIST

5-11. The senior aviation operations sergeant or the aviation operations sergeant supervises the operations of the aviation operations specialist. The duties of the aviation operations specialist are to—
- Update the NOTAM board.
- Interpret and process flight plans.
- Maintain individual flight record folders.
- Post current flight and weather information.
- Maintain the aircrew and aircraft status boards.
- Maintain functional files and type correspondence pertaining to operations.
- Maintain and operate assigned vehicles and equipment.
- Initiate search and rescue procedures for overdue aircraft.
- Post changes to the aircrew reading file.
- Issue, receive, and inventory items as required by the unit SOP.

TACTICAL COMMAND POST

5-12. The TAC CP is established as a temporary C2 organization that directly assists the commander in controlling current operations. It must be able to communicate with higher headquarters, adjacent units, employed subordinate units, and the main CP. The TAC CP is equipped with communications equipment and ATCCS supporting the warfighting functions; including intelligence, movement and maneuver, and FS. It monitors the battalion command and operations and intelligence (O&I) nets and higher headquarters command and O&I nets. The TAC CP assists the commander in controlling current operations by—

- Maintaining the COP and assisting in developing SU.
- Developing combat intelligence of immediate interest to the commander.
- Maneuvering forces.
- Controlling and coordinating FS.
- Coordinating with adjacent units and forward air defense elements.
- Serving as the main CP in the event the main CP is displaced, destroyed, or unable to function.
- Monitoring and communicating sustainment requirements, primarily Classes III and V, to the main CP.

5-13. The TAC CP is small in size and electronic signature to facilitate security and rapid, frequent displacement. Its organizational layout, personnel, and equipment must be in the unit SOP. The TAC CP section must be augmented to operate on a continuous basis.

5-14. The TAC CP is composed of designated personnel from the appropriate staff sections, and is the responsibility of the S-3 section. TAC CP personnel may also include—

- Standardization Pilot (SP), TACOPS officer, and SO.
- Intelligence staff officer (S-2), FSO, air liaison officer, engineer, and civil-military officer, if available.
- Representatives from the logistics cell.

5-15. METT-TC may dictate that an effective TAC CP operate from a C2-equipped UH-60. In this situation, the number of personnel must be reduced.

AVIATION LIAISON TEAM

5-16. Liaison teams from the S-3 liaison element represent the battalion at the headquarters of another unit to facilitate coordination and communication between the units. Preliminary air-ground coordination at brigade combat team (BCT) level is executed by the brigade aviation element (BAE) at the respective BCT headquarters. The liaison team and BAE are not synonymous and perform two unique and different functions. For more information on operations refer to TC 1-400.

5-17. An experienced liaison officer (LNO) heads the team. The LNO must be well versed in all aspects of aviation operations. The team is expected to act as a cell in planning and battle tracking, so operations can continue in the absence of the LNO. The battalion should certify liaison teams via a standard process before deploying to a supported unit.

5-18. LNOs participate in the supported unit's MDMP ensuring aviation is effectively integrated into planning. LNOs ensure supportability of the course of action and relay a clear task and purpose to the parent unit. Battalion commanders must empower LNOs to act on their behalf and ensure liaison teams are fully supported. In return, commanders expect LNOs to maintain positive two-way communication and not commit assets or approve changes to a plan without coordinating with the battalion S-3 or commander. LNOs provide the supported unit with the following:

- Capabilities, limitations, and tactical employment of aviation and ATS assets.
- Assistance in preparing aviation estimates, plans, orders, and reports.
- Assistance in planning aviation missions.
- Coordination with airspace users and the higher AC2 element for airspace management.

- The operational status of aviation assets and their effects on the supported unit's mission.
- Inform appropriate aviation units of current and possible future operations.
- Continuous communications with aviation units supporting the ground unit.

5-19. Liaison teams must have access to current battalion status information to provide the most accurate picture of aviation capabilities. Constant communication with the parent unit is essential for updates on aircraft, maintenance, aircrews, and forward arming and refueling point (FARP) status.

5-20. Liaison teams must be properly equipped and manned to support 24-hour operations. Minimum equipment includes—

- Compatible automation equipment to provide connectivity between supported unit and battalion headquarters.
- Necessary vehicles and equipment required to operate on the move.
- Two single channel air-ground radio system radios and supporting antennas/equipment to monitor command nets and communicate with aviation units.
- Map of the AO with supporting battle-tracking tools and equipment.
- Aviation field manuals (FMs), standing operating procedures (SOPs), charts (equipment weights), and checklists (movement tables) to assist in aviation planning and integration.

FIRE SUPPORT ELEMENT

5-21. The fire support element is organized under the attack/reconnaissance aviation battalions and provides fires planning, coordination, and execution. The principal officer of this section is FSO. The FSO plans, controls, and synchronizes all lethal and nonlethal FS operations and coordinates joint suppression of enemy air defenses. The FSO integrates offensive information operations into FS planning and integrates aviation in the counter firefight. He works with the main command post and the AC2 element regarding final approach firing unit locations and changes to FSCMs and ACMs. The FSO maintains digital and voice communications to supporting artillery. In the absence of a supporting FSO, the S-3 section staff ensures FSO tasks are accomplished.

SECTION II – MISSION SCHEDULING

5-22. Mission scheduling is a major responsibility of the operations section. The S-3 determines which element within the battalion is best qualified to perform the mission; however, missions are normally assigned as required by the SOP. A close working relationship between company commanders and operations personnel ensures the most qualified personnel are assigned missions. Commanders and operations officers must continually update flight crew availability, proficiency, currency, and crew rest requirements.

5-23. The battalion S-3 receives mission requests from supported units and transmits them to the unit flight operations of the tasked unit. These missions are entered on a mission request form maintained by flight operations. Flight operations maintains unit flight schedules for all flights. The S-3 reviews mission requests ensuring they are within unit capabilities and at an acceptable risk.

5-24. Commander reviews mission requests and selects crews for each mission; operations then assigns aircraft for each mission. Operations is responsible for making initial contact with the supported unit and obtaining mission details. Commanders or flight crews follow-up with unit points of contact completing premission coordination. Commanders, platoon leaders, or the authorized briefing officer will—

- Conduct a preliminary premission brief for each crew.
- Analyze missions identifying hazards, assessing risk, and implementing control options to reduce risks to the lowest levels.
- Explain the procedures for aborted missions.
- Keep operations informed of mission progress.

5-25. Aircrews complete after-action reviews (AARs) and forward them to operations. Aircrews use DA Form 5484 (Mission Schedule/Brief) for the AAR vehicle as per AR 95-1. Conflicts are resolved by the S-3 or commanding officer prior to mission assignment.

MISSION BRIEFING

5-26. Missions, including single-ship or single-pilot missions, are briefed by the chain of command (no lower than the platoon leader) or S-3. Pilots must understand the precise nature and execution of the support and command relationships affecting the mission. Aviation units supporting ground or other aviation units are designated attached, OPCON, direct support (DS), or general support (GS) with the command relationships and responsibilities associated with these terms.

5-27. When aircrews are separated from their parent units, supporting and supported unit commanders coordinate and designate command relationships to execute the mission briefing. If there are no significant changes to mission parameters, briefings are not required for each sortie flown. Briefings follow the operations order format and include the information in table 5-1.

Table 5-1. Mission briefing format

Situation
Weather
Current weather.
Forecast weather.
Special environmental considerations
Threat.
Friendly units.
Other aviation operations in the area.
Attached or detached units.
Mission
Mission statement.
Mission unit.
What is to be accomplished.
Mission start time and duration.
Where the mission will take place.
Execution
Describe how the mission will be conducted.
Specify the execution parameters and limits.
Type of mission.
Flight conditions authorized.
Modes of flight authorized.
Aircraft and crew assignment.
Mission specific equipment.
Passenger, cargo, and ammunition loads.
Flight routes.
Restrictions. Brief any restrictions not already covered
Safety
Service support

Table 5-1. Mission briefing format

Refueling and/or rearming locations.
Ration support.
Assembly area, bivouac, and remain overnight locations.
Maintenance support.
Command and signal
Command. Designate the pilot in command, flight commanders.
Chain of command in effect, if other than the normal.
Signal. Brief frequencies, special signals or code words.

MISSION BRIEF-BACK

5-28. Mission brief-backs are given to the original mission briefer by the pilot-in-command (PC) or flight commander. Brief-backs ensure a clear understanding of the mission and execution parameters, verifying all premission planning was accomplished. Brief-backs include—

- Restated mission to include information developed during planning phase causing deviations.
- Weather. Verify current and forecasted weather meet minimums.
- Crew rest status.
- Estimated mission completion time.
- Aircraft status.
- Special mission equipment.
- NOTAMs.
- Passenger, cargo, and ammunition loads.
- Passenger manifests.
- Flight routes.
- Refueling points.

POSTMISSION BRIEFING

5-29. PCs and flight commanders give postmission briefings to the chain of command or S-3. Postmission briefings consist of the following:

- Mission status (mission complete/not complete with explanation including significant changes).
- Weather. Pilot weather report for significant changes from forecasted weather.
- Crew rest status.
- Aircraft status.
- Maintenance.
- Fuel.
- Ammunition.
- Remarks. Provide any information that may impact future missions.

MISSION COMPLETION DEBRIEFING

5-30. On mission completion, aircrews complete AARs and are debriefed by platoon leaders or a designated representative. Debriefings provide commanders with critical information obtained during missions. Debriefs or AARs include—

- Estimate of mission results and degree to which mission was completed.
- Enemy activity encountered (who, what, when, where).
- Damage and casualty report.
- Aircraft damage and personnel casualty report.

- Operations security (OPSEC) violations.
- Safety hazards not previously identified.
- Other information of value.

SECTION III – OPERATIONS TRAINING AND EVALUATION

5-31. Aviation operations specialists should be evaluated when arriving in the unit. This evaluation determines their ability to perform all tasks in Soldier Training Publication (STP) 1-93P24-SM-TG and STP 1-93P1SM-TG for the appropriate skill level. Tasks involving Centralized Aviation Flight Records System (CAFRS) should also be evaluated. Tasks that cannot be adequately performed should be incorporated into a formalized on-the-job training program.

TRAINING

5-32. The operations officer and operations sergeant are responsible for ensuring assigned personnel are adequately trained and competent in all aspects of unit operations. Training must be conducted prior to unit deployments. Training programs include the following.

TACTICAL OPERATIONS TRAINING

5-33. Before the unit conducts operations in a tactical environment, the operations sergeant should develop an operations training plan based on the unit mission essential task list and tactical SOP. The plan should begin with an evaluation of operations personnel identifying training strengths and weaknesses. The operations sergeant is responsible for training assigned personnel in the following duties:

- CP security.
- Setup and teardown of the CP.
- Manual and electronic overlay development and maintenance.
- Correctly completing and timely submission of unit reports.
- Missions review and processing.
- Mission compliance with airspace coordinating measures.
- Proper equipment operation and maintenance.
- Establishing and monitoring search and rescue (SAR) procedures.
- Establishing and monitoring flight-following activities.
- Monitoring and supervising normal administrative flight operations functions.
- Developing a preaccident plan.
- SAR operations.
- Medical evacuation (MEDEVAC) operations.
- Crash rescue and downed aircraft procedures.
- Miscellaneous support operations (such as water, fuel, meals, trash collection, and courier).
- Advance party operations.

PERSONNEL TRAINING

5-34. Shift supervisors are responsible for the training and conduct of aviation operations specialists assigned to their shift. Their training duties include—

- Maintaining DA Form 1594 (Daily Staff Journal or Duty Officer's Log).
- Coordinating flight-following activities.
- Coordinating SAR procedures.
- Maintaining noise, light, and litter discipline.
- Use of proper radio operating procedures.
- Properly maintaining flight records.

- Maintaining control of the command post environment by limiting personnel access.
- Ensuring situation and operations maps are posted and updated in a timely manner. (Printed maps are required for display even though digital systems may depict flight area information)
- Ensuring appropriate records, reports, and other documentation are maintained during training exercises and combat operations per unit SOP. Accuracy and validity of these records and reports are vital for providing commanders with situational awareness and unit status. Reports trained by operations personnel include but are not limited to—
    - CBRN report.
    - Spot report.
    - Weather report.
    - Closing report.
    - Casualty report.
    - Fuel status report.
    - Combat loss report.
    - Vehicle status report.
    - Aircraft status report.
    - Flying-hour report.
    - Ammunition status report.
    - Aircraft accident and incident report.
    - Sensitive item report.
    - Unit FARP location and status report.
    - Downed aircraft report.

AIRSPACE COMMAND AND CONTROL TRAINING

5-35. Selected flight operations personnel should be trained in AC2 procedures. Training is conducted according to FM 3-52 and FM 3-52.2. Personnel should also attend the Joint Firepower Coordinator's Course at Nellis Air Force Base, Nevada.

DRIVER TRAINING

5-36. Drivers and assistant drivers should be trained and licensed in the type of vehicles they will drive. Drivers' training consists of—

- Safety and management of risk.
- Load plans.
- Vehicle preventive maintenance checks and services (PMCS).
- Radio procedures.
- Convoy operations.
- Ambush procedures.
- Vehicle emplacement.
- Cover and concealment.
- Blackout driving procedures.
- Night vision device (NVD) driving.
- CBRN detection and decontamination procedures.
- Vehicle recovery operations and emergency repairs.

GUARD AND GUNNER TRAINING

5-37. Guard and gunner training consists of—

- Range cards.
- Fighting positions.

- Perimeters of fire.
- Air guard procedures.
- Cover and concealment.
- Perimeter guard and command post security.
- Challenge and password procedures.
- Enemy prisoner of war procedures.

RADIO AND ARMY TACTICAL COMMAND AND CONTROL SYSTEM TRAINING

5-38. Radio and ATCCS operators should be trained and proficient in all warfighting function systems available to the unit and radio procedures such as the following:

- Radio net procedures.
- Antenna setup and siting.
- Radio and equipment PMCS.
- Signal operation instructions and secure equipment usage.

POWER GENERATION SYSTEM TRAINING

5-39. Power generation system training includes—

- Generator PMCS.
- Safety procedures.
- Generator operations.
- Setup and siting procedures.

SECTION IV – AVIATION MISSION PLANNING SYSTEM

5-40. AMPS is a mission planning/battle synchronization tool that automates aviation mission planning tasks and generates mission data for use in either hard copy or electronic formats.

5-41. AMPS functions include mission planning, mission management, maintenance management, and transfer of electronic mission data between networked systems and by data transfer device.

5-42. AMPS provides an interface to the ATCCS through an interface with the Tactical Airspace Integration System (TAIS) and Maneuver Control System (MCS). The MCS interface provides the aviation commander with the ability to take a "snapshot" of friendly and enemy situations to rapidly adjust his plan to accomplish the mission.

SYSTEM OBJECTIVES

5-43. AMPS provides the aviation commander, his staff, LNO(s), aviators, and AOBs with the ability to automate all mission planning tasks providing greater accuracy, timeliness, and efficiency over manual processes. The systems objectives can be grouped into two categories providing automated planning and detailed mapping capabilities.

PLANNING

5-44. AMPS planning capabilities include—

- Changing targets, laser codes, signal operating instructions, aircraft data communication information, performance planning variables, weight and balance, routes, waypoints, and FLIP data for both IFR and VFR; and importing weather data from other automated systems.
- Accommodating performance characteristics of all current Army aircraft and growth potential for future aircraft. Calculating changes in aircraft performance due to changes in drag, weight, meteorological conditions, and flight profile.

- Performing mission rehearsals from the cockpit view perspective as seen from various aircraft/pilot vision systems.
- Providing greater accuracy and speed to all planning factors over current manual/semi-automated practices.
- Providing and accepting operational inputs to, from, and through MCS to interface and operate with other Army, joint, and allied mission planning systems.
- Generating, selecting, editing, storing, printing, and recalling an operations order and mission between any two or more points.
- Interfacing with current and future target handover systems using combat net radio Army Common User System and/or local area network (LAN).
- Editing brigade/battalion generated mission.
- Interfacing with the battalion/brigade system through use of a removable hard disk, bulk transfer device, or LAN.
- Providing a functional interface to the TAIS, MCS, and associated networks.
- Providing initial load of SA data and COP graphics.
- Providing a functional interface between Army tactical ATC systems, aviation unit operations, the AOB airfield management element, and the TAGS/AAGS.

MAPPING

5-45. AMPS mapping capabilities include—
- Providing bulk tactical and map data transfer to and from current aircraft systems and communication devices.
- Providing a removable physical means of data storage and transport.
- Maintaining information on a 300 by 300 kilometer area in scales from 1:12,500 to 1:2,000,000.
- Accepting direct input information from any transmission means of National Geospatial-Intelligence Agency digital and digitized data consisting of elevation, terrain features, NAVAIDs, and airfield locations.
- Registering and processing map background and terrain databases.
- Supporting a digital moving map.

LEVELS OF MISSION PLANNING

5-46. The three levels of mission planning are—
- Brigade.
- Battalion.
- Company.

BRIGADE AND BATTALION

5-47. The brigade/battalion mission planner must act as a conduit to bridge the seam between the Force XXI battle command brigade and below systems, of which AMPS is a component, to the ATCCS. The brigade/battalion uses AMPS to perform route generation, set presets and call signs, laser codes, IFF, message setup, validate TERPs, and other tasks to prepare a plan that is supportable and fits in the ground commander's scheme of maneuver. It is also used to transmit these plans into the AC2 system for deconfliction of airspace. The AOB and ATC sections plan the emplacement of mobile ATS equipment and NAVAIDs, and develop emergency recovery procedures with initial TERP data to serve the airfield, airstrip, LZ, or FARP with METT-TC considerations. AMPS provides AOB flight operations personnel a tool to perform their flight service and dispatch tasks. Transient aircrews can also initiate and change flight and mission plans while stopping at an airfield serviced by the AOB.

COMPANY

5-48. The company mission planner is used to conduct rehearsals and select battle positions, routes from the release point, routes to rally points, AOs of fire, and other company details to complete the plan. The company also uses the mission planner to load data cartridges that aircrews take to each individual aircraft to load mission parameters into their aircraft mission computers.

This page intentionally left blank.

Chapter 6

Aviation Flight Records Management

Flight records are permanent DA records for statistical and historical data for all rated aviators, flight surgeons, nonrated personnel (crewmember [CRM] and noncrewmember [NCRM]) and UAS operators. The various forms and records management procedures detailed within this chapter, and chapters seven and eight, must be comprehensively and accurately followed so that Aviation personnel can use records for proof of their flight experience.

SECTION I – FLIGHT RECORDS AUTOMATION

CENTRALIZED AVIATION FLIGHT RECORDS SYSTEM

6-1. Over the next several years, the automated capabilities supporting flight records management will evolve through the fielding of three separate increments of the Centralized Aviation Flight Records System (CAFRS). CAFRS will replace the Automated Flight Record System and the flight management capabilities in the Unit Level Logistics System-Aviation Enhanced.

Contents

6-2. CAFRS will provide up-to-date, accurate information and facilitate, simplify, and standardize the process of compiling, tracking, and analyzing flight records, individual aircrew training folder (IATF), and air ATS records. This system will store information in a centralized repository that can be accessed by the Internet.

6-3. CAFRS will provide units with the ability to support the fully automated mission planning and aviation risk management processes. CAFRS will sustain and improve the management of aviation flight, IATF, and ATS records per current regulations and policies by centralizing and fully automating aviation records through a globally accessible and secure system. Furthermore, the Army's senior-level leadership will maintain visibility over aviation flight operations information to assist in resource, readiness, and personnel management, while commanders will have access to essential aviation information to accomplish effective risk assessment/risk management. Deficiencies and needs will be easily identifiable, providing all parties requiring access with the required data to accomplish tasks in a more accurate and efficient manner.

6-4. The CAFRS help desk may be contacted at cafrs.help@us.army.mil, (256) 842-9808, DSN 788-9808, (256) 842-0261, DSN 788-0261 The CAFRS web site is located at https://www.us.army.mil/suite/page/420577.

USER ROLES/PERMISSIONS

6-5. Users perform different functions within CAFRS based on the unit manning document or the role(s)/permissions assigned when the CAFRS account is created. CAFRS will limit access to data based on user role(s)/permissions. Access privileges to CAFRS data will be constrained by the unit affiliation of the user. All individuals with an IFRF, IATF, or ATC record require a CAFRS account. Normally a unit will appoint two administrators to manage the unit database and assign role(s)/permissions to individuals within their unit.

6-6. The DA Form 759-series is used to maintain flight records and provide the unit commander a means to track total hours while monitoring compliance with aircrew training programs (ATPs). CAFRS is designed to assist flight operations personnel in efficiently managing unit records. Use of the CAFRS is mandatory for all regular Army, U.S. Army Reserve (USAR), and Army National Guard (ARNG) aviation units. A 90 day transition period is provided to units after the fielding of CAFRS. At the end of that period CAFRS will be fully implemented and other automated flight records systems will be excluded from use.

SECTION II – INDIVIDUAL FLIGHT RECORDS FOLDER

6-7. Commanders will maintain individual flight records for all assigned and attached—
- Rated aviators in operational aviation positions.
- All other rated and nonrated crewmembers/noncrewmembers who are authorized to take part in aerial flights, according to AR 600-105 and AR 600-106.
- Aviators in nonoperational aviation positions and those restricted or prohibited by statute from flying Army aircraft. These records are kept in inactive files in either operational aviator files or military personnel records, as specified by major Army Command (AC) commanders.
- Flight/ground personnel performing flight duties, maintenance, or operating mission equipment for UAS. (See AR 95-23, Training Circular [TC] 1-600, and FM 3-04.155 for guidance in preparing UAS training records). An IFRF is not required for RAVEN UAS personnel.

FORMS AND RECORDS

6-8. Forms and other documents used to maintain flight records are filed in DA Form 3513 (Individual Flight Records Folder, United States Army). The following forms are used in conjunction with the IFRF:
- DA Form 759 (Individual Flight Record and Flight Certificate-Army).
- DA Form 759-1 (Individual Flight Record and Flight Certificate-Army) Aircraft Closeout Summary.
- DA Form 759-2 (Individual Flight Record and Flight Certificate-Army) Flying Hours Worksheet.
- DA Form 759-3 (Individual Flight Record and Flight Certificate-Army) Flight Record and Flight Pay Worksheet.
- DA Form 4186 (Medical Recommendation for Flying Duty).
- DA Form 7120-R (Commander's Task List [LRA]) current top page only for each aircraft authorized to fly.
- DA Form 2408-12 (Army Aviator's Flight Record).
- Aeronautical designation orders.
- Aviation service entry date orders.
- Initial aircrew qualification documentation for instructor pilot (IP), standardization pilot (SP), instrument examiner (IE), maintenance pilot (MP), flight engineer (FE), flight instructor (FI), and standardization instructor (SI).
- All flight status orders (issuance/termination/amendments) for active component nonrated crewmembers and ARNG aircrew members.
- Termination notices (120-day) for crewmembers.
- Aviation special-skill badge orders.
- Other documentation, as required by the commander.
- Requests for orders (RFOs) until actual orders are received.

FOLDER LABELING

6-9. Flight records are required to be labeled per Army Records Information Management System (ARIMS), chapter 6 (figure 6-1). Place the personal information label on the top left hand corner and the disposition instructions on the top right hand corner. ARIMS requires the Privacy Act system number found in DA Pam 25-51.

KE 95-1a2. Individual Flight Records Doe, John DOB: 10 FEB 62 RANK: (optional) Privacy Act Sys A 0095-1aTRADOC	DISPOSITION: Forward with person- nel records on reassignment or change of status. Release to individual upon retirement, discharge, or death.

Figure 6-1. Sample of folder labeling system

LOST OR DAMAGED FOLDERS

6-10. When an individual's IFRF is lost or destroyed, reconstruct the record by printing documents needed from CAFRS. Contact the individual's last duty station to obtain a 60 day restore file from the unit's database. Once the CAFRS Central Database (CCDB) is online contact the CAFRS help desk for assistance in recovering the file. Information needed prior to the inception of CAFRS should be obtained from the individual's personal copy of the flight records. To prevent loss due to inaccessible or lost baggage, individuals in transit should not carry their personal copy of flight records in the same container as the original copy. Annotate actions taken to locate missing documentation and methods used to verify flight hours on Part IV of DA Form 759.

FOLDER DISPOSITION

6-11. Forward the IFRF with the individual on reassignment. The records custodian will maintain a log for records that are signed out to individuals for temporary duty, permanent change of station (PCS), or attendance at the Eastern Army Aviation Training Site, Western Army Aviation Training Site, or United States Army Aviation Center of Excellence (USAACE). Charge-out forms will be maintained for records per ARIMS.

6-12. Upon final closeout at unit complete a synchronization with the CCDB to deactivate the record and move it to the CCDB for storage.

FILE ARRANGEMENT

DA FORM 3513

Supplemental Documents

6-13. Post miscellaneous documents in the supplemental documents section. Items such as 120-day notices, ATP extensions/waivers, National Guard Bureau (NGB)/USAR assignment instructions, and other aviation-related documents designated as required by the commander but that do not fall under any other classification.

Note: For units still on legacy systems include an envelope containing the latest closeout file in the IFRF when the records custodian changes. For units on CAFRS place a PCS companion file disk in the IFRF when the custodian changes. Place this disk on top of the DA Form 201A (Field Personnel Divider) labeled "Supplemental Documents."

Medical Documents

6-14. Place DA Form 4186 in the IFRF. Enter effective date and expiration date of DA Form 4186 into CAFRS adding all required remarks. Commanders, individuals, and flight surgeons must complete their areas before it is filed in the IFRF, per AR 40-501. File the commander's copy of DA Form 4186 in the IFRF along with any copies of medical suspensions and subsequent up-slips throughout the year. The annual DA Form 4186 for fitness of flying duty after the completion of the member's medical examination should be maintained in the IFRF throughout the entire year. (See table 6-1 for retention of DA Form 4186.)

Table 6-1. Retention of DA Form 4186

Occurrence	Retention
Completion of annual medical examination	Until expiration date. Maintained in record for entire year
Medical suspension (grounding slip)	Until completion of the next closeout. Filed on top of the annual 4186.
1-calendar month extension	Until the end of the month following the birth month. Filed on top of the annual 4186.
Termination of medical suspension (up slip)	Until completion of the next closeout.
Medical clearance when individual reports to a new duty station	Until completion of an annual medical examination.
Assignment to an operational flying duty position from a nonoperational flying duty position	Until completion of an annual medical examination.
Medical clearance after an aircraft accident	Until completion of an annual medical examination.
Permanent Suspension	Until permanent order is received.
Issue of waiver for medical disqualification	Until permanent order is received.

6-15. Recent guidance for the protection of health information was published under the Health Insurance Portability and Accountability Act (HIPAA). This act requires the safeguard and security of medical information. The retention of medical waivers with personal health information in the IFRF is no longer acceptable. An abbreviated waiver memorandum summarizing the medical waiver, periods of retention, and actions recommended by the medical authority should be filed instead. This memorandum can be obtained from the Flight Surgeon.

Orders

6-16. The following are maintained in the orders section of DA Form 3513 (examples are provided in figure 6-1 (page 6-3) and figure 6-2 (page 6-5):

- Aviation service entry date orders.
- Flying status orders.
- Aeronautical certifications and aircraft qualification course (AQC) certificates.
- Suspension orders (other than for medical disqualification).
- Crewmember/noncrewmember flying status orders.

- Course completion certificates for IP, IE, MP, AQC, nonrated crewmember instructor (FI), and nonrated crewmember SI in this section. When a course completion certificate is not available, use DA Form 1059 (Service School Academic Evaluation Report).
- Current DA Form 7120-R, top page only. Ensure commander and crewmember signatures are present.
- Basic/senior/master aviator badge orders for rated aviators.
  - AR 600-105 contains the procedures for determining eligibility for aeronautical ratings (senior or master Army aviator).
  - Compute aviator's total operational flying duty credit (TOFDC) from his flight records using the definition of TOFDC in AR 570-4.
  - Request a copy of the officer records brief (ORB) from the unit S-1 section.
- Basic/senior/master aviation (or flight surgeon) badge orders for crewmembers/noncrewmembers.
  - AR 600-105 contains the procedures for determining eligibility criteria for aeronautical ratings (senior or master aviation/flight surgeon badge).
  - AR 600-8-22 contains eligibility criteria for these badges.
- RFOs. Maintain RFOs until actual orders are received. Commander approval is required for individuals performing flight duties before receipt of flight orders.

Left Side of DA Form 3513

6-17. Separate subject areas labeled "Supplemental Documents," "Medical," and "Orders." Arrange documents on the left side of the IFRF in chronological order, most recent on top. Figure 6-2 shows examples of the arrangement of documents on the left side of the folder.

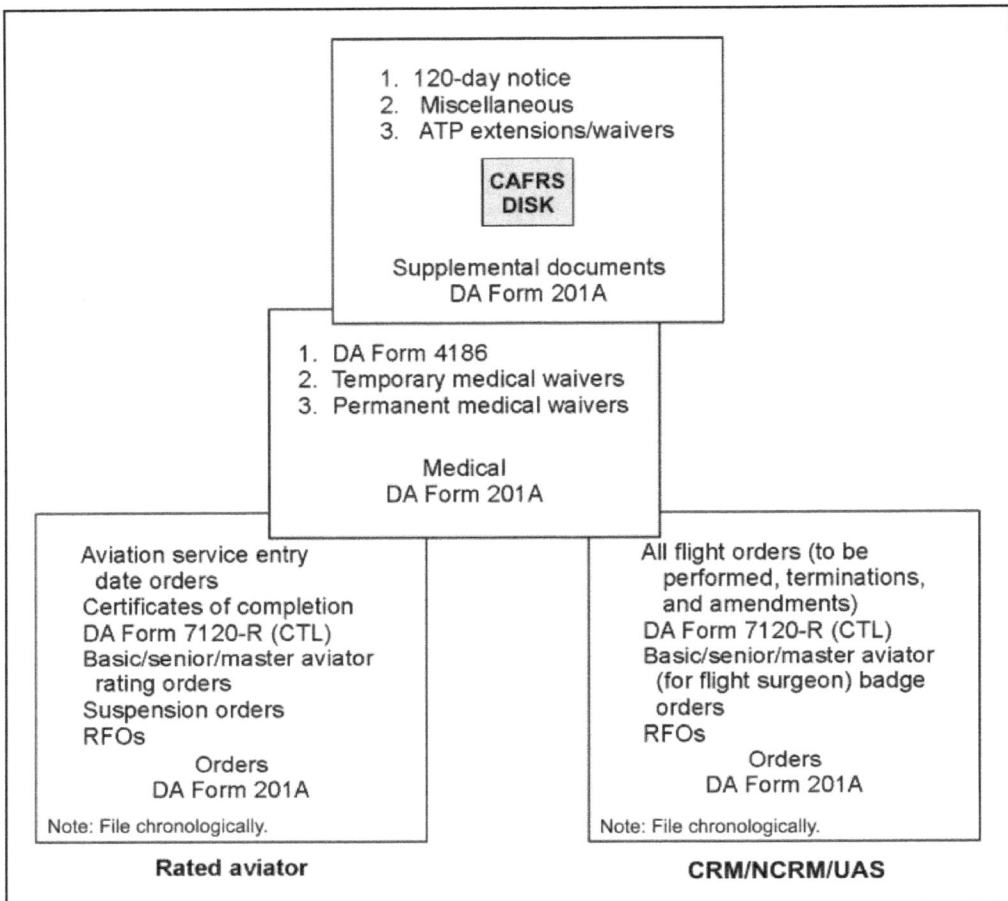

```
                    1. 120-day notice
                    2. Miscellaneous
                    3. ATP extensions/waivers

                         CAFRS
                          DISK

                    Supplemental documents
                       DA Form 201A
```

```
          1. DA Form 4186
          2. Temporary medical waivers
          3. Permanent medical waivers

                    Medical
                  DA Form 201A
```

Aviation service entry date orders Certificates of completion DA Form 7120-R (CTL) Basic/senior/master aviator rating orders Suspension orders RFOs <div align="center">Orders DA Form 201A</div>	All flight orders (to be performed, terminations, and amendments) DA Form 7120-R (CTL) Basic/senior/master aviator (for flight surgeon) badge orders RFOs <div align="center">Orders DA Form 201A</div>
Note: File chronologically.	Note: File chronologically.
Rated aviator	**CRM/NCRM/UAS**

Figure 6-2. Arrangement of DA Form 3513 (left side)

Right Side of DA Form 3513

6-18. Arrange DA Form 759, DA Form 759-1, and DA Form 759-3 for rated and nonrated crewmembers on the right side of the IFRF. Place the most current closeout on top. Label all forms included with a closeout with the series number only. Figure 6-3 shows examples of the arrangement of closeout forms.

DA Form 759-1	Sheet 4
DA Form 759-1	Sheet 4
DA Form 759	Sheet 4
DA Form 759-1	Sheet 5
DA Form 759-1	Sheet 5
DA Form 759	Sheet 5

Rated CRM

DA Form 759-3 Consolidated Worksheet	Sheet 7
DA Form 759-1	Sheet 7
DA Form 759	Sheet 7
DA Form 759-3 Consolidated Worksheet	Sheet 8
DA Form 759-1	Sheet 8
DA Form 759	Sheet 8

Nonrated CRM/NCRM/UAS and Fly for Pay Aviators

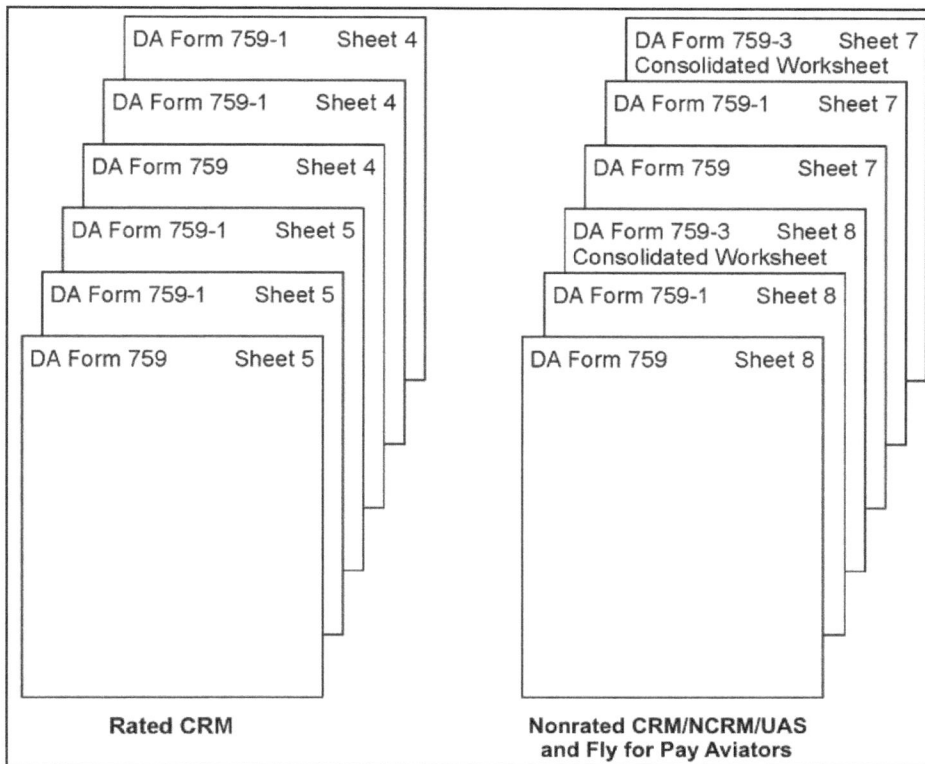

Figure 6-3. Arrangement of DA Form 3513 (right side)

*CLOSING FLIGHT RECORDS

6-19. Prepare DA Form 759 and DA Form 759-1 when the flight records are closed. These forms are required for individuals on flight status. Prepare a consolidated DA Form 759-3 when the records of crewmembers/noncrewmembers, UAS operators, and aviators in a fly-for-pay status are closed. Complete a birth month closeout within 10 working days (active duty) or 30 calendar days (reserve component) from the end of the birth month and provide a copy to the individual. Close records at the following times:

- End of the birth month (also applies to individuals who are in a nonoperational position).
- Upon a change of assignment or attachment governing flying duty. (A closeout is not required when the flight records custodian does not change.)
- Upon termination of flying status.
- Upon a change of designation (noncrewmember to crewmember or vice versa), change of duty status (operational to nonoperational), or change of aviation service (active or reserve).
- When the aviator attends a skill qualification identifier type school (such as MP, IP Course).
- Upon disqualification from flying status.

- When directed by an aircraft accident investigation board.
- Upon death.

Note: The aviator's flight records; CAFRS PCS file and IFRF, will accompany him to the course so flight time and remarks can be entered into the records.

6-20. Number each DA Form 759 consecutively; if an individual's records have been closed three times and this is the fourth closeout, the sheet number will be four.

6-21. At the end of the individual's birth month, forward the commander's task list (CTL), with all enclosures, to the flight records custodian. The custodian will use the CTL to assist with completing Parts III and IV of DA Form 759.

6-22. Upon completion of DA Form 759, the flight records custodian will submit the closeout to the commander for certification. The commander's signature certifies the accuracy of the DA Form 759. The certifying commander is the officer who authorized flight duties on DA Form 7120-R. For units fielded CAFRS the commander must digitally sign the closeout in CAFRS. If the commander is unable to digitally sign the closeout a remark must be added to part IV of the 759.

6-23. The initial closeout that is imported into CAFRS during fielding may be signed by the flight operations officer or NCOIC. The closeout must be signed by the commander in the legacy system.

TRANSCRIBING FLIGHT TIME

6-24. Transcribe flight time from DA Form 2408-12 to DA Form 759-2 and DA Form 759-3. The PC is responsible for accurately completing DA Form 2408-12. DA Pam 738-751 contains procedures for completing DA Form 2408-12. AR 95-1 defines flying duty, mission, and flight condition symbols used in preparing DA Form 2408-12, DA Form 759, DA Form 759-1, DA Form 759-2, and DA Form 759-3. DA Form 2408-12 will become a permanent record in CAFRS. Units using ULLS-A (E) or ELAS maintenance systems may digitally import DA Form 2408-12s into CAFRS using the download tolls of CAFRS.

6-25. Flight time from civilian FW or rotary-wing logbooks is authorized after verification by the operations officer. The operations officer is the approving authority in CAFRS for civilian flight hours. Remarks are required on the next closeout when these times are transcribed.

6-26. Flight hours from previous time as an aeroscout observer or crewmember/noncrewmember are not added to flight time as a rated aviator. Personnel attending a flight school will file their historical records, and a new IFRF will be initiated.

SECTION III – FLYING STATUS MANAGEMENT

RATED AVIATOR

6-27. Army aviators and flight surgeons are authorized flying status per AR 600-105. Flight surgeons are rated officers but are not included in the rated inventory of Army aviators. When using CAFRS identify Flight Surgeons as rated aviators fly for pay.

CREWMEMBER/NONCREWMEMBER

6-28. Crewmembers/noncrewmembers are authorized flying status per AR 600-106. Individuals must meet the criteria outlined in AR 600-106 and pass the appropriate flight physical before orders are requested.

CREWMEMBER/NONCREWMEMBER FLIGHT STATUS POSITIONS

6-29. Operations will maintain a chart reflecting all crewmember/noncrewmember flight slots listed on the modified table of organization and equipment (MTOE) or table of distribution and allowances (TDA), by paragraph and line number. The chart will list individuals in flight positions and contain additional blocks such as—

- Night vision goggles (NVG) qualification.
- Birth month, flight physical.
- PCS date.
- Other information tailored to fit specific unit needs.

6-30. This greatly assists in managing flight slots and replacing outbound individuals. Operations will also work with the S-1 section to ensure the unit manning report reflects individuals filling MTOE or TDA authorized positions.

WRITTEN 120-DAY NOTICE

6-31. A written notice of flight status termination is required for enlisted crewmembers. This notice is given 120 days prior to termination. AR 600-106 discusses requirements for this action. The individual and commander's signature is required prior to placing the notice in the IFRF. Annotate the notification in the remarks section of DA Form 759, part IV, and in the Aviation Personnel Data tab of the Person Editor of CAFRS. If less than 120-days notice is given, file an exception notice stating the reason for the delay.

Note: Only one individual may occupy a paragraph/line number flight position. The 120-day notice is crucial to ensure no crewmember position is "double-slotted." An individual occupies a position until the 120 days has ended. Late notices prevent the commander from using that slot until that time has expired.

FLIGHT PHYSICAL

6-32. Individuals who do not have a current flight physical, or a 1-calendar month extension to complete their annual medical examination documented on DA Form 4186, will be suspended from flying status until medical clearance is given. Commanders will notify the servicing finance and accounting office when personnel are suspended from flight duties.

Note: Valid initial flight physicals may exceed 12 months for personnel completing aviator flight training. AR 40-501 details the frequency and validity of flight physicals and the procedures for completing aircrew member birth month alignments.

MINIMUM FLYING TIME

6-33. Defense Financial Management Regulation (DODFMR) 7000.14-R, volume A outlines the minimum number of monthly flight hours qualifying crewmembers/noncrewmembers for hazardous duty incentive pay (HDIP) and flight surgeons for aviation career incentive pay (ACIP). This regulation also applies to certain fly-for-pay aviators failing to make their 12- or 18-year gate as outlined in AR 600-105. These aviators must qualify monthly to continue receiving ACIP. Flight time is tracked on DA Form 759-3 similar to nonaviators. These times are included at closeout.

6-34. The DOD pay and entitlements manual provides an in-depth discussion of the requirements for HDIP and ACIP and the tracking of flight hours.

6-35. Individual flight records are reviewed each month determining if individuals failed to meet flight requirements or have made up flight requirements from a previous month. DA Form 4730-R (Certificate for Performance of Hazardous Duty) is prepared per AR 37-104-4 and signed by the commander. This certificate is forwarded to finance, and a copy is maintained on file for two years.

SECTION IV – ARMY AVIATOR'S FLIGHT RECORDS

6-36. Information for each flight of an Army aircraft is logged on the flight records. This form contains information about the aircraft, crewmembers, and maintenance information for each flight. DA Pam 738-751 provides guidance for properly filling out DA Form 2408-12. Information includes—

● Aircraft time flown.

● Duty and type of flight performed.

6-37. This information is used to track the amount and type of flying duty crewmembers perform. See example in figure 6-4.

Page _____ of _____				
1. DATE 20020707	2. SERIAL NUMBER 9424235	3. MODEL AH-64A	4. ORGANIZATION A Company, 4-229 AVN	5. STATION Illesheim, GE

6a. FLIGHT 1	DATA FROM Local	TO	TO

TIME	FROM 12:30	TO	TO 15:06	FLT HRS 2.6	LDG: STD 6	AUTO 0	STARTS:#1	#2

MISSION ID	STD T	CONFIG	LOADS: INTERNAL	EXTERNAL	PASSENGERS		CYC	HSF
ROUNDS	7.62	20mm	30mm	40mm	ROCKET	TOW	HELLFIRE	
STATUS	7.62	20mm	30mm	40mm	ROCKET	TOW	HELLFIRE	

HIT CHECK	NO. 1 ENGINE +1	NO. 2 ENGINE +1	APU: STARTS 2	HOURS 0.5	HOUR METER HRS

b.	PERSONNEL DATA			c.	DUTY SYMBOL/FLIGHT SYMBOL/HOURS/SEAT													
NAME	RANK	PID/SSAN		DS	FS	HR	S	DS	FS	HR	S	DS	FS	HR	S	DS	FS	HR	S
Doe, John J.	CPT			PC	D	2.6	B												
Smith, Joe L.	LTC			PI	D	2.6	F												
---------------LAST ENTRY----																			

7.							SERVICING DATA						
FUEL ADDED (GALLONS)	GRADE	IN TANKS	OIL 1	GRADE	OIL 2	GRADE	APU	GRADE	OXY-GEN	ANTI-ICING	SERVICED BY	LOCATION	
191	JP8	300	7	23699	7	23699	2	23699			B. Chaney	Illesheim, GE	
354	JP8	375	1	23699	1	23699	0	23699			B. Chaney	Illesheim, GE	
545			8		8		2					TOTALS	

DA FORM 2408-12, JAN 92
EDITION OF JAN 64 IS OBSOLETE

ARMY AVIATOR'S FLIGHT RECORD USAPPC V2.00
For use of this form, see DA PAM 738-751; the proponent agency is DCSLOG

Figure 6-4. Sample DA Form 2408-12 (front)

6-38. The PC ensures that DA Form 2408-12 is completed properly, and essential information is entered for all crewmembers and noncrewmembers aboard. Passengers will be maintained on a separate manifest.

DEPARTMENT OF THE ARMY FORM 2408-12 COMPLETION

6-39. Information contained on DA Form 2408-12 of special interest for the completion of flight records and other reports generated by flight operations is shown in figure 6-4 and listed below:

- **Block 1**. Date. (Entered by pilot.) Date (YYYYMMDD) of the start of the first flight.
- **Block 2**. Serial Number. Serial number of the aircraft.
- **Block 3**. Model. Aircraft model number.
- **Block 4**. Organization. Unit or activity to which the aircraft is assigned.
- **Block 5**. Station. Aircraft home station.
- **Block 6a**. Flight Data. Information that should be checked carefully because of the effect miscalculated hours have on unit status reports and flying-hour reports. On the row marked "TIME," the block "FLT HRS" represents the total time the crewmember or noncrewmember has logged. The "FROM" time is subtracted from the last "TO" time and the result is entered in the "FLT HRS" block. The time represents the total hours placed on the airframe for that flight. See table 6-2 to convert minutes to partial hours.

Table 6-2. Time conversion for partial hours

Minutes	Hours	Minutes	Hours
0	0	31-36	0.6
1-6	0.1	37-42	0.7
7-12	0.2	43-48	0.8
13-18	0.3	49-54	0.9
19-24	0.4	55-60	1.0
25-30	0.5		

- The next row contains the mission ID. The "STD" block will contain a single character for the mission ID (for example, "S" for service mission). The authorized mission IDs used on DA Form 2408-12 can be found in AR 95-1 and are listed in table 6-3.

Table 6-3. Mission IDs

Mission Symbols	Service Missions
A	Acceptance Test Flight
F	Maintenance Flight
S	Service Mission
T	Training Flight
X	Experimental Test Flight
C	Combat Mission
D	Imminent Danger

- **Block 6b**. Personnel Data. Names, ranks, personal identification data will be entered before flight.
- **Block 6c**. Line to the right of the personnel data provides the duty symbol, flight condition, hours, and seat designation blocks for the crewmembers for that portion of the mission. The following are the authorized entries for these blocks:
    - **DS—Duty symbol**. Duty position the crewmember holds during that portion of the flight.
        - AO–Unmanned aircraft operator (UAS).
        - CE–Crew chief, or aircraft mechanic assigned to a crew chief position.
        - CP—Copilot. Used by an aviator who is at a flight crew station but not qualified or current in the aircraft being flown or who is performing copilot duties at other than a

flight crew station and is undergoing training or evaluation conducted by an IP, SP, IE, UT, or ME (for example NOE navigation, instrument navigation).

- **EO**–External operator (UAS).
- **FE**–Flight engineer.
- **FI**–Nonrated crewmember instructor.
- **IE**–Instrument examiner.
- **IO**–Instructor Operator (UAS).
- **IP**–Instructor pilot.
- **MC**–Mission Commander (UAS).
- **ME**–Maintenance evaluator.
- **MO**–Flight surgeon or other medical personnel.
- **MP**–Maintenance pilot.
- **OR**–Aircraft maintenance personnel, technical observer, firefighter, aerial photographer, gunner, or duties requiring flight.
- **PC–Pilot-in-command.** Designated pilot in command who is performing assigned duties as IP, SP, UT, IE, ME, MP, or experimental test pilot (XP) will not use this symbol. In these cases, the specific symbol will be used to indicate the duty being performed by the PC.
- **PI**–Pilot.
- **PO**–Mission payload operator (UAS).
- **SI**–Nonrated crewmember SI.
- **SO**–Standardization instructor operator (UAS).
- **SP**–Standardization pilot.
- **UT**–Unit trainer.
- **XP**–Experimental pilot.

Note: The only duty symbols that may be logged simultaneously by more than one rated aviator at the controls are MP or XP when authorized by the commander.

- **FS–Flight condition**. Each crewmember will use only one of the following symbols to identify the condition or mode of flight for any time.
- **AA**–Air to air.
- **D–Day.** Between the hours of official sunrise and sunset.
- **DS–Day vision system.** Night vision system installed on aircraft used during the day, also logged when two or more devices are used.
- **H–Hooded** instrument flight/simulated instrument meteorological condition. Vision of the person flying the aircraft is artificially limited from viewing the horizon or earth surface. Aircraft must be controlled using aircraft instruments. An observer is required for all hooded flights.
- **N–Night.** Between the hours of official sunset and sunrise.
- **NG–Night goggles.** Night vision goggles used during the night.
- **NS–Night system.** Night vision system installed on aircraft used during the night, also logged when two or more devices are used simultaneously.
- **W–Weather instrument flight.** Actual weather conditions that do not permit visual contact with the horizon or earth surface. Aircraft attitude must be controlled using aircraft instruments.
- **HR -Hours.** Amount of time spent in the duty position.

- ▪ **S–Seat designation.** In an aircraft requiring designation of seat occupied, the stations will be annotated F for front seat or B for back seat.
- The reverse of the form has two more sets of block 6 for subsequent flights and/or crew changes. An example is shown at figure 6-5. Eighteen flights and eight duty positions IAW DA Form 2408-12 are available in CAFRS.

6a. FLIGHT	2	DATA	FROM				TO				TO					
TIME	FROM	15:30	TO		TO	17:00	FLT HRS 1.5	LDG: STD 6	AUTO 0	STARTS:#1	#2					
MISSION ID	STD T	CONFIG	LOADS: INTERNAL		EXTERNAL		PASSENGERS		CYC		HSF					
ROUNDS	7.62		20mm		30mm		40mm		ROCKET		TOW		HELLFIRE			
STATUS	7.62	20mm	30mm	40mm	RCKT		TOW	HF	APU: STARTS 2		HOURS 0.4		HOUR METER HRS			

b.		PERSONNEL DATA		c.					DUTY SYMBOL/FLIGHT SYMBOL/HOURS/SEAT								
NAME		RANK		PID/SSAN	DS	FS	HR	S	DS	FS	HR	S	DS	FS	HR	S	DS	FS	HR	S
Doe, John J.		CW2			PC	H	1.0	B	PC	D	0.5	B					
Smith, Joe L.		CPT			PI	D	1.5	F									
-------------------LAST ENTRY----																	

6a. FLIGHT	3	DATA	FROM				TO				TO					
TIME	FROM	17:50	TO		TO	18:50	FLT HRS 1.0	LDG: STD 3	AUTO 0	STARTS:#1	#2					
MISSION ID	STD T	CONFIG	LOADS: INTERNAL		EXTERNAL		PASSENGERS		CYC		HSF					
ROUNDS	7.62		20mm		30mm		40mm		ROCKET		TOW		HELLFIRE			
STATUS	7.62	20mm	30mm	40mm	RCKT		TOW	HF	APU: STARTS 2		HOURS 0.4		HOUR METER HRS			

b.		PERSONNEL DATA		c.					DUTY SYMBOL/FLIGHT SYMBOL/HOURS/SEAT								
NAME		RANK		PID/SSAN	DS	FS	HR	S	DS	FS	HR	S	DS	FS	HR	S	DS	FS	HR	S
Jones, Mark F.		CW3			PC	H	0.5	B	PC	D	0.5	B					
Williams, David L.		CW2			PI	D	1.0	F									
-------------------LAST ENTRY----																	

8.	TOTALS	FLIGHT HOURS	5.1	LANDINGS: STD	15	AUTO	0	APU: STARTS	6	HOURS	1.3
HOUR METER HOURS			STARTS: #1		#2			CYCLES		HSF	
ROUNDS	7.62		20mm		30mm		40mm		ROCKET		TOW		HELLFIRE

REVERSE OF DA FORM 2408-12, JAN 92   USAPPC V2.00

Figure 6-5. Sample of DA Form 2408-12 (reverse)

This page intentionally left blank.

Chapter 7

Rated Aviator Flight Records

Management of flight records is a major task accomplished by the unit operations section. Rated aviators have an obligation to maintain a complete and comprehensive set of personal flight records. Flight records can be used by the rated aviator as proof of flight experience. It is imperative these records be comprehensively and accurately maintained. Prior to leaving a unit, the rated aviator should obtain a copy of their most current flight records.

SECTION I – FLYING HOUR WORKSHEET

7-1. DA Form 759-2 is a record of an aviator's flight hours and can be used as both a temporary and consolidation worksheet. It can be arranged in sections allowing entries for different types of aircraft, flight simulators, and/or seat designations. A manual DA Form 759-2 is not required when using CAFRS. It is recommended to help recover information in case of automation loss.

Contents

TEMPORARY WORKSHEET

7-2. Use DA Form 759-2 as both a temporary worksheet and a consolidation worksheet. When used as a temporary worksheet, record the daily flights of rated aviators. Table 7-1 (page 7-3) contains general information for completing the temporary worksheet. Figure 7-1 depicts a sample temporary worksheet.

7-3. Arrange DA Form 759-2 in three sections (A, B, and C). This allows entries for three types of aircraft, flight simulators, and/or seat designations. If an individual flies more than three different aircraft and/or flight simulators during an annual period, use an additional temporary worksheet.

7-4. Take information for the temporary worksheet from DA Form 2408-12. Make entries in pencil. A single line may be used when the date, aircraft, flying duty symbol, flight condition symbol, and mission symbol are the same. The hours flown for these like entries may be combined or listed as separate entries. When any of this information is not the same, use a separate line. Mission symbols containing "C" (combat) and "D" (imminent danger) are the only mission symbols to be used in the mission symbol column.

7-5. Make as many entries on the form as space allows for both daily and monthly use. A new form for each month is not required. Leave a blank line after each month's entries.

7-6. Enter flight time in hours and tenths of hours.

7-7. Do not file the temporary worksheet with DA Form 759 and DA Form 759-1 when the rated aviator's flight records are closed. The unit commander or operations officer determines how long the worksheets are retained (90 days is recommended).

7-8. Initiate a new temporary worksheet each time flight records are closed.

Table 7-1. Instructions for completing DA Form 759-2 temporary worksheet (rated aviator)

Item	Instructions
Block 1	Enter the last name, first name, and middle initial.
Block 2	Enter the rank.
Block 3	Enter the period covered. (DD MMM YY – leave end date open until closeout). Example – (1 JUL 02 – 30 JUN 03)
Note: All references to period covered on all DA Forms 759 will be in this format. The first date will represent either the first day the forms were initiated or the first day after the last DA Form 759 closeout. The second date will represent the last day of the closeout period. Birth-month closeouts will be dated the last day of the birth month.	
Sections A, B, and C	Enter the aircraft mission, type, design, and series or flight simulator and, if applicable, the seat designation. (Example: AH-64A[FS], 2B40[BS])
Note: Complete columns a through e using information from DA Form 2408-12.	
Column a	Enter the date of flight. The first entry in a month will be the month, followed by the day in the space underneath.
Column b	Enter the duty symbol.
Column c	Enter the flight condition symbol.
Column d	Enter mission symbols containing a C (combat) or D (imminent danger) only. For all other mission symbols, leave blank.
Column e	Enter the hours and tenths of hours for each individual entry on DA Form 2408-12. Flights with the same date, duty symbol, flight condition, and mission symbol (if used) may be consolidated into one entry for 1-day's flights only.
Notes: 1. If no time was flown in an aircraft or flight simulator listed in Section A, B, or C for an entire month, enter the month in column a and the comment "No Time Flown" across columns b through d. 2. Enter flight simulator time (military) in the same manner as a separate type of aircraft. 3. Aircraft and flight simulator entries logged by seat designation (DA Form 2408-12, block 6c) will be logged using the appropriate letters. Use a separate section on DA Form 759-2 for each designated (FS, BS) seat position. Example: AH-64A(FS), 2B40(BS).	

INDIVIDUAL FLIGHT RECORD AND FLIGHT CERTIFICATE - ARMY
For use of this form, see AR 95-1, AR 95-23, and FM 3-04.300; the proponent agency is DCS, G-3/5/7.

FLYING HOURS WORKSHEET

1. Name	2. Rank	3 Period
Doe, John D.	CPT	1 Nov 06 - 31 Oct 07

Section A. (AH-64D(BS))					Section B. (AH-64D(FS))					Section C. (2B-64D(FS))				
Date	Duty Sym	Flt Cond	Msn Sym	Hours	Date	Duty Sym	Flt Cond	Msn Sym	Hours	Date	Duty Sym	Flt Cond	Msn Sym	Hours
a.	b.	c.	d.	e.	a.	b.	c.	d.	e.	a.	b.	c.	d.	e.
NOV					NOV					NOV				
1	PC	D		2.0	1	PI	D		2.0	2	PI	W		2.0
					15	PI	NG		1.0					
DEC					15	PI	NS		1.0	DEC				
1	PC	D		2.0						2	PI	W		2.0
15	PC	NG		1.0	DEC					JAN				
15	PC	NS		1.0	1	PI	D		2.0	3	PI	H		2.0
JAN					JAN					FEB	No	Time	Flown	
2	PC	D		1.5	2	PI	D		1.5					
15	PC	D		4.0	15	PI	N		1.0	MAR				
										15	PI	W		1.0
FEB					FEB									
1	PC	D		3.0	15	PI	D		1.0	APR	No	Time	Flown	
					15	PI	N		1.0					
MAR					15	PI	NG		1.0	MAY	No	Time	Flown	
1	PC	D		3.3	15	PI	NS		1.0					
										JUN				
APR					MAR.	No	Time	Flown		15	PI	W		2.0
15	PC	D		3.3	APR	No	Time	Flown						
										JUL	No	Time	Flown	
MAY	No	Time	Flown		MAY									
					1	PI	D		2.0	AUG	No	Time	Flown	
JUN	No	Time	Flown		1	PI	N		1.0					
					1	PI	NG		1.0	SEP	No	Time	Flown	
JUL					1	PI	NS		1.0					
20	PC	D		2.4						OCT	No	Time	Flown	
					JUN	No	Time	Flown						
AUG					JUL	No	Time	Flown						
1	PC	D		4.0										
					AUG	No	Time	Flown						
SEP	No	Time	Flown											
					SEP									
OCT					1	PI	D		2.0					
1	PC	D	D	5.0	1	PI	N		1.0					
					1	PI	NG		1.0					
					1	PI	NS		1.0					
					OCT	No	Time	Flown						

DA FORM 759-2, AUG 2008   PREVIOUS EDITION OF SEP 1986 IS OBSOLETE   APD PE v1.00

Figure 7-1. Sample DA Form 759-2 temporary worksheet (rated aviator)

CONSOLIDATION WORKSHEET

7-9. Table 7-2 contains detailed information for completing a DA Form 759-2 as a consolidation worksheet. Figure 7-2 (page 7-5) depicts a sample consolidation worksheet.

Table 7-2. Instructions for completing DA Form 759-2 consolidated worksheet (rated aviator)

Item	Instructions
Block 1	Enter the last name, first name, and middle initial.
Block 2	Enter the rank.
Block 3	Enter the period covered (DD MMM YY – leave end date open until closeout).
Column a	Enter the month that covers the applicable set of entries to be consolidated from the temporary worksheet.
Columns b, c, d and e	At the end of each month, total the number of hours flown for each group of like flights (same duty, flight condition, and mission symbol [only combat and imminent danger] used from the temporary worksheet). On the consolidation worksheet, make a one-line entry for each group of like flights. Flights that cannot be consolidated will be transferred to the consolidation worksheet as is.

Notes:
1. Procedures for transferring flight simulator time (military) to the consolidation worksheet are the same as those for aircraft flight time.
2. Aircraft and flight simulator entries that are logged by seat designation (DA Form 2408-12, block 6c) will be logged using the appropriate letters. Use a separate section on DA Form 759-2 for each designated (FS, BS) seat position. Example: AH-64A(FS), 2B40(BS).

7-10. Maintain a monthly consolidation worksheet for the aircraft/flight simulator a rated aviator flies during the period covered by DA Form 759-2 temporary worksheet. Arrange the consolidation worksheets in the same order as the temporary worksheets. Complete the consolidation worksheet in pencil.

7-11. Obtain the information needed to complete the consolidation worksheet from the temporary worksheet. At the end of each month, consolidate all like entries in each section (A, B and C) of the temporary worksheet to the consolidation worksheet. Enter the consolidated information as a one-line entry to the consolidation worksheet.

7-12. Consolidate the time by aircraft/simulator type, flying duty, flight condition, and mission symbol. The mission symbol column will be used only for mission symbols containing a "C" (combat) or "D" (imminent danger) flights. All times entered into flight records will be in hours and tenths of hours.

7-13. Be sure the period covered for all entries appearing on the consolidation worksheet is accurately reflected in block 4. Leave a blank space between each month's entries on the consolidation worksheet. For the months in which no hours were recorded, enter the month in column **a**, and the comment "No Time Flown" across columns **b** through **d**.

7-14. A manual DA Form 759-2 does not have to be kept when using CAFRS. However, it is recommended to help recover information in case of automation crashes.

INDIVIDUAL FLIGHT RECORD AND FLIGHT CERTIFICATE - ARMY
For use of this form, see AR 95-1, AR 95-23, and FM 3-04.300; the proponent agency is DCS, G-3/5/7.

FLYING HOURS WORK SHEET

1. Name	2. Rank	3. Period
Doe, John D.	CPT	1 Nov 06 - 31 OcT 07

Section A. (AH-64D(BS)) Section B. (AH-64D(FS)) Section C. (2B-64D(FS))

Date	Duty Sym	Flt Cond	Msn Sym	Hours	Date	Duty Sym	Flt Cond	Msn Sym	Hours	Date	Duty Sym	Flt Cond	Msn Sym	Hours
a.	b.	c.	d.	e.	a.	b.	c.	d.	e.	a.	b.	c.	d.	e.
NOV	PC	D		2.0	NOV	PI	D		2.0	NOV	PI	W		2.0
						PI	NG		1.0					
DEC	PC	D		2.0		PI	NS		1.0	DEC	PI	W		2.0
	PC	NG		1.0										
	PC	NS		1.0	DEC	PI	D		2.0	JAN	PI	H		2.0
JAN	PC	D		5.5	JAN	PI	D		1.5	FEB	No	Time	Flown	
						PI	N		1.0					
FEB	PC	D		3.0	FEB	PI	D		1.0	MAR	PI	W		1.0
MAR	PC	D		3.3		PI	N		1.0	APR	No	Time	Flown	
						PI	NG		1.0					
APR	PC	D		3.3		PI	NS		1.0	MAY	No	Time	Flown	
MAY	No	Time	Flown		MAR	No	Time	Flown		JUN	PI	W		2.0
JUN	No	Time	Flown		APR	No	Time	Flown		JUL	No	Time	Flown	
JUL	PC	D		2.4	MAY	PI	D		2.0	AUG	No	Time	Flown	
						PI	N		1.0					
AUG	PC	D		4.0		PI	NG		1.0	SEP	No	Time	Flown	
						PI	NS		1.0					
SEP	No	Time	Flown		JUN	No	Time	Flown		OCT	No	Time	Flown	
OCT	PC	D	D	5.0	JUL	No	Time	Flown						
					AUG	No	Time	Flown						
					SEP	PI	D		2.0					
						PI	N		1.0					
						PI	NG		1.0					
						PI	NS		1.0					
					OCT	No	Time	Flown						

DA FORM 759-2, AUG 2008   PREVIOUS EDITION OF SEP 1986 IS OBSOLETE   APD PE v1.00

Figure 7-2. Sample DA Form 759-2 consolidation worksheet (rated aviator)

SECTION II – AIRCRAFT CLOSEOUT SUMMARY

7-15. Use DA Form 759-1 as a record of flight time by flying duty and flight condition for each aircraft and/or flight simulator an individual flies during the closeout period. Do not prepare DA Form 759-1 for aircraft not flown during the period covered. CAFRS will automatically prepare a 759-1 for aircraft not flown. This should not be included in the IFRF. Table 7-3 contains instructions for completing DA Form 759-1 as an aircraft closeout summary. See samples provided in figures 7-3 (page 7-8), 7-4 (page 7-9), and 7-5 (page 7-10). General information for completing the aircraft closeout summary follows.

7-16. File DA Form 759-1 with DA Form 759 when an individual's flight record is closed. Type all entries.

7-17. Prepare DA Form 759-1 for each aircraft or simulator listed on the individual's consolidation worksheet (Sections A, B, and C). Aircraft with seat designations require separate DA Form 759-1s for each seat qualification. Total all like entries from the worksheet, by aircraft or flight simulator. Carry the totals forward to DA Form 759-1 when the individual's flight record is closed. Number DA Forms 759-1 the same as DA Form 759 and arrange them in the IFRF according to figure 6-2 (page 6-6).

Table 7-3. Instructions for completing DA Form 759-1 aircraft closeout summary (rated aviator)

Item	Instructions
Note: All required dates will be in the DD MMM YY format. (11 MAR 03)	
Block 1	Enter the chronological sheet number.
Blocks 2 through 4	Enter the appropriate information from blocks 1 through 4 of DA Form 759-2.
Block 5	Enter the aircraft mission, type, design, and series or flight simulator and, if applicable, the seat designation. Separate DA Forms 759-1 are required when tracking seat qualifications/hours.
Lines 6 through 15 and columns a through j	From the corresponding consolidated DA Form 759-2, total the hours for all like entries according to flying duty and flight condition symbols. Enter the totals, in hours and tenths of hours, on the appropriate line in the correct column.
Notes: 1. NV (night vision) time is no longer tracked and has been deleted from DA Form 759-1. Row 11 is reserved for future use and will remain blank. Time in row 11 was previously moved and added into the times in row 10. 2. DS/DG hours, tracked separately on DA Form 759-1, are combined with NS hours on the DA Form 759. 3. TR (terrain) time is no longer tracked as a flight condition according to AR 95-1. Times on line 14 will remain as is.	
Column k	Total the hours across lines 6 through 15 for each flight condition. Enter the totals in hours and tenths of hours in the corresponding lines of column k. Add hours in column k downward and place this total in the block on line 16, column k.
Column l	Enter the sheet number of the previous DA Form 759-1 at the top of this column. Then enter the totals from column m of the previous DA Form 759-1 for the same aircraft mission, type, design, and series or flight simulator and, if applicable, the seat designation.
Column m	Add columns k and l across on lines 6 through 15, and enter the new totals in the corresponding lines of column m (in hours and tenths of hours). Add hours in column m together and place this total in the block on line 18, column m.
Line 16	Total the hours downward in columns a through j. Enter the totals in hours and tenths of hours, in the corresponding column on line 16.
Note: To check the total, add columns a through j across on line 16. This total should agree with the total of column k on line 16.	
Line 17	Enter the same sheet number at the beginning of this line as that entered at the top of column l. Enter the totals from line 18 of the previous DA Form 759-1 to the corresponding columns on this line.
Line 18	Add lines 16 and 17 downward, and enter the totals in hours and tenths of hours, in the corresponding blocks on this line.

Table 7-3. Instructions for completing DA Form 759-1 aircraft closeout summary (rated aviator)

Item	Instructions
Note: To check the total, add columns **a** through **j** across on line 18. This total should agree with the total of column **m** on line 18.	
Line 19 columns a through j	From the corresponding consolidated DA Form 759-2, total the mission symbols containing combat hours for all like entries, according to flying duty symbols. Enter these totals in the corresponding columns on line 19.
Line 20, columns a through j	From the corresponding consolidated DA Form 759-2, total the mission symbols containing imminent danger hours for all like entries, according to flying duty symbols. Enter these totals in the corresponding columns on line 20.
Lines 19 and 20, column k	Add across columns **a** through **j** and enter the total in the corresponding block in lines 19 and 20, column **k**.
Lines 19 and 20, column l	From the previous DA Form 759-1, enter the totals from lines 19 and 20, column **m** into the corresponding block in lines 19 and 20, column **l**.
Lines 19 and 20, column m	Add the totals across in columns **k** and **l** and enter the totals into the corresponding block in lines 19 and 20, column **m**.

INDIVIDUAL FLIGHT RECORD AND FLIGHT CERTIFICATE - ARMY

For use of this form, see AR 95-1, AR 95-23, and FM 3-04.300; the proponent agency is DCS, G-3/5/7.

AIRCRAFT CLOSEOUT SUMMARY

1. Sheet No.
4

2. Name	3. Rank	4. Period	5. Acft/Flt Sim
Doe, John J.	CPT	1 Nov 06 - 31 Oct 07	AH-64D(BS)

FLIGHT COND SYM	FLYING DUTY SYMBOL										k. Total This Sheet	l. From Sheet No. 3	m. Total
	a. CP/ CE/ EO	b. PI/ OR/ AO	c. PC/ PO	d. UT/ MO	e. IP/ FE/ IO	f. IE/ FI	g. SP/ SI/ SO	h. MP	I. ME	J. XP			
6. D			30.5								30.5	150.5	181.0
7. N												40.0	40.0
8. H												10.0	10.0
9. W													
10. NG			1.0								1.0	45.0	46.0
11.													
12. NS			1.0								1.0	34.0	35.0
13. DG/ DS													
14. TR													
15. AA													
16. Total this Sheet			32.5								32.5		
17. From Sheet No.3	50.0	150.0	80.0									280.0	
18. Total	50.0	150.0	112.5										312.5
19. Combat													
20. Imminent Danger			5.0								5.0		5.0

DA FORM 759-1, AUG 2008   PREVIOUS EDITION OF SEP 1986 IS OBSOLETE   APD PE v1.00

Figure 7-3. Sample AH-64A (FS) DA Form 759-1 aircraft closeout summary (rated aviator)

INDIVIDUAL FLIGHT RECORD AND FLIGHT CERTIFICATE - ARMY
For use of this form, see AR 95-1, AR 95-23, and FM 3-04.300; the proponent agency is DCS, G-3/5/7.

AIRCRAFT CLOSEOUT SUMMARY

											1. Sheet No. 4			
2. Name Doe, John D.						3. Rank CPT		4. Period 1 Nov 06 - 31 Oct 07			5. Acft/Flt Sim AH-64D(FS)			
FLIGHT COND SYM	FLYING DUTY SYMBOL										k. Total This Sheet	l. From Sheet No. 3	m. Total	
	a. CP/ CE/ EO	b. PI/ OR/ AO	c. PC/ PO	d. UT/ MO	e. IP/ FE/ IO	f. IE/ FI	g. SP/ SI/ SO	h. MP	i. ME	j. XP				
6. D		10.5									10.5	200.0	210.5	
7. N		4.0									4.0	55.0	59.0	
8. H												10.0	10.0	
9. W														
10. NG		4.0									4.0	30.5	34.5	
11.														
12. NS		4.0									4.0	5.5	9.5	
13. DG/ DS														
14. TR														
15. AA														
16. Total this Sheet		22.5									22.5			
17. From Sheet No. 3	100.0	150.0	51.0									301.0		
18. Total	100.0	172.5	51.0										323.5	
19. Combat														
20. Immi- nent Danger														

DA FORM 759-1, AUG 2008   PREVIOUS EDITION OF APR 1998 IS OBSOLETE   APD PE v1.00

Figure 7-4. Sample AH-64(FS) DA Form 759-1 aircraft closeout summary (rated aviator)

INDIVIDUAL FLIGHT RECORD AND FLIGHT CERTIFICATE - ARMY
For use of this form, see AR 95-1, AR 95-23, and FM 3-04.300; the proponent agency is DCS, G-3/5/7.

AIRCRAFT CLOSEOUT SUMMARY

											1. Sheet No. 4

2. Name Doe, John D.						3. Rank CPT		4. Period 1 Nov 06 - 31 Oct 07			5. Acft/Flt Sim 2B-64D(FS)

FLIGHT COND SYM	\<\<FLYING DUTY SYMBOL\>\>									k. Total This Sheet	l. From Sheet No. 3	m. Total
	a. CP/ CE/ EO	b. PI/ OR/ AO	c. PC/ PO	d. UT/ MO	e. IP/ FE/ IO	f. IE/ FI	g. SP/ SI/ SO	h. MP	i. ME	j. XP		
6. D													
7. N													
8. H	2.0										2.0		2.0
9. W	7.0										7.0	55.5	62.5
10. NG													
11.													
12. NS													
13. DG/ DS													
14. TR													
15. AA													
16. Total this Sheet	9.0										9.0		
17. From Sheet No. 3	55.5											55.5	
18. Total	64.5												64.5
19. Combat													
20. Imminent Danger													

DA FORM 759-1, AUG 2008   PREVIOUS EDITION OF APR 1998 IS OBSOLETE   APD PE v1.00

Figure 7-5. Sample 2B-64D (FS) DA Form 759-1 aircraft closeout summary (rated aviator)

DEPARTMENT OF THE ARMY FORM 759 CLOSEOUT (RATED AVIATOR)

7-18. Prepare DA Form 759 for all individuals on flying status when closing flight records. Detailed instructions for completing DA Form 759 are in table 7-4. At closeout, arrange flight record forms in the DA Form 3513, as shown in figure 6-2 (page 6-6).

7-19. DA Form 759 contains four parts; all parts must be completed and all entries must be typed. The individual's commander must sign and date the form to certify the accuracy of the closeout data. If the individual's commander is not the certifying officer who authorized flight duties on DA Form 7120-R, the certifying officer authorizing flight duties will sign and date the closeout to certify the accuracy of the closeout data. The DA Form 759 must be digitally signed in CAFRS. If the commander is unable to digitally certify within CAFRS a remark must be added to part IV of the 759.

Table 7-4. Instructions for completing DA Form 759 closeout (rated aviator)

Item	Instructions
Part I. Biography/Demographic	
Note: All required dates on all DA Forms 759 will be in the DD MMM YY format (15 JUN 03).	
Block 1thru 4	Enter the appropriate information from blocks 1 through 4 of current DA Form 759-1.
Block 5	Enter the date of birth.
Block 6	Enter the aviation service entry date (the date the aviator received his initial aeronautical certification orders or certificate of completion and aviator wings).
Block 7	Enter the branch of service.
Block 8	Enter the component designation, as shown in table 6-9.
***Block 9**	Enter the unit responsible for the Aircrew Training Program (ATP).
Block 10	Enter the duty MOS. The duty MOS may be obtained from the unit S1 section or modification table of organization and equipment/table of distribution and allowances (MTOE/TDA). DA Pam 600-3 lists commissioned officer MOSs and DA Pam 600-11 lists MOSs for warrant officers. Include additional skill and special qualification identifiers when reflected on MTOE/TDA documentation.
Block 11	Enter the assigned duty position.
Block 12	Indicate if the individual is in an operational flying duty position (yes or no). If yes, place date assigned to that position in block.
Part II. Flight Hours	
Section A. Qualifications	
Column a	Aircraft. The specific DOD aircraft in which the individual is qualified to operate (regardless of whether the individual currently flies) in order by date the individual qualified. The aircraft will be listed by mission, type, design, and series. For each aircraft in which the individual has logged time while using an NVD or night vision system (NVS), enter night system (NS) on the line directly below the aircraft entry in which the NS or DG/DS time was logged. Do not include DG/DS as a separate line entry. For aircraft in which the individual has logged time while using night vision goggles, enter NG on the line directly below NS or the aircraft entry in the absence of NS time.
	Compatible Flight Simulator. List, in the same order as the aircraft, the compatible flight simulator the individual has flown. (AR 95-1 lists the compatible flight simulators.) Leave a blank line between aircraft and flight simulator listings.
	Other Flight Simulators. List any other flight simulators the individual has flown that are not compatible with the aircraft operated.

Table 7-4. Instructions for completing DA Form 759 closeout (rated aviator)

Item	Instructions
	Other Aircraft. Any aircraft flown in which the individual is not qualified to operate and for which a DA Form 759-1 has been completed will be listed following the other flight simulators category. List this time as "RW" for rotary wing or "FW" for fixed-wing. Also, list time flown in aircraft that have been removed from the Army inventory under this category. In CAFRS remove the aircraft qualification date and the time flown will be moved to RW or FW. Leave a blank line between flight simulator and other aircraft listings.
Column b	Transcribe, from the previous DA Form 759 closeout, the date the aviator qualified in the aircraft and/or NS or night goggles (NG) listed. Also, enter the date of any new qualifications and a corresponding comment in Part IV. Leave this column blank for flight simulators and aircraft designated as "Other Aircraft."
Note: Obtain the dates for new aircraft and NVD or NVS qualification from the aviator's aircrew training record.	
Column c	Enter the date the individual completed his most recent flight in the aircraft or simulator and the NS or NVGs used (information from DA Form 759-2, temporary worksheet). Leave this column blank for aircraft designated as "Other Aircraft."
Column d	Aircraft (in which qualified). Enter the total hours flown from line 18, column m, of each DA Form 759-1 on the line that corresponds to the aircraft flown.
	NS: Enter the total hours flown from lines 12 (NS) and 13 (DG/DS), column **m**, of each DA Form 759-1 on the line that corresponds to the NS hours. NG: Enter the total hours flown from line 10 (NG), column **m**, of each DA Form 759-1 on the line that corresponds to the NG hours.
	NS and NG totals will not be included when the total number of flight hours is calculated in Part II Section B.
	Compatible Flight Simulator. Enter the total hours flown from line 18, column **m**, of each DA Form 759-1 on the line that corresponds to the flight simulator flown.
	Other Aircraft (not qualified or retired from Army inventory). Add from DA Form 759-2 any hours flown in an aircraft the individual is not qualified in to the RW or FW time (Part II, Column a) of the previous DA Form 759. Enter the total hours flown.
Notes: 1. When the aviator becomes qualified in the aircraft, subtract hours previously logged in the flight records under "FW" or "RW" from that category at the next closeout and enter as indicated above as a qualified aircraft. 2. When aircraft are removed from the Army inventory, update DA Form 759 at the next closeout. Remove those aircraft from Part II, Section A. Total hours and add to either "FW" or "RW," as noted under "Other Aircraft" above. In CAFRS remove the aircraft qualification date and the time flown will be moved to RW or FW. Do not add time to historical hours.	
Columns e through n	Enter the total hours flown from line 18, columns **a** through **j**, of each DA Form 759-1 in the blocks that correspond to the duty position and aircraft or flight simulator flown. Ensure you carry forward aircraft and simulators from previous DA Forms 759 that were not flown during current period.
Section B. Total Hours	
Note: Section B is a compilation of total aircraft time and does not include flight simulator time. NS time is a part of each respective airframe total hours; therefore, NS time from Part II, Section A, column **d**, is not added to obtain total hours. Blocks in Section B are updated at each closeout of the individual's flight records. Block g, "Historical Hours," is never updated and always remains the same.	
Block a	Enter the cumulative totals of combat hours flown from all DA Forms 759-1, line 19, column **m**. (The total in this block will be updated each closeout only if combat time was flown during the period covered.)
Block b	Enter the cumulative totals of imminent danger hours flown from all DA Forms 759-1, line 20, column **m**. (The total in this block will be updated each closeout only if imminent danger time was flown during the period covered.)
Blocks c and e	The operations officer will verify new civilian flight hours from civilian logbooks. Once verified, add these hours to the total entered on the previous DA Form 759. Explain the verification and the change in hours in Part IV, Remarks.

Table 7-4. Instructions for completing DA Form 759 closeout (rated aviator)

Item	Instructions
Block d	Add all military rotary-wing aircraft totals, to include RW, in Section A, column **d**, and enter the total in this block. Do not include NS, NG, or flight simulator time.
Block f	Add all military FW aircraft totals, to include FW, in Section A, and enter the total in this block. Do not include NS, NG, or flight simulator time.
Block g	Transcribe the historical hours from the previous DA Form 759 closeout to this block. The historical hours block is used to track time prior to 1987 when the change in format of DA Form 759-series became effective.
Block h	Add the hours in blocks **c** through **g** and enter the total in hours and tenths of hours in this block.
Page 2, DA Form 759, Blocks 1 through 4	Transcribe information from Part I, blocks 1 through 4 to this section.
Part III. Aircrew Training Program (ATP)	
Note: ATP requirements include hours, tasks, and iterations identified in the appropriate aircrew training manuals, readiness level progression, and the APART. Failure of an individual to complete any portion of the ATP requires a comment in Part IV, Remarks. The individual's DA Form 7120-R, with enclosures, will be used to assist the flight records clerk with the completion of this section.	
Block 1	Enter flight activity category.
Block 2	For maintenance test pilots (MP, ME), enter the most recent date of the maintenance test pilot's flight evaluation/re-evaluation.
Block 3	Enter the date of the most recent flight physical. If the individual is on a one calendar month extension, use the date from the previous DA Form 759 and make the appropriate remark in Part IV. On the next closeout, annotate in Part IV when the flight physical was completed. The physical examination is an annual requirement according to AR 95-1 and is not considered part of the APART.
Blocks 4 and 5	Enter the date of the most recent training, if applicable.
Block 6	Enter the date the individual completed all Annual Proficiency and Readiness Test (APART) requirements. (This will be the latest date that corresponds to the standardization flight evaluation [Block 9], instrument evaluation [Block 10], or -10 test, which is not shown on the reverse of DA Form 759).
Note: If the individual fails to complete the APART successfully, leave block 6 blank and enter the appropriate comment in Part IV.	
Block 7	Enter the primary aircraft mission symbol, type, design, and series.
Note: TC 1-210 defines the Flight Activity Category. Do not enter seat designation as "FS" or "BS," for example; AH-64A (FS) should be entered as AH-64A.	
Block 8	Enter the appropriate readiness level for the individual's primary aircraft.
Block 9	Enter the date of the most recent standardization flight evaluation for the individual's primary aircraft, if applicable.
Block 10	Enter the date of the most recent instrument evaluation for the individual's primary aircraft.
Block 11	Enter the individual's alternate aircraft, if designated. (For example, if the aviator's primary aircraft is rotary wing, his/her alternate aircraft would be fixed wing, if he/she were rated in both fixed and rotary wing aircraft. If not rated in both, leave blank.)
Block 12	Enter the appropriate readiness level for the individual's alternate aircraft, if designated. Note: TC 1-210 defines flight readiness levels.
Block 13	Enter the date of the most recent standardization flight evaluation for the individual's alternate aircraft, if designated.

Table 7-4. Instructions for completing DA Form 759 closeout (rated aviator)

Item	Instructions
Block 14	Enter the date of the most recent instrument evaluation for the aviator's alternate aircraft, if designated.
Block 15	Enter the individual's additional aircraft, if designated.
Block 16	Enter the appropriate readiness level for the individual's additional aircraft, if designated.
Block 17	Enter the date of the most recent standardization flight evaluation for the individual's additional aircraft, if designated.

Note: If the individual has more than one alternate or additional aircraft designated, list second and subsequent entries in Part IV in the same format as the corresponding categories in Part III.

Part IV. Remarks	
	Enter a historical narrative of the individual's flying status, qualifications, and proficiency if they are not stated elsewhere on the form. Use the remarks in table 6-8 to ensure consistency.
Commander's signature and date	The individual's commander must sign and date the form to certify the accuracy of the closeout data. If the individual's commander is not the certifying officer who authorized flight duties on DA Form 7120-R, the certifying officer authorizing flight duties will sign and date the closeout to certify the accuracy of the closeout data. The DA Form 759 must be digitally signed in CAFRS. If the commander is unable to digitally certify within CAFRS a remark must be added to part IV of the 759.

Notes:
1. Commander's signature block contains name, rank, and branch only.
2. For ARNG and U.S. Army Reserves only, the commander's designated representative may sign the commander's block. This individual must be under assumption of command orders to be designated the commander's representative.

7-20. Mandatory and standard remarks used to complete DA Form 759, part IV, are given in table 7-5.

Table 7-5. Examples of mandatory and standard remarks (rated aviator)

MANDATORY REMARKS
Note: The following remarks are mandatory for every closeout.
1. Records closed (date) (reason).
2. Aviator has completed _____ months of total operational flying duty credit.
Note: Aviator's TOFDC can be verified by requesting a copy of his officer records brief (ORB) through the unit S1 section.
3a. Aviator has completed ATP requirements.
3b. Aviator has not completed ATP requirement(s). (Explain what ATP requirements have not been completed and the actions that have been taken.)
3c. Aviator has no ATP requirements due to _____. (State reasons individual has no requirements.)
Note: When an individual completes or fails to complete ATP requirements, a remark will be annotated on the next DA Form 759 closeout of the result as shown below.
3d. Aviator completed previous ATP requirements on (date).
3e. Previous ATP requirements waived by (as appropriate) commander on (date).
3f. Aviator failed to complete ATP requirements within the additional timeframe. (State action(s) taken.)
4a. ACT-E train the trainer complete.
4b. ACT-E qualification complete.

Table 7-5. Examples of mandatory and standard remarks (rated aviator)

4c. ACT-E refresher complete.
4d. ACT-E instructor qualification complete.
STANDARD REMARKS
Note: When a standard remark applies to a closeout, that remark becomes mandatory. If a situation arises that is not explained in a standard remark, it will be explained in easy-to-understand language.
1. Aviator is temporarily suspended from flying duty from (date) to (date) because of (reason). (This usually is used to explain temporary medical grounding, but may be used for other reasons.)
2. Aviator awarded senior or master aviator badge under provisions of (issuing authority), (date).
3. Aviator completed (type) NVG training on (date).
4. Aviator qualified in (mission, type, design, and series) aircraft on (date). Added (number) hours to this aircraft previously logged under "RW" (or FW) time on DA Form 759.
5. Aviator has successfully completed the U.S. Navy Underwater Egress 9D5A Device Training conducted at (location) on (date).
6. Error sheet (sheet #), Part (part #) (give a detailed description of the error) is incorrect. Reads "(say what is incorrect)," should read "(enter corrected data)." Corrected this sheet.
7. Logging of combat or imminent danger time is authorized under provisions of (issuing authority), (date).
Note: This remark will be used only when adjustments to combat (C) or imminent danger (D) time have been made for the closeout period.
8. Aviator completed, disqualified from, or relieved from (type of aviation course) on (date).
9. Violation of (regulation) on (date). (Briefly describe the violation and the action taken.)
10. Aviator involved in (Class A, B, or C) accident on (date) in (type of aircraft) as (pilot duty station).
Note: If the accident classification is upgraded or downgraded, an entry will be made on the next closeout to reflect the change.
11. Aviator reassigned under provisions (issuing authority) orders number____, dated____. Reassigned to (unit and station).
12. Medical waiver granted effective (date) for (summarize medical condition waived).
13. Aviator must wear corrective lenses when performing duties as a crewmember.
14. Suspension from flying duty on (date) under provisions (authority) for (purpose).
15. Aviator placed before a flying evaluation board for (reason) on (date). (State determination of board.)
16. Operations officer verified (number) hours of civilian (fixed- or rotary-wing) hours flown from (date) to (date).
17. Added (number) hours to "RW" (or FW) time on DA Form 759. (Aircraft) removed from the Army inventory effective (date).
18. Flight record lost on (date). (Enter action to locate missing records) Records reconstructed from ____ on (date).
19. (Aircraft) designated as individual's second (third and so on) additional aircraft effective (date).
20. Aviator has completed initial physiological training prescribed in FM 3-04.301 including hypobaric (low-pressure/high-altitude) chamber qualification on (date).

Table 7-5. Examples of mandatory and standard remarks (rated aviator)

21. Aviator has completed refresher physiological training including hypobaric (low-pressure/high-altitude) chamber qualification on (date).
22. Commander is unable to digitally certify 759 due to_____.

7-21. Table 7-6 provides service component category codes.

Table 7-6. Service component category codes

Code	Component
RA	Regular Army.
USAR	United States Army Reserve.
ARNG	Army National Guard.
DAC	Department of the Army civilian employed for flying in military aircraft.
CIV	Civilian employed by contractor for flying duty in Army aircraft under a specific contract.
FGN	Foreign military student or rated pilot.
OTHER	All other components.

7-22. Examples of completed DA Forms 759 are shown in figure 7-6 (page 7-17) and figure 7-7 (page 7-18).

INDIVIDUAL FLIGHT RECORD AND FLIGHT CERTIFICATE-ARMY
For use of this form, see AR 95-1, AR 95-23, and FM 3-04.300; the proponent agency is DCS, G-3/5/7.

PART I. BIO/DEMOGRAPHIC	1. Sheet No. 4

2. Name			3. Rank
Doe, John D.			CPT

4. Period		5. DOB	6. ASED	7. Branch
1 Nov 06 - 31 Oct 07		13 Oct 1983	30 Aug 2005	AV

8. Component	9. Unit	10. DMOS
RA	A Co 1st Bn 17th Avn Regt	15B

11. Duty Position	12. Operational Position
AH-64D Pilot	Yes 20 Nov 2006

PART II. FLIGHT HOURS
SECTION A. QUALIFICATIONS

a. Acft System	b. Date Qual	c. Last Flight	d. Total Time	e. CP/ CE/ EO	f. PI/ OR/ AO	g. PC/ PO	h. UT/ MO	i. IP/ FE/ IO	j. IE/ FI	k. SP/ SI/ SO	l. MP	m. ME	n. XP
AH-64D(BS)	25 Aug 05	01 Oct 07	312.5	50.0	150.0	112.5							
NG	25 Aug 05	15 Dec 06	46.0										
NS	25 Aug 05	15 Dec 06	35.5										
AH-64D(FS)	25 Aug 05	01 Sep 07	323.5	100.0	172.5	51.0							
NG	25 Aug 05	01 Sep 07	34.5										
NS	25 Aug 05	01 Sep 07	9.5										
2B-64D(FS)		15 Jun 07	64.5		64.5								

SECTION B. TOTAL HOURS

a. Combat	b. Imminent Danger	c. Civilian RW	d. Military RW
	5.0		636.0

e. Civilian FW	f. Military FW	g. Historical Hours	h. Total Hours
			636.0

DA FORM 759, AUG 2008   PREVIOUS EDITION OF APR 98 IS OBSOLETE   Page 1 of 2
APD PE v1.00ES

Figure 7-6. Sample DA Form 759 closeout (rated aviator) (front)

INDIVIDUAL FLIGHT RECORD AND FLIGHT CERTIFICATE--ARMY *(Cont'd)* For use of this form, see AR 95-1, AR 95-23, and FM 3-04.300; the proponent agency is DCS, G-3/5/7.					1. Sheet No. 4
2. Name Doe, John D.				3. Rank CPT	4. Period 1 Nov 06 - 31 Oct 07

PART III. ATP

1. FAC 1	2. MTFE		3. Phys Exam 01 Nov 2006	4. Ejection Seat	5. Alt Chamber	6. APART Completed 20 Oct 2007
7. Primary Acft AH-64D		8. RL 1		9. Std Flt Eval 20 Oct 2007		10. Inst Eval 20 Oct 2007
11. Alternate Acft		12 RL		13. Std Flt Eval		14. Inst Eval
15. Additional Acft		16. RL		17. Std Flt Eval		

PART IV. REMARKS

1. Records closed 31 Oct 2007 due to end of birth month.

2. Aviator has completed 23 months of total operational flying duty credit.

3. Aviator has completed ATP requirements.

4. ACT-E refresher complete.

Commander's Typed Name, Rank, Branch EMMETT C. BOLTON JR CPT, AV	Signature Digitally signed using CAFRS login	Date 20 Dec 2007

DA FORM 759, AUG 2008

Page 2 of 2
APD PE v1.00ES

Figure 7-7. Sample DA Form 759 closeout (rated aviator) (back)

Chapter 8

Crewmember/Noncrewmember, Fly for Pay Aviators, and Unmanned Aircraft System Personnel Flight Records

This chapter details flight records management procedures for personnel performing duties as crewmembers/noncrewmembers, UAS personnel, and rated aviators who do not qualify for continuous aviation career incentive pay (ACIP), commonly referred to as fly for pay aviators. It remains imperative that these records be comprehensively and accurately maintained. Personnel completing flight records should follow the procedures contained within this chapter and refer to the appropriate pay regulations when reporting flight time for pay incentives.

DEPARTMENT OF THE ARMY FORM 759-3

TEMPORARY WORKSHEET

8-1. DA Form 759-3 is used as both a temporary worksheet and a consolidation worksheet for flights performed by a CRM/NCRM, UAS personnel, and fly for pay aviators. It incorporates requirements from AR 37-104-4 to manage monthly flight hours.

8-2. Flight records personnel manage monthly flight requirements for entitlement to HDIP. Table 8-1 (page 8-2) contains instructions for completing DA Form 759-3 as a temporary worksheet. Figures 8-1 (page 8-3) and 8-2 (page 8-4) depict a sample temporary worksheet.

8-3. Take information for the temporary worksheet from DA Forms 2408-12. A single line may be used when the date, aircraft, flying duty symbol, flight conditions, and mission symbol are the same. The hours flown for these like entries may be combined or listed as separate entries. When any of this information is not the same, use a separate line.

8-4. Make as many entries on the form as space allows for daily use. A new form for each month is not required. Leave a blank line after each month's entries.

8-5. Enter flight time with pencil, in hours and tenths of hours.

8-6. For the months in which no hours were recorded, enter the month in column **a** and the comment "No Time Flown" across columns **b** through **d**.

8-7. Do not file the temporary worksheet with DA Form 759, DA Form 759-1, and DA Form 759-3 when the crewmember/noncrewmember's, UAS personnel's, and fly for pay aviator's flight records are closed. The unit commander or operations officer determines how long the worksheets are retained (90 days are recommended). Initiate a new temporary worksheet each time the flight records are closed.

Table 8-1. Instructions for completing DA Form 759-3 temporary worksheet (crewmember/noncrewmember, and unmanned aircraft personnel)

Item	Instructions
Note: All required dates will be in the DD MMM YY format (11 MAR 03).	
Block 1	Leave blank (sheet number not required).
Block 2	Enter the last name, first name, and middle initial.
Block 3	Enter the rank.
Block 4	Enter the period covered (DD MMM YY—leave end date open until closeout).
Block 5	Enter the type of flying status (CRM/NCRM).
Block 6	Enter the effective date from the flight orders.
Column a	Enter the date of flight. The first entry will be the month, followed by the day in the space underneath. (Figure 6-16.)
Column b	Enter the aircraft mission, type, design, and series recorded on DA Form 2408-12.
Column c	Enter the flying duty symbol recorded on DA Form 2408-12.
Column d	Enter the flight condition symbol recorded on DA Form 2408-12.
Column e	Enter the mission symbol recorded on DA Form 2408-12.
Note: Mission symbols are necessary to ensure the hours recorded on DA Form 2408-12 are consistent with the duties performed as described in the original flight orders. Example: A maintenance supervisor should not expect HDIP for hours logged with a mission symbol other than "F." (See AR 600-106.)	
Column f	Enter the hours flown in hours and tenths of hours.
Column g through k,	Leave blank. These blocks will be completed at the end of the month on the consolidation worksheet.
Blocks 7 through 15	Leave blank.

INDIVIDUAL FLIGHT RECORD AND FLIGHT CERTIFICATE - ARMY

For use of this form, see AR 95-1, AR 95-23, and FM 3-04.300; the proponent agency is DCS, G-3/5/7.

FLIGHT RECORD AND FLIGHT PAY WORKSHEET

1. Sheet No.

2. Name	3. Rank
Doe, James D.	CPT

4. Period	5. Flying Status	6. Effective Date
1 Nov 06 - 31 Oct 07	CRM	01 Jan 2002

Date/ Month	Acft	Flying Duty Sym	Flt Cond Sym	Msn Sym	Hours Flown	Entitle-ment Yes or No	Based on Hours Flown During	Excess Hours This Month	Excess Hours Accum	Remarks
a	b	c	d	e	f	g	h	i	j	k
NOV										
20	UH-60L	MO	D	T	4.0					
DEC										
18	UH-60L	MO	D	T	4.0					
JAN	No	Time	Flown							
FEB										
10	UH-60L	MO	D	T	6.0					
15	UH-60L	MO	D	T	2.0					
MAR										
15	UH-60L	MO	D	D	5.0					
APR	No	Time	Flown							
MAY	No	Time	Flown							
JUN										
20	UH-60L	MO	D	D	6.0					
JUL	No	Time	Flown							
AUG										
12	UH-60L	MO	D	T	2.0					
SEP	No	Time	Flown							
OCT	No	Time	Flown							

Total Hours This Sheet	7.	Hours From Sheet No.	10.	Total Hours to Date	13.
Total Combat Hours This Sheet	8.	Combat Hours From Sheet No.	11.	Total Combat Hours to Date	14.
Total Imminent Danger Hours This Sheet	9.	Imminent Danger Hours From Sheet No.	12.	Total Imminent Danger Hours to Date	15.

DA FORM 759-3, AUG 2008   PREVIOUS EDITION OF AUG 93 IS OBSOLETE   APD PE v1.00

Figure 8-1. Sample DA Form 759-3 temporary worksheet (flight surgeon)

INDIVIDUAL FLIGHT RECORD AND FLIGHT CERTIFICATE - ARMY

For use of this form, see AR 95-1, AR 95-23, and FM 3-04.300; the proponent agency is DCS, G-3/5/7.

FLIGHT RECORD AND FLIGHT PAY WORKSHEET										1. Sheet No.
2. Name Smith, John A.										3. Rank SFC
4. Period 1 Nov 06 - 31 Oct 07							5. Flying Status CRM			6. Effective Date
Date/ Month	Acft	Flying Duty Sym	Flt Cond Sym	Msn Sym	Hours Flown	Entitle- ment Yes or No	Based on Hours Flown During	Excess Hours		Remarks
								This Month	Accum	
a	b	c	d	e	f	g	h	i	j	k
NOV	No	Time	Flown							
DEC										
10	RQ-7B	PO	D	T	3.3					
16	RQ-7B	SI	D	T	9.8					
JAN	No	Time	Flown							
FEB										
06	RQ-7B	SI	D	T	4.3					
MAR										
08	RQS-7B	PO	N	T	7.2					
APR										
14	RQS-7B	AO	D	T	9.4					
MAY	No	Time	Flown							
Jun	No	Time	Flown							
Jul										
14	RQS-7B	SI	D	T	7.3					
25	RQS-7B	SI	N	T	5.6					
Aug	No	Time	Flown							
SEP	No	Time	Flown							
OCT										
25	RQS-7B	AO	D	T	4.8					

Total Hours This Sheet	7.	Hours From Sheet No.	10.	Total Hours to Date	13.
Total Combat Hours This Sheet	8.	Combat Hours From Sheet No.	11.	Total Combat Hours to Date	14.
Total Imminent Danger Hours This Sheet	9.	Imminent Danger Hours From Sheet No.	12.	Total Imminent Danger Hours to Date	15.

DA FORM 759-3, AUG 2008   PREVIOUS EDITION OF AUG 93 IS OBSOLETE   APD PE v1.00

Figure 8-2. Sample DA Form 759-3 temporary worksheet (unmanned aircraft system crewmember)

CONSOLIDATION WORKSHEET

8-8. DA Form 759-3 will also be used as the consolidation worksheet for flights performed by a crewmember/noncrewmember and fly for pay aviators. Table 8-2 contains instructions for completing DA Form 759-3 as a consolidation worksheet. Figure 8-3 (page 8-6) and figure 8-4 (page 8-7) show examples of consolidation worksheets. The following is general information for completing the consolidation worksheet.

8-9. File DA Form 759-3 consolidated worksheet with DA Form 759 and DA Form 759-1 when an individual's flight records are closed.

8-10. Number the consolidated worksheet the same series as the DA Form 759. For example, if this is the fifth closeout, label the consolidated worksheet sheet number 5.

8-11. Maintain DA Form 759-3 and calculate flight entitlements throughout the period. When the flight records are closed, type the information in the form using the temporary worksheets that pertain to the period covered and the previous DA Form 759-3 consolidation worksheet or worksheets.

8-12. For each month, consolidate the time by aircraft, flying duty symbol, flight condition symbol and, mission symbol (only combat or imminent danger). Enter the total time in hours and tenths of hours.

8-13. Type all entries. Make as many entries to the form as space allows. Leave a blank line after each month's entries.

8-14. For the months in which no hours were recorded, enter the month in column **a** and the comment "No Time Flown" across columns **b** through **d**.

**Table 8-2. Instructions for completing DA Form 759-3
consolidation worksheet (crewmember/noncrewmember and unmanned aircraft system
personnel)**

Item	Instructions
Note: All required dates will be in the DD MMM YY format (11 MAR 03).	
Block 1	Enter the chronological sheet number.
Blocks 2 through 6	Transcribe information to these blocks from the individual's temporary worksheet.
Column a	Enter the month that covers each set of entries to be consolidated from the temporary worksheet.
Columns b through f	At the end of each month, total the number of hours flown for each group of like flights from the temporary worksheet or worksheets. Enter the totals in these columns. Column e will be filled out only if it pertains to mission symbols containing a "C" or "D."
Column g	For each month in which the minimum flight requirements have been met, enter "Yes." If the flight requirements have not been met and excess hours are not sufficient to meet these requirements, enter "No."
Note: Excess time from the previous 5 months starting with the fifth previous month may be used to qualify for entitlement of HDIP or ACIP for the month in which minimum hours were not met. If time cannot be recovered from the previous 5 months, a 3-month grace period will start. (Refer to DODFMR 7000.14-R, Volume 7A for further information on 90-day grace periods.)	
Column h	Leave blank if individual qualified for HDIP or ACIP during that month. If excess hours are needed to qualify for entitlement to HDIP or ACIP, enter the month or months and the number of excess hours used from each month to meet that requirement.
Column i	Enter any excess flight time, in hours and tenths of hours, for the current month. If there is no excess time, leave blank.

**Table 8-2. Instructions for completing DA Form 759-3
consolidation worksheet (crewmember/noncrewmember and unmanned aircraft system
personnel)**

Item	Instructions
Column j	Enter any accumulated excess flight time, in hours and tenths of hours. Determine accumulated hours as follows: 1) If column l is used, add it to the previous month's accumulated time. If there is any excess time remaining from the fifth previous month, subtract it from the new total. 2) If column h is used, subtract the amount used from the previous month's accumulated time. If there is any excess time remaining from the fifth previous month, subtract it from the new total. 3) If columns h and i are not used, subtract any excess time remaining from the fifth previous month from the previous month's accumulated time.
	Note: This block is used to quickly determine an individual's amount of excess time available for the next month.
Column k	Explain any adjustments made to the total in column j. Use "for" to note hours used for another month. Use "from" to note that excess time from the fifth previous month, which can no longer be used, has been subtracted. Also, explain any temporary restriction from flying duty in which flight hours or entitlement is affected.
	Note: It is not necessary to list hours brought forward from previous closeouts in column k. Instead, add these hours to column j, as necessary.
Block 7	Total the hours in column f, and enter the total in this block.
	Note: When the consolidation worksheet requires two or more pages, place the cumulative total in block 7 of the last sheet.
Block 8	Total the hours in column f with the mission symbols containing a "C" (combat) and place total in this block.
Block 9	Total the hours in column f with the mission symbols containing a "D" (imminent danger) and place total in this block.
Block 10	Enter the total hours from block 13 of the previous consolidated DA Form 759-3. Indicate the sheet number of the previous consolidated DA Form 759-3 in the space provided.
Block 11	Enter the total hours from block 14 of the previous consolidated DA Form 759-3. Indicate the sheet number of the previous consolidated DA Form 759-3 in the space provided.
Block 112	Enter the total hours from block 15 of the previous consolidated DA Form 759-3. Indicate the sheet number of the previous consolidated DA Form 759-3 in the space provided.
Block 13	Add block 7 to block 10. Enter the total in hours and tenths of hours.
Block 14	Add block 8 to block 11. Enter the total in hours and tenths of hours.
Block 15	Add block 9 to block 12. Enter the total hours and tenths of hours.

INDIVIDUAL FLIGHT RECORD AND FLIGHT CERTIFICATE - ARMY

For the use of this form, see AR 95-1, AR 95-23, and FM 3-04.300; the proponent agency is DCS, G-3/5/7.

FLIGHT RECORD AND FLIGHT PAY WORKSHEET

1. Sheet No.
4

2. Name	3. Rank
Doe, James D.	CPT

4. Period	5. Flying Status	6. Effective Date
1 Nov 06 - 31 Oct 07	CRM	01 Jan 2002

Date/ Month	Acft	Flying Duty Sym	Flt Cond Sym	Msn Sym	Hours Flown	Entitle-ment Yes or No	Based on Hours Flown During	Excess Hours This Month	Excess Hours Accum	Remarks
a	b	c	d	e	f	g	h	i	j	k
NOV	UH-60L	MO	D		4.0	YES			0.0	
DEC	UH-60L	MO	D		4.0	YES			0.0	
JAN	No	Time	Flown			YES	FEB 4.0		0.0	
FEB	UH-60L	MO	D		8.0	YES		4.0	0.0	-4.0 for JAN
MAR	UH-60L	MO	D	D	5.0	YES		1.0	1.0	-1.0 for AUG
APR	No	Time	Flown			NO			1.0	
MAY	No	Time	Flown			NO			1.0	
JUN	UH-60L	MO	D	D	6.0	YES		2.0	3.0	-1.0 for AUG
JUL	No	Time	Flown			NO			3.0	
AUG	UH-60L	MO	D		2.0	YES	MAR 1.0 JUN 1.0		1.0	
SEP	No	Time	Flown			NO			1.0	
OCT	No	Time	Flown			NO			1.0	

	7.	Hours From Sheet No.	10.	Total Hours to Date	13.
Total Hours This Sheet	29.0	3	100	Total Hours to Date	129.0
Total Combat Hours This Sheet	8.	Combat Hours From Sheet No.	11.	Total Combat Hours to Date	14.
Total Imminent Danger Hours This Sheet	9. 11.0	Imminent Danger Hours From Sheet No.	12.	Total Imminent Danger Hours to Date	15. 11.0

DA FORM 759-3, AUG 2008   PREVIOUS EDITION OF AUG 93 IS OBSOLETE   APD PE v1.00

Figure 8-3. Sample DA Form 759-3 consolidated worksheet (flight surgeon)

INDIVIDUAL FLIGHT RECORD AND FLIGHT CERTIFICATE - ARMY
For use of this form, see AR 95-1, AR 95-23, and FM 3-04.300; the proponent agency is DCS, G-3/5/7.

FLIGHT RECORD AND FLIGHT PAY WORKSHEET										1. Sheet No. 8
2. Name Smith, John A.										3. Rank SFC
4. Period 1 Nov 06 - 31 Oct 07							5. Flying Status CRM			6. Effective Date

Date/ Month	Acft	Flying Duty Sym	Flt Cond Sym	Msn Sym	Hours Flown	Entitle-ment Yes or No	Based on Hours Flown During	Excess Hours		Remarks
								This Month	Accum	
a	b	c	d	e	f	g	h	i	j	k
NOV	No	Time	Flown							
DEC	RQ-7B	SI	D		9.8					
DEC	RQS-7B	PO	D		3.3					
JAN	No	Time	Flown							
FEB	RQ-7B	SI	D		4.3					
MAR	RQS-7B	PO	N		7.2					
APR	RQS-7B	AO	D		9.4					
MAY	No	Time	Flown							
Jun	No	Time	Flown							
Jul	RQS-7B	SI	D		7.3					
Jul	RQS-7B	SI	N		5.6					
Aug	No	Time	Flown							
SEP	No	Time	Flown							
OCT	RQ-7B	AO	D		4.8					

Total Hours This Sheet	7. 51.7	Hours From Sheet No. 7	10. 605.5	Total Hours to Date	13. 657.2
Total Combat Hours This Sheet	8. 0	Combat Hours From Sheet No. 7	11. 222.8	Total Combat Hours to Date	14. 222.8
Total Imminent Danger Hours This Sheet	9. 0	Imminent Danger Hours From Sheet No. 7	12. 0	Total Imminent Danger Hours to Date	15. 0

DA FORM 759-3, AUG 2008	PREVIOUS EDITION OF AUG 93 IS OBSOLETE	APD PE v1.00

Figure 8-4. Sample DA Form 759-3 consolidated worksheet (unmanned aircraft system crewmember)

DEPARTMENT OF THE ARMY FORM 759-1

AIRCRAFT CLOSEOUT SUMMARY

8-15. Use DA Form 759-1 as a record of flight time, by flying duty and flight condition, for each aircraft (and/or flight simulator for flight surgeons) in which an individual performs duties during the closeout period. Table 8-3 provides detailed instructions. Figure 8-5 (page 8-11), figure 8-6 (page 8-12), and figure 8-7 (page 8-13) provide examples. The following are general instructions for completing the aircraft closeout summary.

8-16. File DA Form 759-1 with a DA Form 759 when an individual's flight record is closed. Type all entries.

8-17. Prepare DA Form 759-1 for each aircraft (and/or flight simulator for flight surgeons) listed on the individual's DA Form 759-3 consolidation worksheet. Total all like entries from the worksheet, by aircraft. Carry the totals forward to DA Form 759-1 when the individual's flight record is closed.

Number DA Forms 759-1 the same as DA Form 759 and arrange them in the IFRF according to figure 6-2 (page 6-6).

Table 8-3. Instructions for completing DA Form 759-1 aircraft closeout summary (crewmember/noncrewmember and unmanned aircraft system personnel)

Item	*Instructions*
Note: All required dates will be in the DD MMM YY format (11 MAR 03).	
Blocks 1 through 4	Enter the appropriate information from blocks 1 through 5 of DA Form 759-3, consolidated worksheet.
Block 5	Enter the aircraft mission, type, design, and series.
Lines 6 through 15 and columns a through g	From the corresponding consolidated DA Form 759-3, total the hours for all like entries according to flying duty and flight condition symbols. Enter the totals in hours and tenths of hours on the appropriate line in the correct column.
Notes:1. Columns **c** and **h** through **j** are reserved for aviators. 2. HO (Hands-On) and TR (Terrain) time are no longer logged on DA Form 2408-12 or DA Form 759-1 as a flight condition, according to AR 95-1. Previous time logged on lines 9 and 15 of DA Form 759-1 will remain as is. 3. NV (Night Vision) time is no longer tracked and has been deleted from DA Form 759-1. Row 11 will remain blank, reserved for future use. Time in row 11 was previously moved and added into the times in row 10.	
Column k	Total the hours across lines 6 through 15 for each flight condition, and enter the totals in hours and tenths of hours in the corresponding lines of column **k**. Add hours in column **k** downward, and place this total in the block on line 16, column **k**.
Column l	Enter the sheet number of the previous DA Form 759-1 at the top of this column. Then enter the totals in hours and tenths of hours from column **m** of the previous DA Form 759-1 for the same aircraft mission, type, design, and series or flight simulator.

Table 8-3. Instructions for completing DA Form 759-1 aircraft closeout summary (crewmember/noncrewmember and unmanned aircraft system personnel)

Item	Instructions
Column m	Add columns **k** and **l** across on lines 6 through 15, and enter the new totals in the corresponding lines of column m (in hours and tenths of hours). Add hours in column **m** together and place this total in the block on line 18, column **m**.
Line 16	Total the hours downward in columns **a** through **g**. Enter the totals in hours and tenths of hours in the corresponding column on line 16.
	Note: To check the total, add columns **a** through **g** across on line 16. This total should agree with the total of column **k** on line 16.
Line 17	Enter the sheet number (same as that entered at the top of column l) at the beginning of this line. Enter the totals (in hours and tenths of hours) from line 18 of the previous DA Form 759-1 to the corresponding columns of this line.
	Note: To check the total, add columns **a** through **g** across on line 17. This total should agree with the total of column **l** and 17.
Line 18	Add lines 16 and 17 downward, and enter the totals (in hours and tenths of hours) in the corresponding blocks on this line.
	Note: To check the total, add columns **a** through **g** across on line 18. This total should agree with the total of column **m** on line 18.
Line 19, columns a through g	From the corresponding consolidated DA Form 759-3, total the mission symbols containing combat hours for all like entries, according to flying duty symbols. Enter these totals (in hours and tenths of hours) in the corresponding columns on line 19.
Line 20, columns a through g	From the corresponding consolidated DA Form 759-3, total the mission symbols containing imminent danger hours for all like entries, according to flying duty symbols. Enter these totals (in hours and tenths of hours) in the corresponding columns on line 20.
Lines 19 and 20, column k	Add across columns a through **g** and enter the total (in hours and tenths of hours) in the corresponding block in lines 19 and 20, column **k**.
Lines 19 and 20, column l	From the previous DA Form 759-1, enter the totals (in hours and tenths of hours) from lines 19 and 20, column **m** into the corresponding block in lines 19 and 20, column **l**.
Lines 19 and 20, column m	Add the totals across in columns **k** and **l** and enter the totals (in hours and tenths of hours) into the corresponding block in lines 19 and 20, column **m**.

INDIVIDUAL FLIGHT RECORD AND FLIGHT CERTIFICATE - ARMY

For use of this form, see AR 95-1, AR 95-23, and FM 3-04.300; the proponent agency is DCS, G-3/5/7.

AIRCRAFT CLOSEOUT SUMMARY

1. Sheet No.
4

2. Name	3. Rank	4. Period	5. Acft/Flt Sim
Doe, James D.	CPT	1 Nov 06 - 31 Oct 07	UH-60L

FLIGHT COND SYM	FLYING DUTY SYMBOL										k. Total This Sheet	l. From Sheet No. 3	m. Total
	a. CP/ CE/ EO	b. PI/ OR/ AO	c. PC/ PO	d. UT/ MO	e. IP/ FE/ IO	f. IE/ FI	g. SP/ SI/ SO	h. MP	i. ME	j. XP			
6. D				29.0							29.0	100.0	129.0
7. N													
8. H													
9. W													
10. NG													
11.													
12. NS													
13. DG/ DS													
14. TR													
15. AA													
16. Total this Sheet				29.0							29.0		
17. From Sheet No. 3				100.0								100.0	
18. Total				129.0									129.0
19. Combat													
20. Imminent Danger				11.0							11.0		11.0

DA FORM 759-1, AUG 2008   PREVIOUS EDITION OF APR 1998 IS OBSOLETE   APD PE v.1.00

Figure 8-5. Sample UH-60L DA Form 759-1 aircraft closeout summary (flight surgeon)

INDIVIDUAL FLIGHT RECORD AND FLIGHT CERTIFICATE - ARMY

For use of this form, see AR 95-1, AR 95-23, and FM 3-04.300; the proponent agency is DCS, G-3/5/7.

AIRCRAFT CLOSEOUT SUMMARY											1. Sheet No. 8-1

2. Name						3. Rank		4. Period		5. Acft/Flt Sim
Smith, John A						SFC		1 Nov 06 - 31 Oct 07		RQ-7B

FLIGHT COND SYM	a. CP/ CE/ EO	b. PI/ OR/ AO	c. PC/ PO	d. UT/ MO	e. IP/ FE/ IO	f. IE/ FI	g. SP/ SI/ SO	h. MP	i. ME	j. XP	k. Total This Sheet	l. From Sheet No. 7-1	m. Total
6. D		4.8	3.3				14.1				22.2	35.3	57.5
7. N													
8. H													
9. W													
10. NG													
11.													
12. NS													
13. DG/ DS													
14. TR													
15. AA													
16. Total this Sheet		4.8	3.3				14.1				22.2		
17. From Sheet No. 7-1		8.5	6.8				20.0					35.3	
18. Total		13.3	10.1				34.1						57.5
19. Combat													
20. Imminent Danger													

DA FORM 759-1, AUG 2008   PREVIOUS EDITION OF APR 1998 IS OBSOLETE   APD PE v.1.00

Figure 8-6. Sample RQ-7B DA Form 759-1 aircraft closeout summary (unmanned aircraft system crewmember)

INDIVIDUAL FLIGHT RECORD AND FLIGHT CERTIFICATE - ARMY
For use of this form, see AR 95-1, AR 95-23, and FM 3-04.300; the proponent agency is DCS, G-3/5/7.

AIRCRAFT CLOSEOUT SUMMARY

											1. Sheet No. 8-2
2. Name Smith, John A				3. Rank SFC	4. Period 1 Nov 06 - 31 Oct 07						5. Acft/Flt Sim RQS-7B

FLIGHT COND SYM	a. CP/CE/EO	b. PI/OR/AO	c. PC/PO	d. UT/MO	e. IP/FE/IO	f. IE/FI	g. SP/SI/SO	h. MP	i. ME	j. XP	k. Total This Sheet	l. From Sheet No. 7-1	m. Total
6. D		9.4					7.3				16.7	87.5	104.2
7. N			7.2				5.6				12.8	64.6	77.4
8. H													
9. W													
10. NG													
11.													
12. NS													
13. DG/DS													
14. TR													
15. AA													
16. Total this Sheet		9.4	7.2				12.9				29.5		
17. From Sheet No. 7-1		28.7	22.5		82.4		18.5					152.1	
18. Total		38.1	29.7		82.4		31.4						181.6
19. Combat													
20. Imminent Danger													

DA FORM 759-1, AUG 2008   PREVIOUS EDITION OF APR 1998 IS OBSOLETE   APD PE v.1.00

Figure 8-7. Sample RQS-7B DA Form 759-1 aircraft closeout summary (unmanned aircraft system crewmember)

DEPARTMENT OF THE ARMY FORM 759

CLOSEOUT

8-18. Prepare a DA Form 759 when closing flight records of all individuals on flying status. Detailed instructions for completing DA Form 759 are in table 8-4. At closeout, arrange flight record forms in the DA Form 3513, as shown in figure 6-2 (page 6-6). Examples of completed DA Forms 759 are shown in figure 8-8 (page 8-19) and figure 8-9 (page 8-20). Figure 8-10 (page 8-21), and figure 8-11 (page 8-22) show examples of a completed closeout.

8-19. DA Form 759 contains four parts; complete all parts. Type all entries. The DA Form 759 must be signed by the individual's unit commander to be valid.

Table 8-4. Instructions for completing DA Form 759 closeout (crewmember/noncrewmember)

Item	Instructions
Part I. Biography/Demographic	
Note: All required dates on DA Form 759 will be in the DD MMM YY format (15 JUN 03).	
Block 1 thru 4	Enter the appropriate information from blocks 1 through 4 of current DA Form 759-1sheet number.
Block 5	Enter the date of birth.
Block 6	Enter the date the individual was awarded his original aviation badge (or flight surgeon badge) from the individual's basic aviation badge orders, maintained in the orders section in the IFRF. Operations personnel will use this date to determine eligibility for senior and master aviation badges. For non-aviation personnel such as door gunners that have not been awarded an aviation badge enter the effective date of their flight orders.
Block 7	For flight surgeons and other officers, enter the branch of service. For all others, leave blank.
Block 8	Enter the component designation, as shown in table 6-9.
*Block 9	Enter the unit responsible for the Aircrew Training Program (ATP).
Block 10	Enter the duty MOS. The duty MOS may be obtained from the unit S1 section or modification table of organization and equipment/table of distribution and allowances (MTOE/TDA). Include additional skill and special qualification identifiers when reflected on MTOE/TDA documentation.
Block 11	Enter the current assigned duty position.
Block 12	Leave blank.
Part II. Flight hours	
Section A. Qualifications	
Column a	Aircraft. Enter the specific DOD aircraft in which the individual is qualified to perform duties (regardless of whether the individual currently flies) in order by date the individual qualified. List the aircraft by mission, type, design, and series. For each aircraft in which the individual has logged time while using an NVD or NVS, enter NS on the line directly below the aircraft entry in which the NVD or NVS time was logged. For aircraft in which the individual has logged time while using night vision goggles, enter NG on the line directly below NS or the aircraft entry in the absence of NS time.
Note: When aircraft are removed from the Army inventory, update DA Form 759 at the next closeout. Then remove those aircraft from Part II, Section A. Total hours and add to either "FW" or "RW." In CAFRS remove the qualification date and the time will be moved to RW or FW. Do not add time to historical hours.	
	Compatible Flight Simulator (flight surgeons only). List, in the same order as the aircraft, the compatible flight simulator that the individual has flown. (AR 95-1 lists the compatible flight simulators.)

Table 8-4. Instructions for completing DA Form 759 closeout (crewmember/noncrewmember)

Item	Instructions
Column b	For nonrated crewmembers/noncrewmembers: Enter the date the individual qualified to perform his duty position or was progressed to RL 1. This date reflects the first time the nonrated crewmember attained RL 1 in a particular aircraft. Also, enter the date of any new qualifications and a corresponding comment in Part IV.
	For flight surgeons: This date will reflect the date the flight surgeon was placed on aviation service orders by The Surgeon General; Commander, U.S. Army Personnel Center; or Chief, National Guard Bureau .
Note: The dates for new aircraft and NVD qualification are obtained from the individual's aircrew training record.	
Column c	Enter the date the individual completed the most recent flight in the aircraft and the NVD used (information taken from the DA Form 759-3 [temporary worksheet]).
Note: all time will be entered in hours and tenths of hours	
Column d	Aircraft. Enter the total hours flown from line 18, column **m**, of each DA Form 759-1 on the line that corresponds to the aircraft flown.
	NS: Enter the total hours flown from lines 10 and 13, column **m**, of each DA Form 759-1 on the line that corresponds to NS hours.
	NG: Enter the total hours flown from line 13, column **m**, of each DA Form 759-1 on the line that corresponds to NG hours.
	NS and NG totals will not be included when the total number of flight hours is calculated in Part II Section B.
	Compatible Flight Simulator (flight surgeons only). Enter the total hours flown from line 18, column **m**, of each DA Form 759-1 on the line that corresponds to the flight simulator flown.
Columns e through k	Enter the total hours flown from line 18, columns **a** through **j**, of each DA Form 759-1 in the blocks that correspond to the duty position and aircraft flown.
Section B. Total hours	
Note: Section B is a compilation of total aircraft time and does not include flight simulator time. NS time is already a part of each respective airframe total hours. NS time from Part II, Section A, column d is not added to total hours. Blocks in Section B are updated at each closeout of the individual's flight records. Block **g** historical hours are never updated and always remain the same.	
Block a	Enter the cumulative total combat hours flown from DA Form 759-3 (consolidation worksheet), block 14. (The total in this block will be updated each closeout only if combat time was flown during the period covered.)
Block b	Enter the cumulative total imminent danger hours flown from DA Form 759-3 (consolidation worksheet), block 15. (The total in this block will be updated each closeout only if imminent danger time was flown during the period covered.)
Blocks c and e	Leave blank.
Block d	Add all military rotary-wing aircraft totals, to include RW, in Section A, column **d**, and enter the total in this block. Do not include NS, NG, or simulator time.
Block f	Add all military FW aircraft totals, to include FW, in Section A, column **d**, and enter the total in this block. Do not include NS, NG, or simulator time.
Block g	Transcribe the historical hours from the previous DA Form 759 closeout to this block. The historical hours block is used to track time prior to 1987 when the change in format of the DA Form 759 series became effective.
Block h	Add the hours in blocks **d**, **f**, and **g** and enter the total in hours and tenths of hours in this block.
Page 2, DA Form 759, Blocks 1 through 4	Transcribe information from Part I, blocks 1 through 4 to this section.

Table 8-4. Instructions for completing DA Form 759 closeout (crewmember/noncrewmember)

Item	Instructions
Part III. ATP	
Note: ATP requirements include hours, tasks, and iterations identified in the appropriate aircrew training manuals, readiness level progression, and the APART). Failure of an individual to complete any portion of the ATP requires a comment in Part IV, Remarks. The individual's DA Form 7120-R with enclosures will be used to assist the flight records clerk with the completion of this section. Flight surgeons do not have APART requirements. The only block that applies to a flight surgeon in Part III is Block 3, Physical Exam.	
Block 1	Leave blank.
Block 2	Leave blank.
Block 3	Enter the date of the most recent flight physical. If the individual is on a one calendar month extension, use the date from the previous DA Form 759 and make the appropriate remark in Part IV. On the next closeout, annotate in Part IV when the flight physical was completed. The physical examination is an annual requirement according to AR 95-1 and is not considered part of the APART.
Blocks 4 and 5	Enter the date of the most recent training, if applicable.
Block 6	Enter the date the individual completed all APART requirements, if applicable.
Note: If the individual fails to complete APART successfully, leave block 6 blank and enter the appropriate comment in Part IV.	
Block 7	Enter the primary aircraft mission symbol, type, design, and series.
Block 8	Enter the appropriate readiness level for the individual's primary aircraft, if applicable.
Block 9	Enter the date of the most recent standardization flight evaluation for the individual's primary aircraft, if applicable.
Block 10	Leave blank.
Block 11	Enter the individual's alternate aircraft, if designated.
Block 12	Enter the appropriate readiness level for the individual's alternate aircraft, if designated.
Block 13	Enter the date of the most recent standardization flight evaluation for the individual's alternate aircraft, if designated.
Block 14	Leave blank.
Block 15	Enter the individual's additional aircraft, if designated.
Block 16	Enter the appropriate readiness level for the individual's additional aircraft, if designated.
Block 17	Enter the date of the most recent standardization flight evaluation for the individual's additional aircraft if designated.
Part IV. Remarks	
Enter a historical narrative of the individual's flying status, qualifications, and proficiency if they are not stated elsewhere on the form.	
Commander's signature and date	The individual's commander must sign and date the form to certify the accuracy of the closeout data. If the individual is an ATP Commander, the next higher commander within the chain of command must verify and sign the flight records. The DA Form 759 must be digitally signed in CAFRS. If the commander is unable to digitally certify within CAFRS a remark must be added to part IV of the 759
Notes: 1: Commander's signature block contains name, rank, and branch only. 2. For ARNG and U.S. Army Reserves only, the commander's designated representative may sign the commander's block.	

8-20. Table 8-5 lists the mandatory and standard remarks used to complete Part IV of DA Form 759 .Table 7-6 (page 7-15) shows the service component designations for Part I, block 9.

Table 8-5. Examples of mandatory and standard remarks (DA Form 759 closeout)

MANDATORY REMARKS
Note: The following remarks are mandatory for every closeout.
1. Records closed (date) (reason).
2. Individual has completed (total) months flying duty.
3a. Individual has completed all ATP requirements.
3b. Individual has not completed ATP requirement(s). (Explain what ATP requirement(s) have not been completed and the actions that have been taken.)
3c. Individual has no ATP requirements due to _____. (State reasons why individual has no requirements.)
Note: When an individual completes, or fails to complete, ATP requirements, annotate the results with a remark on the next DA Form 759 closeout. The following are example remarks.
3d. Individual completed previous ATP requirements on (date).
3e. Previous ATP requirements waived by (as appropriate) commander on (date).
3f. Individual failed to complete ATP requirements within the additional timeframe. (State action(s) taken.)
4a. ACT-E train the trainer complete.
4b. ACT-E qualification complete.
4c. ACT-E refresher complete.
4d. ACT-E instructor qualification complete.
STANDARD REMARKS
Note: When a standard remark applies to a closeout, that remark becomes mandatory. If a situation arises that is not explained in a standard remark, explain it in easy-to-understand language.
1. Individual is temporarily suspended from flying duty from (date) to (date) because of (reason). (This is usually used to explain temporary medical grounding, but may be used for other reasons.)
2. Individual awarded senior or master aviation badge under provisions of (issuing authority), (date).
3. Individual completed (type) NVG training on (date).
4. Individual mission qualified in (mission, type, design, and series) aircraft on (date).
5. Individual has successfully completed the U.S. Navy Underwater Egress 9D5A Device Training conducted at (location) on (date).
6. Error sheet (sheet #), Part (part #), (give a detail description of the error) is incorrect. Reads "(say what is incorrect)," should read "(enter corrected data)," corrected this sheet.
7. Logging of combat or imminent danger time is authorized under provisions of (issuing authority), (date). Note: This remark will be used only when adjustments to combat (C) or imminent danger (D) time have been made for the closeout period.
8. Individual completed, disqualified from, or relieved from (type of aviation course) on (date).
9. Individual reassigned under provisions (issuing authority) orders number____, dated_____. Reassigned to (unit and station).
10. Medical waiver granted effective (date) for (summarize medical condition waived).
11. Individual must wear corrective lenses when performing as a crewmember/noncrewmember.
12. Individual terminated from flying status on (date) under provisions (authority) orders number_____, dated_____, effective date_____.
13. Added (number) hours to "RW" (or FW) time on DA Form 759. (Aircraft) removed from the Army inventory effective (date).
14. Flight record lost on (date). (Enter action to locate missing records) Records reconstructed from ____ on (date).

Table 8-5. Examples of mandatory and standard remarks (DA Form 759 closeout)

15. Individual placed on (crewmember/noncrewmember) flying status under provisions (issuing authority) orders number ____, dated ____, effective date ____.
16. 120-day notice for removal from flight status given on (date).
20. (Aircraft) designated as individual's second (third and so on) additional aircraft effective (date).
21. Individual has completed aircrew coordination training - enhanced on (date) according to Directorate of Evaluation and Standardization guidance and U.S. Army Aviation Center (USAAVNC) Aircrew Coordination Exportable Training Package.
22. Suspension from flying duty on (date) under provisions (authority) for (purpose).
23. Commander is unable to digitally certify 759 due to_____.

INDIVIDUAL FLIGHT RECORD AND FLIGHT CERTIFICATE-ARMY
For use of this form, see AR 95-1, AR 95-23, and FM 3-04.300; the proponent agency is DCS, G-3/5/7.

PART I. BIO/DEMOGRAPHIC

1. Sheet No.	4

2. Name		3. Rank	
Doe, John D.		CPT	

4. Period		5. DOB	6. ASED	7. Branch
1 Nov 06 - 31 Oct 07		13 Oct 1983	30 Aug 2005	MC

8. Component	9. Unit	10. DMOS
RA	A Co 1st Bn 17th Avn Regt	61N9C

11. Duty Position	12. Operational Position
Flight Surgeon	No

PART II. FLIGHT HOURS
SECTION A. QUALIFICATIONS

a. Acft System	b. Date Qual	c. Last Flight	d. Total Time	e. CP/ CE/ EO	f. PI/ OR/ AO	g. PC/ PO	h. UT/ MO	i. IP/ FE/ IO	j. IE/ FI	k. SP/ SI/ SO	l. MP	m. ME	n. XP
UH-60L	25 Aug 05	12 Aug 07	129.0				129.0						

SECTION B. TOTAL HOURS

a. Combat	b. Imminent Danger	c. Civilian RW	d. Military RW
	11.0		129.0

e. Civilian FW	f. Military FW	g. Historical Hours	h. Total Hours
			129.0

DA FORM 759, AUG 2008   PREVIOUS EDITION OF APR 98 IS OBSOLETE   Page 1 of 2
APD PE v1.00ES

Figure 8-8. Sample DA Form 759 closeout (flight surgeon) (front)

INDIVIDUAL FLIGHT RECORD AND FLIGHT CERTIFICATE--ARMY *(Cont'd)* For use of this form, see AR 95-1, AR 95-23, and FM 3-04.300; the proponent agency is DCS, G-3/5/7.					1. Sheet No. 4

2. Name Doe, John D.				3. Rank CPT	4. Period 1 Nov 06 - 31 Oct 07

PART III. ATP

1. FAC NA	2. MTFE	3. Phys Exam 01 Nov 2006	4. Ejection Seat	5. Alt Chamber	6. APART Completed
7. Primary Acft UH-60L		8. RL 1	9. Std Flt Eval		10. Inst Eval
11. Alternate Acft		12 RL	13. Std Flt Eval		14. Inst Eval
15. Additional Acft		16. RL	17. Std Flt Eval		

PART IV. REMARKS

1. Records closed 31 Oct 2007 due to end of birth month.

2. Aviator has completed 12 months of total opertional flying duty credit.

3. Aviator has completed ATP requirements.

4. ACT-E refresher complete.

Commander's Typed Name, Rank, Branch EMMETT C. BOLTON JR CPT, AV	Signature Digitally signed using CAFRS login	Date 20 Dec 2007

DA FORM 759, AUG 2008

Page 2 of 2
APD PE v1.00ES

Figure 8-9. Sample DA Form 759 closeout (flight surgeon) (back)

INDIVIDUAL FLIGHT RECORD AND FLIGHT CERTIFICATE-ARMY
For use of this form, see AR 95-1, AR 95-23, and FM 3-04.300; the proponent agency is DCS, G-3/5/7.

PART I. BIO/DEMOGRAPHIC

1. Sheet No.	8

2. Name		3. Rank
Smith, John A.		SFC

4. Period	5. DOB	6. ASED	7. Branch
1 Nov 06 - 31 Oct 07	13 Oct 1983	30 Aug 2005	MI

8. Component	9. Unit	10. DMOS
RA	A Co 1st Bn 17th Avn Regt	96U

11. Duty Position	12. Operational Position
UAS CRM	

PART II. FLIGHT HOURS
SECTION A. QUALIFICATIONS

a. Acft System	b. Date Qual	c. Last Flight	d. Total Time	e. CP/ CE/ EO	f. PI/ OR/ AO	g. PC/ PO	h. UT/ MO	i. IP/ FE/ IO	j. IE/ FI	k. SP/ SI/ SO	l. MP	m. ME	n. XP
RQ-7B		25 Oct 07	18.9		4.8	3.3				14.1			
RQ-5A	11 Oct 96	06 Aug 97	36.8	33.3						3.5			
RQ-7A	07 Jul 04	20 Apr 06	533.4	111.2	154.3	0.6		236.2		31.1			
RQS-7B		25 Jul 07	32.8		9.4	7.2				16.2			
RQS-5B		04 Aug 97	13.2				4.5	8.7					
RQS-7A		20 Apr 06	160.1	6.0	16.9	17.9				82.4			

SECTION B. TOTAL HOURS

a. Combat	b. Imminent Danger	c. Civilian RW	d. Military RW
222.8			

e. Civilian FW	f. Military FW	g. Historical Hours	h. Total Hours
	657.2		657.2

DA FORM 759, AUG 2008　　PREVIOUS EDITION OF APR 98 IS OBSOLETE　　　Page 1 of 2 / APD PE v1.00ES

Figure 8-10. Sample DA Form 759 closeout (unmanned aircraft system crewmember) (front)

INDIVIDUAL FLIGHT RECORD AND FLIGHT CERTIFICATE--ARMY *(Cont'd)* For use of this form, see AR 95-1, AR 95-23, and FM 3-04.300; the proponent agency is DCS, G-3/5/7.					1. Sheet No. 8

2. Name
   Smith, John A.
			3. Rank
			   SFC
				4. Period
				1 Nov 06 - 31 Oct 07

PART III. ATP

1. FAC 2	2. MTFE	3. Phys Exam 01 Oct 2007	4. Ejection Seat	5. Alt Chamber	6. APART Completed 25 Oct 2007
7. Primary Acft RQ-7B	8. RL 1		9. Std Flt Eval 25 Oct 2007	10. Inst Eval	
11. Alternate Acft	12 RL		13. Std Flt Eval	14. Inst Eval	
15. Additional Acft	16. RL		17. Std Flt Eval		

PART IV. REMARKS

1. Records closed 31 Oct 2007 due to end of birth month.

2. Individual has completed 24 months flying duty.

3. Individual has completed ATP requirements.

4. ACT-E refresher complete.

5. Individual must wear corrective lenses when performing as a crewmember.

Commander's Typed Name, Rank, Branch JOE B. JONES CPT, AV	Signature Digitally signed using CAFRS login	Date 21 Nov 2007

DA FORM 759, AUG 2008	Page 2 of 2 APD PE v1.00ES

Figure 8-11. Sample DA Form 759 closeout (unmanned aircraft system crewmember) (back)

8-21. Figures 8-12 through 8-18 (pages 8-26 through 8-32) depict DA Form 759 series in complete closeout.

INDIVIDUAL FLIGHT RECORD AND FLIGHT CERTIFICATE-ARMY
For use of this form, see AR 95-1, AR 95-23, and FM 3-04.300; the proponent agency is DCS, G-3/5/7.

PART I. BIO/DEMOGRAPHIC

2. Name Doe, Jane D.	**1. Sheet No.** 4

			3. Rank SGT

4. Period		5. DOB	6. ASED	7. Branch
1 Nov 06 - 31 Oct 07		13 Oct 1983	30 Aug 2005	MC

8. Component	9. Unit	10. DMOS
RA	A Co 1st Bn 17th Avn Regt	15T

11. Duty Position	12. Operational Position
UH-60L Crew Chief	

PART II. FLIGHT HOURS
SECTION A. QUALIFICATIONS

a. Acft System	b. Date Qual	c. Last Flight	d. Total Time	e. CP/ CE/ EO	f. PI/ OR/ AO	g. PC/ PO	h. UT/ MO	i. IP/ FE/ IO	j. IE/ FI	k. SP/ SI/ SO	l. MP	m. ME	n. XP
UH-60L	25 Aug 05	12 Aug 07	237.9	237.9									
NG	25 Aug 05	05 Aug 07	36.0										

SECTION B. TOTAL HOURS

a. Combat	b. Imminent Danger	c. Civilian RW	d. Military RW 237.9
e. Civilian FW	f. Military FW	g. Historical Hours	h. Total Hours 237.9

DA FORM 759, AUG 2008   PREVIOUS EDITION OF APR 98 IS OBSOLETE   Page 1 of 2 APD PE v1.00ES

Figure 8-12. Sample DA Form 759 in complete closeout (front)

INDIVIDUAL FLIGHT RECORD AND FLIGHT CERTIFICATE--ARMY *(Cont'd)* For use of this form, see AR 95-1, AR 95-23, and FM 3-04.300; the proponent agency is DCS, G-3/5/7.					1. Sheet No. 4	

2. Name Doe, Jane D.				3. Rank SGT	4. Period 1 Nov 06 - 31 Oct 07

PART III. ATP

1. FAC 2	2. MTFE	3. Phys Exam 01 Nov 2007	4. Ejection Seat	5. Alt Chamber	6. APART Completed 20 Oct 2007
7. Primary Acft UH-60L	8. RL 1		9. Std Flt Eval 20 Oct 2007		10. Inst Eval
11. Alternate Acft	12 RL		13. Std Flt Eval		14. Inst Eval
15. Additional Acft	16. RL		17. Std Flt Eval		

PART IV. REMARKS

1. Records closed 31 Oct 2007 due to end of birth month.

2. Individual has completed 24 months flying duty.

3. Individual has completed ATP requirements.

4. ACT-E refresher complete.

5. Individual must wear corrective lenses when performing as a crewmember.

Commander's Typed Name, Rank, Branch EMMETT C. BOLTON JR CPT, AV	Signature Digitally signed using CAFRS login	Date 20 Dec 2007

DA FORM 759, AUG 2008

Page 2 of 2
APD PE v1.00ES

Figure 8-13. Sample DA Form 759 in complete closeout (back)

INDIVIDUAL FLIGHT RECORD AND FLIGHT CERTIFICATE - ARMY

For use of this form, see AR 95-1, AR 95-23, and FM 3-04.300; the proponent agency is DCS, G-3/5/7.

AIRCRAFT CLOSEOUT SUMMARY

											1. Sheet No. 4
2. Name Doe, Jane D.						3. Rank SGT		4. Period 1 Nov 06 - 31 Oct 07			5. Acft/Flt Sim UH-60L

FLIGHT COND SYM	FLYING DUTY SYMBOL										k. Total This Sheet	l. From Sheet No. 3	m. Total
	a. CP/ CE/ EO	b. PI/ OR/ AO	c. PC/ PO	d. UT/ MO	e. IP/ FE/ IO	f. IE/ FI	g. SP/ SI/ SO	h. MP	i. ME	j. XP			
6. D	32.4										32.4	120.0	152.4
7. N	4.5										4.5	45.0	49.5
8. H													
9. W													
10. NG	6.0										6.0	30.0	36.0
11.													
12. NS													
13. DG/ DS													
14. TR													
15. AA													
16. Total this Sheet	42.9										42.9		
17. From Sheet No. 3	195.0											195.0	
18. Total	237.9												237.9
19. Combat													
20. Imminent Danger													

DA FORM 759-1, AUG, 2008	PREVIOUS EDITION OF APR 1998 IS OBSOLETE	APD PE v1.00

Figure 8-14. Sample DA Form 759-1 in complete closeout

INDIVIDUAL FLIGHT RECORD AND FLIGHT CERTIFICATE - ARMY

For use of this form, see AR 95-1, AR 95-23, and FM 3-04.300; the proponent agency is DCS, G-3/5/7.

FLIGHT RECORD AND FLIGHT PAY WORK SHEET

1. Sheet No. 4										
2. Name Doe, Jane D.								**3. Rank** SGT		
4. Period 1 Nov 06 - 31 Oct 07						**5. Flying Status** CRM		**6. Effective Date** 01 Nov 2006		

Date/ Month	Acft	Flying Duty Sym	Flt Cond Sym	Msn Sym	Hours Flown	Entitle-ment Yes or No	Based on Hours Flown During	Excess Hours		Remarks
								This Month	Accum	
a	b	c	d	e	f	g	h	i	j	k
NOV										
01	UH-60L	CE	D	T	3.0					
15	UH-60L	CE	D	T	2.0					
15	UH-60L	CE	N	T	1.0					
15	UH-60L	CE	NG	T	1.0					
DEC										
05	UH-60L	CE	D	T	2.6					
20	UH-60L	CE	D	T	3.0					
JAN	No	Time	Flown							
FEB										
08	UH-60L	CE	D	T	2.0					
08	UH-60L	CE	N	T	1.0					
08	UH-60L	CE	NG	T	1.0					
20	UH-60L	CE	D	T	2.6					
MAR	No	Time	Flown							
APR										
01	UH-60L	CE	D	T	5.0					
MAY										
01	UH-60L	CE	D	T	1.5					
01	UH-60L	CE	N	T	1.0					
01	UH-60L	CE	NG	T	2.0					
JUN										
15	UH-60L	CE	D	T	4.0					

Total Hours This Sheet	7.	Hours From Sheet No.	10.	Total Hours to Date	13.
Total Combat Hours This Sheet	8.	Combat Hours From Sheet No.	11.	Total Combat Hours to Date	14.
Total Imminent Danger Hours This Sheet	9.	Imminent Danger Hours From Sheet No.	12.	Total Imminent Danger Hours to Date	15.

DA FORM 759-3, AUG 2008   PREVIOUS EDITION OF AUG 93 IS OBSOLETE   APD PE v1.00

Figure 8-15. Sample DA Form 759-3 in complete closeout (temporary worksheet)

INDIVIDUAL FLIGHT RECORD AND FLIGHT CERTIFICATE - ARMY
For use of this form, see AR 95-1, AR 95-23, and FM 3-04.300; the proponent agency is DCS, G-3/5/7.

FLIGHT RECORD AND FLIGHT PAY WORK SHEET

1. Sheet No.	
	4

2. Name											3. Rank	
Doe, Jane D.											SGT	

4. Period					5. Flying Status		6. Effective Date	
1 Nov 06 - 31 Oct 07					CRM		01 Nov 2006	

Date/ Month	Acft	Flying Duty Sym	Flt Cond Sym	Msn Sym	Hours Flown	Entitle-ment Yes or No	Based on Hours Flown During	Excess Hours		Remarks
								This Month	Accum	
a	b	c	d	e	f	g	h	i	j	k
JUL	No	Time	Flown							
AUG										
05	UH-60L	CE	D	T	1.5					
05	UH-60L	CE	N	T	1.5					
05	UH-60L	CE	NG	T	2.0					
SEP	No	Time	Flown							
OCT										
10	UH-60L	CE	D	T	2.0					
20	UH-60L	CE	D	T	3.2					

Total Hours This Sheet	7.	Hours From Sheet No.	10.
Total Combat Hours This Sheet	8.	Combat Hours From Sheet No.	11.
Total Imminent Danger Hours This Sheet	9.	Imminent Danger Hours From Sheet No.	12.

Total Hours to Date	13.	
Total Combat Hours to Date	14.	
Total Imminent Danger Hours to Date	15.	

DA FORM 759-3, AUG 2008   PREVIOUS EDITION OF AUG 93 IS OBSOLETE   APD PE v1.00

Figure 8-16. Sample DA Form 759-3 in complete closeout (temporary worksheet [continuation])

INDIVIDUAL FLIGHT RECORD AND FLIGHT CERTIFICATE - ARMY
For use of this form, see AR 95-1, AR 95-23, and FM 3-04.300; the proponent agency is DCS, G-3/5/7.

FLIGHT RECORD AND FLIGHT PAY WORK SHEET										1. Sheet No. 4
2. Name Doe, Jane D.										3. Rank SGT
4. Period 1 Nov 06 - 31 Oct 07						5. Flying Status CRM				6. Effective Date 01 Nov 2006
Date/ Month	Acft	Flying Duty Sym	Flt Cond Sym	Msn Sym	Hours Flown	Entitle- ment Yes or No	Based on Hours Flown During	Excess Hours		Remarks
								This Month	Accum	
a	b	c	d	e	f	g	h	i	j	k
NOV	UH-60L	CE	D		5.0	YES		3.0	3.0	-3.0 for JAN
	UH-60L	CE	N		1.0					
	UH-60L	CE	NG		1.0					
DEC	UH-60L	CE	D		5.6	YES		1.6	4.6	-1.0 for JAN
										-0.6 for MAR
JAN	No	Time	Flown			YES	NOV 3.0		0.6	
							DEC 1.0			
FEB	UH-60L	CE	D		4.6	YES		2.6	3.2	-2.6 for MAR
	UH-60L	CE	N		1.0					
	UH-60L	CE	NG		1.0					
MAR	No	Time	Flown			YES	DEC 0.6		0.0	
							FEB 2.6			
							APR 0.8			
APR	UH-60L	CE	D		5.0	YES		1.0	0.2	-0.8 for MAR
MAY	UH-60L	CE	D		1.5	YES		0.5	0.7	
	UH-60L	CE	N		1.0					
	UH-60L	CE	NG		2.0					
JUN	UH-60L	CE	D		4.0	YES			0.7	
JUL	No	Time	Flown			NO			0.7	
AUG	UH-60L	CE	D		1.5	YES		1.0	1.7	
	UH-60L	CE	N		1.5					
	UH-60L	CE	NG		2.0					

Total Hours This Sheet	7.	Hours From Sheet No.	10.	Total Hours to Date	13.
Total Combat Hours This Sheet	8.	Combat Hours From Sheet No.	11.	Total Combat Hours to Date	14.
Total Imminent Danger Hours This Sheet	9.	Imminent Danger Hours From Sheet No.	12.	Total Imminent Danger Hours to Date	15.

DA FORM 759-3, AUG 2008   PREVIOUS EDITION OF AUG 93 IS OBSOLETE   APD PE v1.00

Figure 8-17. Sample DA Form 759-3 in complete closeout (consolidation)

INDIVIDUAL FLIGHT RECORD AND FLIGHT CERTIFICATE - ARMY

For use of this form, see AR 95-1, AR 95-23, and FM 3-04.300; the proponent agency is DCS, G-3/5/7.

FLIGHT RECORD AND FLIGHT PAY WORK SHEET

	1. Sheet No. 4

2. Name	3. Rank
Doe, Jane D.	SGT

4. Period	5. Flying Status	6. Effective Date
1 Nov 06 - 31 Oct 07	CRM	01 Nov 2006

Date/ Month	Acft	Flying Duty Sym	Flt Cond Sym	Msn Sym	Hours Flown	Entitle- ment Yes or No	Based on Hours Flown During	Excess Hours		Remarks
								This Month	Accum	
a	b	c	d	e	f	g	h	i	j	k
SEP	No	Time	Flown			NO			1.5	-0.2 from APR
OCT	UH-60L	CE	D		5.2	YES		1.2	2.2	-0.5 from MAY

Total Hours This Sheet	7. 42.9	Hours From Sheet No. 3	10. 195	Total Hours to Date	13. 237.9
Total Combat Hours This Sheet	8.	Combat Hours From Sheet No.	11.	Total Combat Hours to Date	14.
Total Imminent Danger Hours This Sheet	9.	Imminent Danger Hours From Sheet No.	12.	Total Imminent Danger Hours to Date	15.

DA FORM 759-3, AUG 2008   PREVIOUS EDITION OF AUG 93 IS OBSOLETE   APD PE v1.00

Figure 8-18. Sample DA Form 759-3 in complete closeout consolidation (continuation)

This page intentionally left blank.

PART THREE

Installation Airfield Operations

Chapter 9

Airfield Operations

The safe and efficient management of airfields enhances operations and allows Army aviation units to concentrate on mission readiness and training. The ratio of military to civilian airfield operations personnel varies greatly from one installation to the next. This chapter describes organization and staffing for both military and civilian airfield operations positions; however, the command for each airfield will ultimately determine personnel requirements necessary for daily operations.

ORGANIZATION

9-1. Figure 9-1 (page 9-2) depicts a standard airfield organization. Most installation Army airfields are owned and operated by the Installation Management Command (IMCOM). The command element of the airfield has supervisory/management authority for airfield functions. Day-to-day operations of the ATC facility are under the control

Contents

and authority of the IMCOM airfield chain of command or ATC parent unit depending on the airfield's mission and location.

AIRFIELD DIVISION

9-2. The airfield division consists of airfield operations, airfield safety office, ATC maintenance, and ATC branches. The airfield division chief is overall responsible for all airfield functions at primary and secondary airfields and heliports/helipads within the division. Normally, the airfield division chief is the airfield manager for the primary airfield. In this situation, the airfield division chief performs all functions and tasks as noted below.

9-3. The airfield division's staff consists of an airfield manager (at secondary airfields), airfield operations officer, airfield safety officer, ATC maintenance chief, and ATC chief. Appropriate administrative staff may also be assigned. When there is only one airfield at the installation, the airfield division chief performs all functions of the airfield manager.

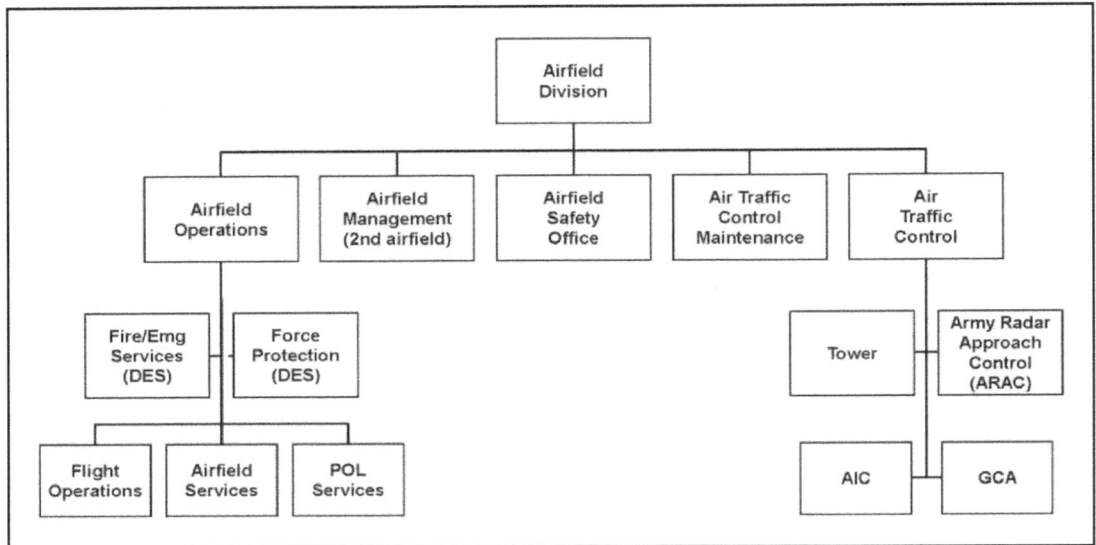

Figure 9-1. Standard airfield organization

Airfield Division Chief/Commander/Manager

9-4.   The airfield division chief/commander/manager should have military or civilian aviation experience with prior airfield management experience and/or military/civilian airfield management schooling. The airfield commander/manager is responsible for tasks stated in AR 95-2, including but not limited to—

- Supervising and managing the airfield.
- Publishing the Airfield Operations Manual (AOM).
- Attending installation planning committee meetings and providing input on issues affecting the airfield.
- Attending installation flight standardization committee meetings and providing input on issues affecting the airfield and local flying area.
- Working with local civil authorities, public relations personnel, and liaison officers concerning public relations matters (such as noise complaints, environmental issues, public events, and aircraft accidents or incidents).
- Working with local contracting offices on airfield services not provided by permanent airfield facilities or personnel (such as cutting grass, removing snow, painting the airfield, testing electrical grounds, and performing other periodic or routine maintenance).
- Working with the Directorate of Human Resources and Civilian Personnel Advisory Center on matters relating to hiring, terminating, transferring, and evaluating civilian employees.
- Recommending and implementing airfield policy and providing guidelines for use of airfield property by tenant organizations (such as parking areas, hours of operation, airfield services, complaint procedures, and interorganization working agreements).
- Maintaining accountability of airfield installation property.
- Developing air crash, search, and rescue requirements in coordination with the airfield safety officer, medical personnel, firefighters, and other appropriate authorities.
- Providing area map coverage.

Secondary Airfield Management Branch

9-5.   The airfield management branch consists of an airfield manger position for secondary airfield at installations with more than one airfield. The airfield manager works directly for the airfield division chief and manages the secondary airfield under that authority.

Airfield Operations Branch

9-6.   The airfield operations branch consists of a flight operations section, airfield services section, and petroleum, oils, and lubricants (POL) services section.

Airfield Operations Officer

9-7.   The airfield operations officer should be an experienced aviator (civilian or military) in one or more of the aircraft normally flown at the airfield and appointed by the airfield commander or hired through the civilian personnel system. The airfield operations officer is responsible for—
- Providing input to the AOM that pertains to aircrew procedures such as—
    - Filing flight plans.
    - Use of airfield services.
    - Joint use of airspace.
    - Airfield facility use.
    - Night operation agreements.
    - Noise abatement.
    - Other special interest areas.
- Supervising the flight operations section, airfield services section and POL services section.
- Ensuring local hazard maps are current. Printed maps are required for display even though digital systems may depict hazard area information.
- Ensuring airfield facilities are adequate and in good repair.
- Developing preaccident plans in cooperation with the ATC chief/senior sergeant, airfield safety officer, airfield operations sergeant, flight operations sergeant, and other personnel from responding agencies.
- Reviewing personnel training programs for flight operations section, airfield services section, and POL services section.
- Recommending personnel for appointment to accomplish specific duties not covered in the general duty description.

Flight Operations Section

Airfield Operations Sergeant (when assigned)

9-8.   The airfield operations sergeant must be a graduate of the Aviation Operations Specialist Basic Noncommissioned Officer Course, have knowledge of flight operations/dispatch procedures, and completed the Aviation Accident Prevention Course. Airfield operations sergeant responsibilities include—
- Performing airfield NCOIC duties.
- Assisting the airfield operations officer.
- Assisting the airfield safety officer.
- Supervising the flight operations section.
- Writing SOPs for the airfield operations division and the flight operations branch.
- Assisting in the development of OLs and LOAs.
- Developing and conducting training programs.
- Ensuring that required publications are current and available.
- Maintaining accountability for flight operation and dispatch installation property.

- Coordinating section activities under supervision of the airfield operations sergeant/officer.
- Supervising and training aviation operations specialists in their assigned duties.
- Serving as the assistant airfield operations sergeant.
- Providing flight-planning services to include—
  - Current publications.
  - Maps and charts.
  - NOTAM display.
  - Weight and balance forms on each assigned Class II aircraft.
- Preparing work schedules for aviation operations specialists and ensuring adequate coverage during peak periods.
- Ensuring the section SOP provides for immediate notification of the operations officer of an impending or actual emergency or OPSEC violation.
- Processing required reports concerning airspace violations caused by kites, balloons, model airplanes, and drones.
- Developing training programs for newly assigned personnel.
- Ensuring airfield advisory procedures are established per Federal Aviation Administration Order (FAAO) 7110.10.
- Ensuring ground personnel operating near or on taxiways or runways are briefed on two-way radio communication procedures and are familiar with the ATC light signals found in the Aeronautical Information manual and FAA Order JO 7110.65.
- Establishing and maintaining a FLIP account outlined in AR 95-2.

Airfield Operations Specialist/Dispatcher

9-9. The aviation operations specialist/dispatcher—

- Posts and disseminates NOTAMs.
- Transmits and records flight data.
- Advises the local control tower on proposed departures and arrivals.
- Notifies the operations sergeant when an arriving flight is overdue, as required by the local SOP and overdue aircraft procedures.
- Notifies airfield services of estimated arrival and departure times to ensure timely servicing of aircraft.
- Notifies operations sergeant of arriving and departing very important persons (VIPs) so proper honors can be extended.
- Disseminates severe weather warnings to appropriate individuals or agencies according to local SOPs and emergency plans.
- Informs the operations sergeant of any OPSEC violations.
- Inspects airfield (including runways and taxiways) at least once during the shift for maintenance, police, OPSEC considerations and requirements, and FOD.
- Provides advisory service when the ATC tower facility is closed or not available.

Airfield Safety Office Branch

9-10. The airfield safety office branch consists of an airfield safety officer (AFSO), who works directly for the airfield division chief/commander/manager, and may include an assistant airfield safety officer at installations with more than one airfield or high operations volume. The airfield safety officer implements the airfield safety program for all airfields, heliports/helipads within the airfield division.

Airfield Safety Officer

9-11. The AFSO is rated by the airfield division chief/commander/manager, should be a GS-0018 (when civilian) and a graduate of the Aviation Safety Officer's Course or completed equivalent training. Airfield safety officer responsibilities include—

- Representing the airfield division chief/manager/commander on all safety-related matters.
- Performing duties outlined in AR 385-10, DA Pam 385-40, and TC 1-210.
- Investigating accidents or incidents involving aircraft or airfield personnel or equipment.
- Assisting the operations officer in writing the aircraft mishap plans.
- Conducting airfield safety inspections.
- Advising airfield personnel on safety-related matters.
- Scheduling and conducting safety meetings.
- Advising the airfield division chief/manager/commander of potential problem areas.
- Providing safety input to the local flying rules.

Air Traffic Control Branch

9-12. The ATC branch consists of an ATC chief and facility chiefs for each type facility located at the installation (such as, control tower, Army radar approach control [ARAC]), AIC, and/or GCA). The organization of the ATC branch depends on the number and type of NAVAIDs and services provided by the airfield. At ATC facilities operated by the military, an ATC chief or senior sergeant will fill the ATC facility chief position. At IMCOM-managed airfields, a Department of the Army civilian (DAC) may occupy the facility chief position.

Air Traffic Control Chief/Senior Sergeant

9-13. AR 95-2 outlines the qualification requirements for the ATC chief/senior sergeant. The ATC chief/senior sergeant is responsible for—

- Supervising all ATC activities on and around the airfield including notifying the flight operations branch of outages in navigational or communication systems so it can notify aircrews operating in the area.
- Providing input to the AOM on ATC-related matters.
- Developing and reviewing operations letters (OLs), LOA.
- Establishing ATC training programs.
- Coordinating with the operations division so aircrews fly maneuvers needed for ATC currency requirements.
- Nominating ATC control tower operator and ATC specialist examiners.
- Assisting the operations officer in writing aircraft (or other) mishap plans.
- Maintaining accurate air traffic records. These records help personnel investigate aircraft accidents or incidents, operational hazard reports and missing aircraft.
- Administering ATC facilities per AR 95-2 and FM 3-04.303.
- Advising the air traffic and airspace (AT&A) officer on airspace matters and assisting him in performing his duties.

Air Traffic Control Maintenance Branch

9-14. The ATC maintenance branch consists of an ATC maintenance chief and additional airfield maintenance personnel as required.

Air Traffic Control Maintenance Chief

9-15. The ATC maintenance chief is responsible for all ATC equipment maintenance.

Air Traffic and Airspace Officer (when assigned)

9-16. At Army airfields where unit missions impact the national airspace or host nation national airspace system, the appropriate commander will designate an installation AT&A officer per AR 95-2. The appointed person should be a member of the installation planning board. The AT&A officer's responsibilities include representing the installation on all airspace-related matters such as—

- Joint-use airspace.
- Special-use airspace (SUA).
- Altitude restrictions.
- Restricted areas.
- Range restrictions.
- Training areas.
- ATC procedures in areas of overlapping control.
- Joint service agreements.
- Providing input to the local flying rules on airspace-related matters.
- Maintaining liaison with local FAA and/or host government agencies.

PERSONNEL CONSTRAINTS

9-17. Personnel organization and duties performed depend on the size and structure of aviation units the airfield supports. Airfields not having all positions outlined in the preceding paragraphs may combine positions and functional areas. Consolidation of functions can be accomplished only when the personnel selected meet all requirements of the position, and the size and traffic density of the airfields are compatible with a smaller staff. Over-consolidation can become a safety hazard and cause degradation of services. The following are typical consolidations and are recommended for small airfields:

- Airfield commander and an operations officer.
- AT&A officer and the ATC chief position.
- Aviation safety NCO and airfield operations sergeant.

Chapter 10

Flight Planning and Operations

An Army airfield is normally the hub for aviation support operations and tactical aviation training activities of the command. Flight planning and operations provides a link for the aviation units and the airfield management and its organizations, ensuring the necessary and responsive airfield services are available to the aviation units.

SECTION I – ORGANIZATION

WEATHER SECTION

10-1. Air Weather Service (AWS) facilities provide weather forecasting and briefings to aircrews. If AWS support is part-time or not available, a direct landline or Defense Switched Network (DSN) line to an AWS or other AC-approved weather facility is required. National Weather Service forecast offices or flight service stations (FSSs) may be contacted when use of an AWS facility is not practical. The airman's information manual contains additional information on alternate means of obtaining weather briefings.

Contents

10-2. When weather services are not available, flight operations personnel will contact the nearest weather servicing facility to obtain local area hourly weather reports. These reports will be updated immediately when weather conditions occur that were not forecasted. Aircrews planning to fly outside the coverage area will contact the servicing weather facility for specialized weather briefings.

10-3. Local area weather briefings contain the following information:
- Date and valid times in universal time coordinated (UTC).
- Cloud layers in hundreds of feet and sky coverage.
- Visibility (in local format) and obstructions to visibility.
- Surface wind direction and speed.
- Any forecast changes during the valid period, when changes are expected to occur, and any pertinent remarks.
- Area covered by the report in nautical miles.
- Weather warnings or advisories.
- Maximum surface temperature and pressure altitude.
- Minimum ceiling and visibility.
- Forecast surface turbulence and altitude where turbulence ends.
- Forecast icing at surface or low altitude.
- Forecaster's and flight operations dispatcher's initials.

10-4. Specialized weather reports may be required to provide the following information:
- Wind direction and speed and temperature data at intervals of 1,000 feet from the surface. (This information should be provided up to the highest altitude flown by aircraft operating in the area covered by the report.)

- Freezing level.
- Maximum temperature, pressure altitude, and density altitude in Fahrenheit and Celsius.
- Minimum temperature in Fahrenheit and Celsius.
- Sunrise and sunset times.
- Moonrise and moonset times and percentage of illumination.

AIRFIELD OPERATIONS BRANCH

10-5. An Army airfield is normally the hub for aviation operational and tactical aviation training activities of the command. The airfield operations branch functions as the coordination link for the aviation units and each branch in the airfield organization. The airfield operations branch executes specific responsibilities assigned to it as part of the airfield operations organization. This chapter discusses functions and responsibilities of the airfield operations branch.

FLIGHT OPERATIONS SECTION

10-6. The flight operations section must be located near main aircraft parking areas and runways. All flight operations services are normally located in the same building. This allows for better coordination and services provided to airfield uses. The flight planning room, pilots' ready area, VIP lounge, weather and flight operations section are normally collocated or within close proximity to each other. The flight operations section is responsible for processing flight plans and other air traffic related data through national and international air traffic systems.

Staffing

10-7. The number of specialists assigned to the flight operations section depends on the services provided, hours of operation, TOE and TDA for the airfield.

10-8. A minimum of two persons shall be on duty during hours of operation. The AC, NGB, or Headquarters, Department of the Army may modify this requirement during periods of critical manning or as necessary. Shift personnel must not be scheduled for additional duties and details outside the scope of the flight dispatch function unless the above requirement has been met. This does not excuse or preclude personnel from completing military training requirements. Other important considerations/procedures include—

- Individuals working in the flight operations section must be assigned two-letter operating initials for use during daily operations.
- Comprehensive procedures are established to ensure a thorough shift change briefing is given to incoming shift personnel.
- Maintenance of a DA Form 1594 that is used to record significant incidents occurring during each tour of duty. Airfield commanders must specify the items or issues that require documentation and must review each entry.

Assignment of Operating Initials

10-9. Flight operations personnel are assigned two-letter operating initials to use when identification of the individual is necessary. The flight operations sergeant assigns the operating initials and maintains a current list. No two people should be assigned the same operating initials. Operating initials usually are based on the first and last letters of the individual's last name.

Recommended Equipment

10-10.   The recommended equipment for the flight operations section includes—

- Four-wheel drive or suitable vehicle for off-road use for the Airfield Manager and/or Airfield Safety Office and staff.
- Frequency modulated (FM), UHF, and VHF radios for pilot-to-dispatcher communications with personnel operating on the airfield (such as disaster response agencies, civil engineers, and the control tower).
- Emergency lighting equipment with an automatic back-up power generation system.
- Telecommunications equipment to process flight data and other air traffic information.
- Console with direct voice line communication with control tower, radar approach control, FAA and rescue agencies, supported aviation units, additional administrative circuits, as required and primary and secondary crash alarm system.
- Classified materiel facilities capable of storing, issuing, and receiving.
- Current set of operating instructions and ready reference files available, as required by the airfield commander. These publications must have detailed operating instructions so airfield operations specialists can complete actions without referring to other directives.
- Flight operations personnel must maintain local checklists, logs, or similar documentation to support functional area responsibilities. Examples of local instructions include procedures for airfield inspections, inbound and outbound aircraft, distinguished visitors, aircraft requiring special handling (such as air evacuation or hazardous cargo), airfield restrictions (such as prior permission required), crash alarm system, FLIPs, weather warnings and advisories, in-flight advisories and bird strike hazard responses.

Flight Planning Room

10-11.   The airfield operations officer is responsible for establishing and operating a flight planning room to include its general appearance, efficient administration, and operation. The flight planning room is a separate work area suitable for aircrew briefings and mission planning located near the weather office and flight operations dispatch desk. The area must be equipped with current aeronautical information enabling aircrews to complete self-briefings and flight planning. Aviation operations specialists are available to assist pilots and provide briefings on local arrival and departure procedures.

10-12.   Physical space and equipment availability dictates how the flight planning room is furnished. The following equipment and furnishings are recommended:

- An installation telephone available for authorized use by aircrews.
- Direct line access to the nearest weather facility.
- An installation and local telephone directory.
- A chart listing important telephone numbers (billeting, transportation, mess hall, flight surgeon, maintenance, operations officer, and safety officer).
- One clock with dual time (UTC and local) or two clocks (one set on UTC and the other on local time).
- A flight-planning table large enough to lay out an entire en route chart or sectional navigational chart.

Planning Table

10-13.   The table should be tilted up slightly with Plexiglas or glass mounted on the table and a local area en route chart and sectional chart placed under the glass. Other items that could be placed under the glass for aircrew convenience are—

- Sample flight plans.
- Sample weight and balance forms.
- Other appropriate sample forms.

10-14. Table 10-1 provides a list of planning resources to be located at the flight-planning table.

Table 10-1. Flight planning resources

Blank Forms	Reference publications
DA Form 2696 (Operational Hazard Report).	DOD FLIPs
DD Form 175 (Military Flight Plan)	Local airfield SOP
DD Form 175-1 (Flight Weather Briefing)	Aeronautical charts
DD Form 365-4 (Weight and Balance Clearance Form F Transport)	Airfield reading file
	FAA regulations
DD Form 1801 (DOD International Flight Plan)	Aircrew training manuals
Performance planning cards	Aircraft operator's manuals for each type of aircraft that normally uses the airfield
E6B computers and flight plotters	
Note: These are only a sample of reference publications. The local operational area may dictate additional materials be available.	

Wall Displays and Charts

10-15. Wall displays and charts for planning and other aeronautical information pertinent to the airfield should also be located in the flight planning area. Printed maps are required for display even though digital systems may depict flight area information. Examples include—

- Crash rescue map.
- Traffic pattern diagrams.
- VFR/IFR planning chart of the CONUS.
- Sectional aeronautical chart depicting the local flying area, military operating areas, special VFR corridors and altitudes, and traffic routes to and from other airports that may conflict with local or transient traffic.
- A 1:50,000 map of the installation showing range information, flight and wire hazards, and NOE and instrument training areas. (This map should be updated, at a minimum, every 30 days. The latest date the map was updated should be posted on or near the map.)
- NOTAM system as prescribed in AR 95-10.
- Large-scale airfield diagram depicting runways, taxiways, ramps, aprons, field elevation, controlled movement area, precision approach critical areas, traffic pattern directions and altitudes, airfield obstructions, and other pertinent airfield information.
- Planning charts with a cord-type mileage indicator that shows statute and nautical miles.
- Weather briefings.
- Radio frequencies for ground control, tower, approach control, ground-controlled approach, and departure control.
- Nondirectional radio beacon frequencies for use in radio checks.
- Bulletin boards or displays containing pertinent flight information and reference materiel such as:
  - Local IFR recovery procedures.
  - Lost communication procedures.

Other Considerations

10-16.   An airfield safety bulletin board containing current safety-related publications and posters should also be displayed. Other items included in the flight planning room are an ear protection dispenser and pencil sharpener.

Pilot Ready Room

10-17.   The pilot ready room should be established in an area easily accessible to the flight planning and dispatch facilities. It should be furnished with comfortable furniture. If a snack bar or eating facility is not available in the immediate vicinity, food- and drink-dispensing machines should be placed in the ready room. Class A telephones should be made available with installation phone numbers displayed.

10-18.   Flight operations personnel in the base operations are responsible for—

- Transmitting flight plan proposals by Service B or F to the regional flight service facility.
- Providing airfield advisory service to aircraft that use the airfield when the control tower is nonoperational.
- Transmitting flight movement messages per AR 95-11 and FAA Order JO 7110.10. Military and civilian CONUS-based airfields use FAA communication systems.

10-19.   Military airfields based outside the continental United States (OCONUS) may have additional requirements placed on them by host nation air traffic procedures. In those cases, a host nation LOA pertaining to air traffic service support may be required. The flight service communications system is a series of microprocessors located at air route traffic control centers (ARTCCs) nationwide. The microprocessors are connected by high-speed circuits to the aeronautical fixed telecommunications network computer in Kansas City, Missouri. Remote base operations (BASEOPS) and FSS users are connected to a microprocessor at their host ARTCC. These microprocessors are known as Service B. Service B is part of the National Airspace Data Interchange Network. Service F is a system of interphone circuits used as a backup system to Service B or when a BASEOPS or FSS does not have a Service B capability. Service B or interphone circuits interconnect all stations. Military airfield tie-in services are described in FAA Order JO 7350.8. Military BASEOPS send flight movement messages to the appropriate military BASEOPS and tie-in FSS. The tie-in FSS relays movement messages to and from the sending BASEOPS when necessary.

SECTION II – AIRFIELD MANAGEMENT RESPONSIBILITIES

AIRFIELD FACILITY RECREATIONAL USE

10-20.   AR 215-1 prescribes procedures that govern the participation of Army personnel in sport parachuting. It also describes required procedures for establishing and operating military sport parachuting clubs. When an Army flying club is established, the airfield operations officer may be responsible for carrying out supervisory and administrative duties. AR 215-1 contains the rules that govern the operation of these clubs. The operations officer will assist the flying club in establishing local flying rules and safety programs. He ensures FAA rules and regulations are followed. Airfield operations will provide the flying club DOD FLIPs at the level authorized by AR 95-2.

AUTHORIZATION TO LAND FOREIGN OWNED/OPERATED AIRCRAFT AT ARMY AIRFIELDS

10-21.   All foreign aircraft operators landing at Army installations in the United States must obtain an aircraft landing authorization number (ALAN). AR 95-2 outlines the required procedures for obtaining an ALAN. This requirement ensures security, diplomatic coordination, customs control, and liability protection. If an unauthorized foreign aircraft lands at an Army installation, the following information is relayed to the U.S. Army Aeronautical Services Agency for coordination with the state department:

- Type of aircraft.

- Tail number (if known).
- Call sign.
- Name of pilot.
- Total number of personnel in crew.
- Total number of passengers (also identify VIPs or special passengers and any honors or special requests).
- Purpose of trip.
- Aircraft itinerary, estimated time of arrival (ETA), location, and estimated time of departure (ETD) for each stop. (Identify location of U.S. customs stop.)
- Hazardous cargo and number of weapons onboard for each leg of flight.
- Requirements for fuel or services at each stop.
- Method of payment for fuel and services.
- Additional remarks or special requirements (such as hotel reservations or ground transportation requests).
- Point of contact and telephone number.

JOINT-USE AIRFIELDS

10-22. A joint-use airfield is an Army installation where agreements exist between the Army and civil authorities for civil aviation use of Army airfield facilities. AR 95-2 contains information on the policies and procedures for joint-use airfields. Civil aircraft are not permitted to use an Army airfield unless they possess an approved Civil Aircraft Landing Permit (CALP). AR 95-2 outlines requirements for obtaining CALPs. Operations personnel should require the pilot of a civil aircraft to fax an approved CALP to operations before granting a PPR.

AIRFIELD MARKINGS

10-23. FAA Advisory Circular 1 50/5340-1J and UFC 3-260-05A contain criteria for marking airfields. These publications dictate the proper procedures for layout and marking of a new airfield. This section covers specific information on repainting existing markings.

COLOR MARKINGS

10-24. Runways will be marked with white reflective paint. Taxiways will be marked with yellow reflective paint. Paint used to mark or re-mark runway and taxiway pavement will conform to the criteria in UFC 3-260-05A. Markings will be painted on paved areas only after the pavements have been allowed to cure thoroughly. The pavement surface must be dry and clean before the paint is applied.

10-25. Markers and markings will be used to indicate usable limits of snow-covered runways. Markers will be spaced at intervals of not more than 330 feet and located symmetrically about the axis of the runway along the sides of the usable portion. Sufficient markers will be placed to indicate the runway threshold. Markers must be kept free of snow and grime.

SNOW AND ICE REMOVAL

10-26. At installations where snow and ice may constitute a hazard, AR 420-1 requires establishment of a snow removal and ice control plan. This plan will include instructions and procedures for—

- Establishing priorities for prompt removal or control of snow, ice, and slush on each movement area.
- Positioning snow from movement area surfaces so aircraft propellers, engine pods, rotors, and wingtips will clear any snowdrift and snow bank as the aircraft landing gear traverses any full-use portion of the movement area.

- Selecting and applying approved materials for snow and ice control to ensure they adhere to snow and ice sufficiently to minimize engine ingestion.
- Beginning snow and ice control operations in a timely manner.
- Identifying equipment to be used.
- Listing quantities and storage location of materials (such as snow fences, chemicals, and abrasives).
- Scheduling training of equipment operators and supervisors.
- Scheduling preseason operational trial run sessions.
- Ensuring around-the-clock cooperation with weather authorities for notification of forecasts of snow and ice storm intensities and durations.

10-27. Calcium chloride, sodium chloride, and abrasives will not be used on airfield or heliport pavements. Only materials that do not corrode aircraft will be used on airfield or heliport pavements.

COMPASS-SWINGING BASES

10-28. Compass-swinging bases are not required on Army airfields. However, when constructed and operational, they must be equipped according to UFC 3-260-05A. These bases align an aircraft for the precise calibration of all types of air navigation equipment. The compass-swinging base pad will be marked with precision alignment indicators that are accurate to within 0.25 percent of 1 degree. A minimum distance of 275 feet will be provided from the center of the compass-swinging base pad to the nearest significant quantity of iron and taxiway or engine run-up area. The same distance will be allowed from the center of the pad to the nearest parking area or hardstand for aircraft, vehicles, or equipment. Compass-swinging bases will be painted with nonreflective white paint.

AIR NAVIGATION OBSTRUCTION MARKING AND LIGHTING

10-29. Obstruction marking and lighting will be limited to objects that penetrate the clearance planes and surfaces described in UFC 3-260-05A and, by their nature and position, constitute a hazard to navigation.

10-30. Obstruction markings should never be placed on objects that are not obstructions. Obstruction marking will be made with aviation surface orange or a combination of aviation surface orange and aviation surface white. Obstruction marking patterns may be solid orange, alternate bands of orange and white, checkerboard pattern, or beach ball pattern. FAA Advisory Circular 70/7460-1 contains specific instructions on which pattern to use. Obstruction lighting will be according to UFC 3-260-05A and FAA Advisory Circular 70/7460-1. Wheel chocks will be marked on all sides with a yellow reflective paint or tape.

FIRE HYDRANTS

10-31. Fire hydrants will be painted per the installation design manual.

FIRE EXTINGUISHERS

10-32. All fire extinguisher containers will be red or the color required by local fire prevention standards. Each extinguisher will be marked with a symbol designating the class of fire for which it is intended. (Class A, B, C, or D fires will be marked as established in National Fire Protection Association [NFPA] Standard 10.) Multiple symbols will be placed on the extinguisher if it is suitable for more than one class of fire. The symbols must conform to the configurations in NFPA Standard 10. Fire extinguishers placed in an area that has aircraft movement will be marked near the top by a 4-inch-wide strip of reflective tape encircling the extinguisher. If a fire extinguisher is stored in a shelter that adjoins areas used by aircraft or aircraft-servicing vehicles, the shelter will be painted with nonreflective red paint and marked with a 4-inch-wide strip of reflective tape along its length.

AIRFIELD MAINTENANCE

10-33. Housekeeping of the grounds around the operations building and parking areas will be accomplished to ensure FOD materials are policed and disposed of properly. The first impression of an airfield is often a lasting impression; therefore, a neat and orderly appearance of the airfield and facilities must be maintained. Important considerations include—

- Fire extinguishers should be checked for broken seals and proper charging. They must be taken annually to the firefighting facility for recharging. Other checks will be conducted according to TB 5-4200-200-10.
- Aircraft tie-down ropes and anchors will be inspected periodically for serviceability. Besides securing parked aircraft during periods of high ground winds, these anchors ground the aircraft electrically to preclude fire generated from static sparks. Anchors and grounding rods will be maintained according to FM 10-67-1.

10-34. A plan should be established for periodic sweeping of runways, taxiways, and ramp areas. This plan should include procedures for mowing grass on the airfield.

AIRFIELD INSPECTION

10-35. Daily and periodic airfield inspections will be conducted and documented per AR 95-2 to ensure quality service and facility maintenance. Inspection checklists should include those items essential to maintaining a well-organized and functional airfield. The checklists should be expanded or modified to suit the airfield. Checklists should be furnished to the branch chiefs to ensure they fully understand their duties.

10-36. Department of Public Works personnel should inspect the extended runway centerline annually. They will resolve any disparity between the painted runway numbers and actual magnetic heading of the extended runway centerline. Air traffic facility managers will annually review and update runway centerline heading information. They will also review any local departure procedures that might be affected by heading changes.

VEHICLE MOVEMENT AND MARKINGS

10-37. Vehicle movement on the runway should be held to the minimum required for runway inspection and maintenance. All vehicles should be properly marked.

10-38. Airfield operations/management and airfield safety vehicles that operate regularly on the airfield shall be equipped with a rotating beacon or strobe light system atop the vehicle. Other vehicles that operate on the airfield shall have, at minimum, a flag displayed atop the vehicle to assist aircraft crew and/or air traffic controllers in identifying the vehicle. ATC light signals descriptions will be displayed on the dashboard of vehicles that regularly operate on the airfield. Vehicle operation near POL and aircraft refueling areas should be closely supervised. Sparks from the exhaust systems of these vehicles can create a hazardous situation. FM 10-67-1 describes the use of spark arresters for internal combustion engines.

10-39. The maximum speed limit for all vehicles on the flight line is 15 mph (excluding emergencies). The maximum speed limit for all vehicles operating within 25 feet of an aircraft is 5 mph, however, the speed of vehicles will not exceed 3 mph (walking speed) when within 10 feet of the aircraft, to include movement inside the aircraft. Drivers of vehicles that operate on ramps, taxiways, or runways should have on file evidence of satisfactorily passing a written examination. The examination should include clearance requirements between aircraft and vehicles, light signals, and radio procedures if vehicles are so equipped. All drivers for the Airfield Services Branch should possess the appropriate military driver's license and special authority to operate on the airfield movement area. Equipment other than vehicles may be required by the Airfield Services Branch and will be authorized on the TDA or TOE, as appropriate. Any vehicle that is required and can be justified can usually be obtained for the airfield. Items that may be needed include the following:

- Snow removal equipment.
- Auxiliary ground power units.

- Decontamination equipment.
- Illuminated marshalling wands.
- Flashlights.
- Forklift.
- Fuel contamination detector.
- Goggles.
- Hearing protection.
- Magnetic sweeper.
- Portable light sets.
- Radio equipment.
- Runway and taxiway sweeper.
- Maintenance procedures.
- Decelerometer.

10-40.   Good preventive maintenance procedures enhance efficient operations. AR 420-1contains criteria and responsibilities for initiating and accomplishing preventive maintenance programs. TM 1-1500-204-23-1 and TM 1-1500-204-23-2 contains standard inspection and maintenance procedures for auxiliary power units, maintenance workstands, portable air compressors, aircraft jacks, and other ground support equipment.

SECTION III – FLIGHT PLANNING PROCEDURES

FLIGHT PLANS

10-41.   AR 95-1, paragraph 5-2d states, "Aircraft will not be flown unless a flight plan (military or civil) has been filed or an operation's log completed. Local commanders will establish policies specifying the flight plans to be used." FAA Order JO 7110.10, Aeronautical Information Manual, and DOD FLIP general planning (GP) provide details on flight plan procedures. Specific information transmitted depends on the type of flight plan and agency to receive it. The information in table 10-2 will be sent to the agencies listed when filing a flight plan CONUS or sending flight information internationally.

Table 10-2. Flight plan information

Proposal to tower		
Type of proposal (VFR or IFR)	Proposed time of departure	
Aircraft identification	Destination	
Aircraft designation/transmitter distributor (TD) code	VIP code; pertinent remarks	
	Operating initials	
IFR flight plan (proposal) message to ARTCC		
Type of message (IFR flight plan)	Initial cruising altitude	
Aircraft identification	Standard instrument departure and route of flight (first leg only)	
Aircraft designation/TD code	Destination (first stop)	
Estimated true airspeed	Estimated time en route	
Point of departure	Remarks (capabilities and limitations of the	
Proposed departure time	Operating initials	
Outbound to the FSS		
Type of outbound (VFR or IFR)	Destination	Aircraft identification

Table 10-2. Flight plan information

Estimated time of arrival	Aircraft designation/TD code	VIP code, pertinent marks
Point of departure	Operating initials	
Outbound with stopover to FSS		
Type of outbound (VFR or IFR with stopover)	Destination (first stopover)	
Aircraft identification	Estimated time of arrival for first stopover	
Aircraft designation/TD code	Remarks applicable to this leg only	
Point of departure	Slant (This word is interpreted by the FSS subsequent legs are to follow)	
On VFR flight plan		
Destination (subsequent to first leg)	Void time (date-time group in six digits)	
Estimated time en route	Repeat from the slant as necessary for subsequent VFR legs	
Remarks (applicable to this leg, then to the entire flight)	Operating initials	
On IFR flight plan		
True airspeed	Estimated time en route	
Point of departure	Remarks (capabilities and limitations of the	
Proposed departure time	Void time (date-time group in six digits)	
Altitude	Repeat of IFR steps, to include the slant, as necessary, for subsequent IFR legs	
Standard instrument departure and route of flight	Operating initials	
Destination		
Inbound from the FSS		
Type of inbound (IFR or VFR)	Destination (only if servicing more than one)	
Aircraft identification	Estimated time of arrival	
Aircraft designation/TD code	Remarks	
Point of departure	Their operating initials (reply with yours)	
Inbound to tower		
Type of inbound (VFR or IFR)	Estimated time of arrival	
Aircraft identification	VIP code, pertinent remarks	
Aircraft designation/TD code	Your operating initials	
Point of departure		
Arrival from tower (of previous inbound)		
Type of arrival (IFR or VFR)	Actual time of arrival	
Aircraft identification	Their operating initials (reply with yours)	
Arrival to FSS (of previous inbound)		
Type of arrival (IFR or VFR)	Actual time of arrival	Aircraft identification
Point of arrival	Point of departure	Your operating initials

FAA FLIGHT SERVICE STATIONS

10-42. Regional FSSs are operated by the FAA and perform the services described below for Army aviation personnel.

Receiving Air Traffic Control Clearances

10-43. When filing an IFR flight plan, the dispatcher transmits it by Service B to the ARTCC servicing the departure area. If Service B is not available, the dispatcher transmits the flight plan by telephone to the tie-in FSS or ARTCC servicing the departure area. The IFR clearance is then delivered directly by Service B by the host ARTCC to the tower. It may also be delivered indirectly by Service B to the appropriate approach control or FSS who, in turn, will relay the clearance by interphone to the tower or BASEOPS.

Forward Departure and Inbound Messages

10-44. After the aircraft departs a military installation, the dispatcher transmits the VFR and/or IFR departure message to the appropriate military BASEOPS or tie-in FSS. If required, the FSS relays the departure and/or inbound message to the destination of intent. Local flights do not require a departure message.

Receive and Coordinate In-Flight Changes to Destination

10-45. If a change in the destination is made in flight, the pilot transmits this information to the nearest FSS. The FSS advises the original point of destination, new point of destination, and point of departure.

Destination Operations Office

10-46. Destination operations offices acknowledge receipt of inbound flight messages from the destination FSS or military BASEOPS. It then—

- Transmits the actual arrival time of VFR and/or IFR aircraft to the tie-in FSS, if the destination is not equipped with Service B, so the flight plan may be closed.
- Advises the tie-in FSS, if the destination is not equipped with Service B, a part of a VFR and/or an IFR stopover flight plan may be closed.
- Notifies tower of the impending arrival.
- Advises the pilot of hazardous conditions that have developed at the pilot's destination. The destination operations office for military airports, or FAA for civilian airports, initiates an in-flight advisory.
- Sends the advisory through ATC en route or terminal facilities to the pilot, for IFR flights, and sends the advisory through the FSS or terminal ATC facilities for VFR flights.
- Conducts a local search of all adjacent flight plan area airports and communications search when an aircraft is overdue.

Message Priority

10-47. Multiple messages require transmission by priority. Priority 1 and 2 messages are transmitted within 5 minutes after receipt of the required information. The following is a description of priority 1, 2, 3, and 4 messages:

- **Priority 1:** Emergency messages include essential information on aircraft accidents or suspected accidents. After an actual emergency, give a lower priority to messages relating to the accident.
- **Priority 2:** Clearance and control messages.
- **Priority 3:** Movement and control messages in the following order:
  - Progress reports.
  - Departure/arrival reports.

- ■ Flight plans.
- ■ Movement messages on IFR aircraft.
- ● **Priority 4:** Movement messages on VFR aircraft.

10-48. When transmitting an emergency or control message, use "emergency" or "control" to interrupt lower priority messages. FAA Order JO 7110.65 and FAA Order JO 7110.10 outlines procedures for transmission of movement control messages.

Remain Overnight Messages

10-49. When transmitting remain overnight (RON) messages to the tie-in FSS, only the following information will be sent in the order shown:

- ● Base or bases to receive the message (name or location identifier).
- ● Other addressees at the base of delivery.
- ● Aircraft identification.
- ● Aircraft designation.
- ● Pilot's last name.
- ● The term "RON."
- ● Location identifier of base where aircraft will remain overnight.
- ● Date or dates.
- ● Remarks (keep to absolute minimum).

10-50. The FAA transmits RON messages to BASEOPS. BASEOPS is responsible for delivering final or multiple RON messages to additional addressees at the same station. RON messages regarding VIPs require immediate delivery.

Service B Message

10-51. AR 95-11 and FAA Order JO 7110.10 contain information on the transmission of flight movement messages within both the national and international airspace systems via Service B.

MILITARY AIRCRAFT IDENTIFICATION

10-52. Military aircraft are identified according to FM 3-01.80 and DOD FLIP GP. The following is a description of some of the aircraft mission identification procedures.

Special Mission Aircraft

10-53. When special mission aircraft cannot be identified by their call sign, explain under "REMARKS" in the flight plan. For example, if Air Force Systems Command (AFSC) aircraft are engaged in flight test operations, enter "AFSC flight test mission" in the remarks section of each flight plan or message.

Military Search and Rescue Flights

10-54. When military aircraft are on a SAR flight, insert the word "Rescue" between the service prefix and prescribed markings; for example, "Air Force Rescue 12345".

Military Code System

10-55. DOD FLIP GP contains information on flight plan, mission, and service codes.

FLIGHTS NEAR SENSITIVE BORDERS

10-56. Commanders responsible for flight operations near politically sensitive borders will publish specific and detailed instructions. These instructions prescribe—

- ● Procedures for border orientation flights, pilot proficiency qualifications, currency requirements for both visual and instrument flight procedures, and all OPSEC procedures.

- Detailed emergency procedures for all foreseeable contingencies (such as equipment malfunction and pilot disorientation).
- Sufficient map and chart coverage of the general area for the planned flight route. Minimum requirements for preflight briefings and flight planning.
- Periodic review of operating instructions in FLIPs to preclude inadvertent border overflights.
- Publication requirements for instrument and radio navigation.

Restricted Area Usage

10-57. Restricted areas may be used when a request is sent through diplomatic or North Atlantic Treaty Organization (NATO) channels by the visiting nation or NATO command, as a result of an in-flight emergency, or through bilateral agreements between NATO nations.

Distinguished Visitor and Transient Services

10-58. The operations officer is responsible for ensuring proper courtesies and services are provided to distinguished visitors/VIPs and transient personnel using airfield facilities. The flight operations sergeant or designated representative is responsible for ensuring VIP and transient facilities are clean, comfortable, and properly equipped. The lounge should be equipped with comfortable and convenient furnishings. Many times, VIPs will be required to wait while their aircraft is serviced or until it arrives for their pickup. Regardless of how well the airfield functions, a visitor's most lasting impression of an airfield may be of the available facilities. There are no established criteria for a VIP lounge; however, comfort and convenience should be the primary consideration in establishing this facility.

This page intentionally left blank.

Chapter 11

Airfield Services and Safety

The airfield services/POL services branch is responsible for the servicing of aircraft and inspection and general policing of the airfield and its facilities. This chapter briefly discusses the branch responsibilities, criteria for marking airfields, and airfield maintenance.

SECTION I – PERSONNEL AND RESPONSIBILITIES

PERSONNEL

AIRFIELD SERVICES BRANCH

11-1. The Airfield Services Branch includes the following positions:

- The branch chief—

Contents

  - Coordinates branch activities under supervision of the operations officer.
  - Prepares an SOP that outlines duties and responsibilities of branch personnel.
  - Ensures branch personnel are properly trained and qualified to perform their assigned duties.
  - Assigns specific personnel responsibilities and ensures duty rosters and performance records are properly maintained.
  - Ensures a daily inspection of the airfield is conducted.
- Shift supervisors—
  - Inspect the airfield (including runways and taxiways) for maintenance, police, FOD, and OPSEC considerations and requirements, at least once during the shift.
  - Supervise and train assigned personnel in their duties.
  - Coordinate with other branches concerning VIPs, transient and assigned aircraft, transportation requirements, and airfield conditions.
- Aircraft service personnel—
  - Provide and operate vehicles, as required, and perform operator maintenance in compliance with applicable technical manuals.
  - Maintain FOD controls while performing their duties.
  - Stand fireguard for all aircraft starting, if required.
  - Look for and report OPSEC violations.
  - Serve as aircraft ground guides and marshals.

11-2. Personnel organization and duties performed depend on size and structure of the airfield and size of the unit or units the airfield supports. As a general rule, a minimum of two airfield services personnel are required per shift during airfield operating hours to satisfy operational requirements.

Ground Handling

11-3. When directing aircraft movements during land operations, aircraft service personnel (guides or marshals) should use the appropriate hand and arm (marshaling) signals in FM 21-60 and NATO Standardization Agreement (STANAG) 3117. When available, signal flags may be used with hand and arm signals during daylight hours. Ground guides or marshals should wear hearing and eye protection when guiding fixed- and rotary-wing aircraft. At night, a ground guide will signal with a lighted baton (wand) in each hand. The intensity of these lights will vary, depending on whether the aircrew is aided or unaided. Signals given with wands will be identical to the day signals unless stated otherwise in FM 21-60. Wands should remain lighted at all times during use. During surface taxiing and parking, the pilot will stop immediately when one or both of the ground guide wands fail.

11-4. When required, a flagman will be stationed so as to be clearly visible to approaching aircraft. This person will direct the pilot to the ground guide. The ground guide will indicate when he or she is ready to guide the aircraft. The position of the ground guide for a FW aircraft is on a line extending forward of, and at an oblique angle from, the left (port) wing. The pilot's eyes must be visible to the ground guide from this position. The position of the ground guide for a rotary-wing aircraft is relatively the same as a FW aircraft. However, the ground guide may be on either side of the aircraft as long as the pilot's eyes are visible to him.

11-5. To ensure the safety of aircraft and vehicles on the airfield movement area, two-way radio communication is mandatory for tower controllers. The SOP must require pilots and vehicle drivers to obtain tower clearance before they proceed onto the aircraft movement area.

POL PERSONNEL AND RESPONSIBILITIES

11-6. The POL services branch includes the following positions:
- The branch chief—
  - Coordinates branch activities under supervision of the operations officer.
  - Prepares an SOP that outlines duties and responsibilities of branch personnel.
  - Ensures personnel are properly trained and qualified to perform their assigned duties.
  - Assigns specific personnel responsibilities and ensures duty rosters and performance records are properly maintained.
  - Ensures POL handlers are checked semiannually for body contamination.
  - Inspects POL facilities daily.
  - Ensures supplies of aviation fuels, oils, and lubricants are adequate to meet current and emergency operational requirements.
- Shift supervisors—
  - Inspect POL facilities at least once during a shift.
  - Supervise and train assigned personnel in their duties.
  - Coordinate with other branches concerning VIPs and assigned and transient aircraft refueling requirements.
- Petroleum storage specialists—
  - Provide refueling and other related services for assigned and transient aircraft and ensure transient aviators complete DD Form 1898 (Fuel Sale Slip) for credit-card purchases.

- Receive, store, and inspect all petroleum products delivered to the storage area.
- Use appropriate safety equipment specified in FM 10-67-1.
- Perform operator maintenance on lines, tanks, pumps, and valves in the POL storage area.

Aircraft Refueling

11-7. Normally, refuelers (refuel vehicles) are used to refuel aircraft on the flight line. They should be used when it is more practical to take fuel to the aircraft than to bring the aircraft to the fuel. Due to the inherent dangers of rapid refueling operations, a refueler is used only in unusual situations. FM 10-67-1 discusses operating procedures to follow in such a case.

Staffing

11-8. A minimum of two persons are required for refueling from a tank vehicle. If only the vehicle operator and his assistant are present, the operator should attend the pump and the assistant should handle the nozzle. A fire extinguisher should be within reach of each. Where possible, the aircraft crew chief should be present to oversee the entire operation and another member of the aircraft or ground crew should man the fire extinguisher at the nozzle.

11-9. A minimum of three persons are required for rapid refueling or hot refueling of an aircraft. One person operates the fuel nozzle, the second remains at the emergency fuel shutoff valve, and the third mans a suitable fire extinguisher. The third person stands outside the main rotor disk of the aircraft at a point where he or she can see both the pilot at the controls and the refueler with the nozzle. This person may be from the FARP or one of the aircraft crewmembers. In a combat situation, METT–TC may override the availability of a third person to operate the fire extinguisher.

AIRCRAFT FIREFIGHTING AND CRASH AND RESCUE SERVICES

11-10. Aircraft firefighting and rescue services may be provided by installation engineers or personnel, and equipment may be assigned under direct supervision of the airfield operations division. These are critical functions that must be closely coordinated with the branches of the operations division. AR 420-1 establishes basic procedures and responsibilities for crash and rescue operations at airfields under DA jurisdiction.

11-11. The installation commander having jurisdiction over an airfield is responsible for maintaining an effective organization of trained personnel and adequate and reliable equipment. The commander ensures the airfield provides emergency protective services for flight activities and the types of aircraft operating at that airfield. These services include publishing detailed procedures for emergency firefighting, crash rescue, and handling of hazardous cargo and defueling operations as outlined in AR 420-1. These procedures should be posted at each location where emergency calls are received.

SECTION II – AIRFIELD SAFETY

11-12. Commanders and leaders are responsible for managing risks inherent to aviation operations. Developing and implementing an integrated, imaginative and comprehensive accident prevention program will ensure identification of hazards and implementation of appropriate control measures. This section discusses aircraft accident prevention and describes preaccident and contingency plans. It also outlines requirements for aircraft accident investigations and describes the operational hazard report. This section also references several safety regulations and procedures for handling hazardous materiel.

AIRCRAFT ACCIDENT PREVENTION

11-13. Accident prevention is a command responsibility. Commanders must establish and ensure a safety program that involves all personnel, equipment, and activities of the organization. Commanders establish a formal process to identify, assess, and control risks in aviation operations. Management of risk is an operations function of a unit.

11-14.   Command levels from ACs through aviation companies have a TOE or TDA-authorized, full-time position for a qualified aviation safety officer (ASO). The ASO assists in administering the aviation accident prevention program. A safety-trained NCO will be appointed to assist the ASO at brigade level and below. These appointments are made according to AR 385-10.

PREACCIDENT PLAN

11-15.   A preaccident plan lists actions to be taken if an accident occurs. A good plan includes care for injured personnel, security of the accident scene, and procedures for safe airfield operations during a crash rescue/recovery operation. A preaccident plan will be developed and maintained for each operational Army airfield, heliport, and aviation activity. The ASO is responsible for rehearsing and reviewing the unit preaccident plan with the operations officer (quarterly, at a minimum). The airfield operations officer is responsible for preparing, disseminating, and testing the preaccident plan.

EMERGENCY PLANS

11-16.   Emergency plans should provide enough guidance to ensure immediate issue of vital information to personnel who have responsibilities during an emergency.

Hurricane and High Wind Plan

11-17.   During a hurricane evacuation, Army commanders of airfields and flight activities will, at their discretion, evacuate assigned aircraft and impose temporary restrictions on use of flight facilities under their control. A detailed plan should be outlined in the local SOP and implemented when a hurricane or high wind warning is received. The plan should include but not be limited to—

- Evacuation, storage, or tiedown of aircraft. (Tiedown instructions in the aircraft operator's manual must be followed.)
- Removal of loose objects from parking areas (for example, chocks, fire extinguisher, boarding ramps, toolboxes, FOD containers, and work platforms).
- Protection of window glass and interiors by using prefabricated window covers. (To allow for pressure equalization, the building should not be made airtight.)
- Conducting checks on backup power sources to ensure efficient operation and availability of required fuel and oil.

Air Crash, Search, and Rescue Map

11-18.   All Army airfields are required to develop and maintain an air crash, search, and rescue (ACS&R) map according to AR 385-10 and AR 420-1. Both air and ground rescue personnel use the map to locate and reach the site of an aircraft accident. All personnel who assist in the rescue must be familiar with the map and area depicted.

11-19.   The ACS&R map will be marked with concentric circles with a minimum radius of 7 nautical miles. An appropriate grid method for navigation reference will be provided as an overlay or overprint. The grid overlay or template will be issued for rapid exchange of information between personnel involved in rescue operations using a common map.

11-20.   The ACS&R map will be coordinated with rescue agencies of adjacent airfields to ensure a compatible design for effective rescue operations. The airfield commander is responsible for ensuring all agencies providing emergency assistance are given a standardized map. Failure to provide a standardized scale map to each agency may cause confusion and unnecessary delay when emergency assistance is required.

11-21.   Airfield diagrams should be sectioned off in the alphanumeric format or have predetermined crash response points indicated. These diagrams are provided to each agency for easy airfield reference when responding to emergencies.

AIRCRAFT ACCIDENT INVESTIGATION

11-22.   A successful aircraft accident investigation requires proper planning and organization, a vital part of which is the preaccident plan. These plans ensure personnel and equipment will be effectively used. DA Pam 385-40 provides instruction for conduct of an aircraft accident investigation.

11-23.   Commanders ensure all Army accidents that result in injury, occupational illness, or property damage are investigated, analyzed, reported, and recorded as prescribed in AR 385-10.

OPERATIONAL HAZARD REPORT

11-24.   Operational hazards are any condition or act that affects, or may affect, the safety of Army aircraft or associated personnel and equipment. DA Form 2696 is used to report a hazard or unsafe condition or act. AR 385-10 contains information on preventing accidents caused by operational hazards. Operational hazards include inadequacies, deficiencies, or unsafe practices in—

- ATC.
- Airways and NAVAIDs.
- Controller procedures and techniques.
- Near midair collisions between aircraft or near collisions between aircraft and other objects in the air or on the ground.
- Aircraft operations.
- Aircraft maintenance or inspection.
- Weather services.
- Airfields and heliports (facilities or services).
- Flight or maintenance training and education.
- Regulations, directives, and publications issued by DOD agencies, the FAA, International Civil Aviation Organization, and host nations.

11-25.   Occupational Hazard Reports (OHRs) are not submitted after corrective action has been taken for materiel failure of aircraft components and ground support equipment. See DA Pam 738-751 for handling these occurrences.

11-26.   Commanders will establish procedures for reporting operational hazards and ensure all such reports are investigated and hazardous conditions are corrected.

11-27.   OHRs will be submitted to the ASO or Army flight operations office at the unit or installation where the hazard was observed, or at the home airfield or next airfield at which the reporting individual lands. The ASO will immediately forward the OHR to the installation concerned. The ASO will thoroughly investigate the report and submit recommendations to the commander. When corrective action cannot be taken at unit level, the report will be forwarded through channels to the command level at which appropriate corrective action can be taken.

11-28.   Commanders will ensure procedures are established to manage the OHR system including signing and returning completed OHRs to the ASO within 10 working days of receiving the report. The completed action will be returned to the originator within 20 working days of receipt.

11-29.   Reports that have worldwide application will be forwarded to Commander, U.S. Army Combat Readiness Center, Fort Rucker, Alabama 36362-5363. Information copies of all OHRs not correctable at or below AC level and reports that indicate possible involvement or deficiency of FAA personnel or facilities should also be forwarded to the U.S. Army Combat Readiness Center. OHRs concerning Army ATC procedures will be forwarded to Commander, U.S. Army Aviation Warfighting Center, ATTN: ATZQ-ATC Fort Rucker, Alabama 36362-5265.

HAZARDOUS MATERIEL

11-30. Hazardous materiel is defined as any materiel that is flammable, corrosive, explosive, toxic, radioactive, nuclear, unduly magnetic, biologically infective, or acts as an oxidizing agent. It also includes any other materiel that may endanger human life or property due to its quantity, properties, or packaging. Special storage, use, handling, and shipment procedures and protocols must be followed to help protect against accidental exposure.

TRANSPORT

11-31. Flight operations personnel must comply with special procedures governing the transport of hazardous materiel. AR 95-27 outlines the operational procedures for aircraft transporting hazardous materiel. AR 200-1, AR 420-1, FM 4-01.11, and TM 38-250 contain additional information on the transport of hazardous materiel. Before takeoff, the supported unit briefs the aircrew on special handling requirements. Aircraft loaded with ammunition or fuel requesting takeoff or landing will notify ATC with the following information—

- Quantity and type of load.
- Classification of the load.

11-32. Should the contents be classified, the pilot will inform ATC he or she is unable to divulge aircraft contents due to its sensitive nature. Procedures for handling these aircraft remain the same as any aircraft carrying hazardous cargo.

Chapter 12

National Airspace System Requirements

Whether based CONUS or OCONUS, Army aviation requires special-use airspace (SUA) to conduct training requirements. Training, disaster relief, and homeland security operations within U.S. airspace requires that Army aviation operate in the National Airspace System (NAS). Army aviators, airspace managers, and airfield managers must understand SUA and the NAS and its requirements to ensure aviation and airfield operations are conducted safely and within Army and FARs.

SECTION I – NATIONAL AIRSPACE SYSTEM DEFINED

12-1. The NAS is defined as a common network of:
- U.S. NAVAIDs.
- Equipment and services.
- Airports or landing areas.
- Aeronautical charts.
- Airways.
- Information.
- Services.
- Rules.
- Procedures.
- Technical information.
- Manpower.
- Material.

Contents

12-2. Included in the NAS are components and facilities shared jointly by the military and civilians and the SUA used by the military.

HIERARCHY OF AIRSPACE

12-3. The hierarchical layout of airspace within the NAS is classified as follows.

CLASS A

12-4. Class A is the most restrictive airspace and requires all aircraft to operate under IFR. Airspace starts at 18,000 feet mean sea level (MSL) and goes to flight level 600 (60,000 feet MSL). Class A airspace overlays the entire United States.

CLASS B

12-5. Class B airspace is generally from surface to 10,000 feet MSL, located around the nation's busiest airports and is tailored for each airport. The exact dimensions are depicted on VFR sectionals and airport terminal charts.

CLASS C

12-6. Class C airspace is from surface to 4,000 above ground level (AGL) and depicted in MSL. Airspace surrounds airports that have operational control tower and radar approach control. Airports must meet certain traffic density requirements.

CLASS D

12-7. Class D airspace dimensions are generally from surface to 2,500 feet and depicted in MSL. It surrounds airports with operational control towers. The configuration is individually tailored for each airport and is displayed on VFR charts.

CLASS E

12-8. Class E airspace consists of any controlled airspace that is not Class A, B, C, or D. Airspace has no defined vertical limit until reaching Class A airspace. Class E airspace may begin at the surface or at a designated altitude. If there is no other designated lower altitude, Class E airspace starts at 14,500 feet MSL and is not less than 1,500 feet AGL. This airspace may be designated to start at a lower altitude to provide controlled airspace for en route airways. Class E airspace designated to start below 14,500 feet MSL is depicted on VFR charts. It may be further lowered to start at either 700 or 1,200 feet AGL. This provides controlled airspace for transitioning to or from the terminal or en route environment. The 700-foot transition area is depicted on VFR charts. The 1,200 feet transition area is depicted if it borders Class G airspace. Surfaced-based Class E airspace occurs in two situations where Class E will be designated to start at the surface.

- The airspace will be configured to contain all instrument approach procedures.
- Areas that serve as extensions to Class B, C, or D surface areas. This provides controlled airspace without imposing a communications requirement for the VFR pilot. Surface-based Class E airspace is depicted on VFR charts.

CLASS G

12-9. This is uncontrolled airspace not designated A, B, C, D, or E. IFR operations are authorized in Class G airspace. Weather requirements for VFR operations depend on the altitude being flown.

AIR TRAFFIC COORDINATION REQUIREMENTS

12-10. Air traffic coordination requirements for operation in Class A, B, C, D, E, and G airspace are located in table 12-1.

Table 12-1. Air traffic control requirements

Class A
Operating in Class A airspace requires all aircraft operate under an IFR clearance and are under radar positive control from the ground.
Aircraft must be equipped for IFR operations as outlined in AR 95-1 and FAR part 91.
Class B
ATC clearance is required regardless of the weather.
IFR operations require very (high frequency) omnidirectional range or tactical air navigation receiver.

VFR operations in Class B airspace requires:
    Three statute miles visibility and remain clear of clouds.
    Two-way radio communications with ATC is required.
    Transponder with automatic altitude encoding.

Table 12-1. Air traffic control requirements

Class C
Two-way radio communications with ATC is required prior to entering and while operating in Class C airspace.
Weather requirements are three statute miles visibility and basic cloud clearance for VFR operations.
Transponder with automatic altitude encoding.
Class D
Two-way radio communications must be established with ATC prior to entering and while operating in Class D.
Weather requirements are three statute miles visibility and basic cloud clearance.
Class E
Two-way radio communications are required in Class E airspace when there is an operational ATC tower within the Class E airspace.
Operating VFR in Class E airspace below 10,000 ft MSL flight visibility must be three statute miles with a cloud clearance of 1,000 ft above, 2,000 ft horizontal, and 500 ft below.
Operating VFR in Class E airspace at or above 10,000 ft flight visibility must be five statute miles with a cloud clearance of 1,000 ft above, one statute mile horizontally, and 1,000 ft below.
Class G
To operate VFR in Class G airspace above 1,200 ft AGL, but below 10,000 ft MSL, flight visibility must be at least one statute mile during the day and three statute miles during the night with a cloud clearance of 1,000 ft above, 2,000 ft horizontal, and 500 ft below.
To operate VFR in Class G at or above 1,200 ft AGL and at or above 10,000 ft MSL, flight visibility must be at least five statute miles with a cloud clearance of 1,000 ft above, one statute mile horizontally, and 1,000 ft below.
Two-way radio communications are required in Class G airspace when there is an operational ATC tower.

SECTION II – SPECIAL-USE AIRSPACE

12-11.   SUA has limitations that may be imposed on aircraft. Except for controlled firing areas, SUA areas are depicted on aeronautical charts. The following are SUA types.

TEMPORARY FLIGHT RESTRICTIONS

12-12.   Temporary flight restrictions (TFRs) are added to the airspace system through the national NOTAM system. This type of SUA is depicted on sectionals and may appear with little notice. The most common uses for TFRs are—

- Presidential visits or movements.
- Other high level government officials' visits or movements.
- Major sporting events.
- Firefighting.

PROHIBITED AREAS

12-13.   Prohibited areas are established for security or other reasons associated with national welfare. No flights are allowed in these areas. (These areas are depicted on sectional charts.)

RESTRICTED AREAS

12-14. Restricted areas are established when determined necessary to confine or segregate activities considered hazardous to nonparticipating aircraft. The following denotes the existence of hazards to aircraft such as:

- Artillery firing.
- Aerial gunnery.
- Guided missile ranges.

12-15. Entering a restricted area without authorization from the using or controlling agency may be hazardous to flight. Before entering these areas, contact the controlling authority through the FAA flight service station. Restricted areas are depicted on sectional charts.

WARNING AREAS

12-16. Warning areas contain activities that may be hazardous to nonparticipating aircraft. These areas extend from three nautical miles outward from the coast of the United States. Warning areas are depicted on sectional charts.

MILITARY OPERATIONS AREAS

12-17. Military operations area (MOAs) are designated to contain nonhazardous military flight activities including, but not limited to, air combat maneuvers, air intercepts and low altitude tactics. Most military flight training activities necessitate acrobatic or abrupt flight maneuvers. Pilots operating under VFR should exercise extreme caution while flying within an MOA when military activity is being conducted. The active/inactive status of MOAs may change frequently. Pilots should contact any FSS within 100 miles of the area to obtain the MOA hours of operation. Pilots should contact the controlling agency for traffic advisories before entering an active MOA.

ALERT AREAS

12-18. Alert areas exist to inform pilots of areas that may contain a high volume of pilot training or an unusual type of aerial activity. Pilots should be particularly alert for other traffic when flying in these areas. Alert areas are depicted on sectional charts.

VICTOR AIRWAYS

12-19. Victor airways are aerial highways that connect electronic NAVAIDs. Victor airways carry a high volume of VFR and IFR traffic. Flight near these airways requires extra vigilance to see and avoid other air traffic. Victor airways are 12 nautical miles wide (4 miles wide primary area and 2 miles wide secondary area) and are depicted on sectional charts.

MILITARY TRAINING ROUTES

12-20. Military training routes (MTRs) are usually established below 10,000 feet MSL for operations at speeds in excess of 250 knots. Route segments may be defined at higher altitudes for purposes of route continuity. Operations on IFR MTRs are conducted in compliance with IFR regardless of weather conditions. VFR MTRs operate under VFR rules.

Appendix A

Contingency Airfield Opening Checklists

TAOGs and AOBs must be airfield opening experts. For this to occur, AOBs must be aggressively involved during seizure planning when identifying airfields that meet requirements. Engineers are also an important element when evaluating airfields. The engineer assessment and future airfield needs must be incorporated into the overall intelligence collection plan as this information determines the feasibility of the airfield and the tasks required for the airfield opening force. The airfield assessment and opening plan should be developed as soon as the mission is assigned. Many tools are available to engineers and the AOB to begin airfield assessment prior to actual arrival at the field. After arrival, the airfield assessment team verifies the information gained during premission planning, collects additional data, and provides a recommendation to the airfield opening force. This appendix details the numerous checklists necessary for adequate airfield assessment and the duties required for airfield opening.

AIRFIELD ASSESSMENT CHECKLISTS

A-1. Tables A-1 through A-11 provide airfield assessment checklists categorized by airfield functional areas.

A-2. Table A-1 is an example of an airfield data checklist.

Table A-1. Airfield data checklist

Item	Remarks
Airfield name	
Runway data/condition 　　　Usable/unusable 　　　Damaged 　　　UXO present 　　　Drainage problems 　　　Rutting 　　　Runway length 　　　Runway width 　　　Surface type 　　　Weight bearing capability 　　　Slope gradient 　　　• Longitudinal lateral transverse gradient 　　　Glide – slope 　　　Runway markings 　　　• Centerline 　　　• Runway edge 　　　• Distance Note: For semiprepared (dirt) surfaces, determine runway friction factor for C-17.	

Table A-1. Airfield data checklist

Item	Remarks

Lighting
    Edge
    Approach
    Threshold
    VASI/PAPI
Note: PCN values should be based on 50,000 C-17 passes.	

Shoulder width	

Overrun data
    Length
    Surface type
    Condition
    Slope	

Arresting system
    Type
    Location	

Obstructions
    Approach illusions
    Visual terrain
    Zero city lights	

Engine blast information	

Obstacles on airfield
    Height
    Location	

Graded area
    Width
    Slope
    Obstacles	

Maintained area
    Width
    Slope
    Obstacles	

Clear area
    Obstacles
    Glide slope	

Approach area
    Obstacles
    Clearance slopes	

Hazards to flight	
Capability to support airlift operations	
Maximum on ground by aircraft type	

A-3.   Table A-2 is an example of a taxiway assessment checklist.

Table A-2. Taxiway assessment checklist

Item	Remarks

Status
   Unusable
   Damaged
   Check for UXO	

Width	
Surface type	
Weight bearing capability/source	
Markings	
Lighting	
Runway hold lights	
Shoulders stabilized	
Obstructions	
Serve as emergency LZ	

Aircraft (fixed/rotary wing) movement on ground
   Identify any area not accessible to aircraft
   Identify any specific taxi routes for aircraft	

A-4.   Table A-3 is an example of a helipad assessment checklist.

Table A-3. Helipad assessment checklist

Item	Remarks
Dimensions	
Surface type	
Hot landing area location(s)	
FARP location(s)	
Existing approach plan	
Existing departure plan	
Existing emergency egress plan	
Hazards to flight	

A-5. Table A-4 is an example of an air traffic assessment checklist.

Table A-4. Air traffic assessment checklist

Item	Remarks
Field elevation	
Traffic patterns Altitudes Type Prevailing wind	
Departure procedures Radar handoff Nonradar handoff Heading	Call sign, FIX, altitude, frequency, location
Reporting points (VFR/IFR) Location Altitude Pattern Missed approach MSA	
Jettison/bailout/fuel dump areas Location Altitude	
TERPS	
NOTAMs	
Alternate airfields	
NAVAIDs Location Type Identifier Frequency	
Obstacles in Class D airspace	

A-6.   Table A-5 is an example of a parking area assessment checklist.

Table A-5. Parking area assessment checklist

Item	Remarks
Maximum on ground	
Designation	
Dimensions	
Surface types	
Weight bearing capability/source	
Tie down rings	
Grounding points	
Lighting	
Obstructions	

Special parking pads
   HOTPAD
   Explosive/HAZMAT storage
   Engine run clearance area
   Hot refuel
   Arm/de-arm	

Slope of ramp	
Breakaway	
Taxi power requirements	
Taxi area for parking	
Factors that may affect aircraft operations	

A-7.   Table A-6 is a lighting assessment checklist.

Table A-6. Lighting assessment checklist

Item	Remarks
Significant local lighting	
Surrounding area lighting	
Location of airport lighting controls	
Point of contact for turning on and off lights	Telephone number

A-8. Table A-7 is an example of a pavement analysis checklist.

Table A-7. Pavement analysis checklist

Item	Remarks
Runway/Taxiway Identified	
Pavement Type	
Pavement Condition Index	
Soil Structure	
Load Classification Number	See AFCESA engineering letter 02-19
Aircraft Classification Number	See AFCESA engineering letter 02-19
Pavement Classification Number (PCN)	See AFCESA engineering letter 02-19

A-9. Table A-8 is an example of an airfield support requirements checklist.

Table A-8. Airfield support requirements checklist

Item	Remarks
Control Tower Facility	
Operational	
Unrestricted vision of all approaches, departures, runways, and taxiways	
Electrical power available	
Radio blind spots	
Base Operations	
Facilities	
Bird aircraft strike hazard level history	
Bird strike hazard/Bird avoidance model program	
Bird hazard reporting signals/system	
Airfield photos and maps	
Operations Facilities	
Rooms or building available	
Space available for operations tents	
Sanitation accommodations	
Trash disposal	
Portable airfield lighting/marking	
Power Generation	
Weather Support	
Equipment	
Observation capability	
Forecast capability	
Conditions reporting capability	
Braking action reporting capability	

Table A-8. Airfield support requirements checklist

Item	Remarks
Communications	
UHF	
VHF	
HF	
FM	
SATCOM	
Telephones	
Commercial	
DSN	
Friendly forces communications list	
Crash, Fire, and Rescue	
Equipment	
Capacity	
Water/foam rates	

A-10. Table A-9 is an example of a transportation/logistics checklist.

Table A-9. Transportation/logistics checklist

Item	Remarks
Aerial Port Facility Requirements	
Covered space available	
Dimensions	
Outside storage space available Location Dimensions Fencing Lights	
Hazardous cargo buildup area	
Passenger service area	
Aircraft Support	
Fire bottles	
Power units	
Light carts	
Aerospace Ground Equipment	
MX stands	
MX hangers available	
Revetments available	
Fuels	
Aircraft type supported	
Jet fuel storage facilities	
Jet fuel dispensing capabilities	
Refueling vehicles	
Liquid oxygen	
Gaseous oxygen	
Gaseous nitrogen	
Oil and lubricants	
Transportation	
Materials handling equipment available	
Host nation support	
Contact transportation assets	
Assets available from support agencies	
Location of movement control center	
Availability of local road maps	
Identified A/DACG procedures	
Identified seaport of debarkation Location Route Procedures	

A-11. Table A-10 is an example of a base support checklist.

Table A-10. Base support checklist

Item	Remarks
Base Support Facilities	
Billeting area	
Messing facilities	
Hospital and Medical Support	
Location of medical facilities Capabilities	
Location of area support medical company	
Emergency evacuation procedures	
Location of civilian medical facilities Capabilities	
Availability of emergency medical transportation	
Hours medical services available	
Water	
Suitability of local water sources	
Source of the local drinking water	
Location of potable water points	
Location of nonpotable water points	
Firefighting Support	
Manpower	
Facilities	
Equipment	
Location/response time	
Host nation firefighting support	
Procedures to request firefighting	

Aircraft support
    Type of aircraft
    Time duration	

Fire/Rescue point of contact	Telephone number/radio frequency
Field Sanitation	

Field latrines
    Locations
    Servicing
    Status	

Contract portable latrine facilities Service agreements in place	
Theater specific health concerns	
Preventive measures identified	
Trash collection procedures	

Table A-10. Base support checklist

Item	Remarks
Burn procedures	
Power Generation	
Status of commercial power	
Augmentation status of commercial power to tactical power	
Structure of power limitations	

A-12. Table A-11 is an example of a security/disaster preparation assessment checklist.

Table A-11. Security/disaster preparation assessment checklist

Item	Remarks

Airfield security force
    Nationality
    Strength
    Point of contact	

Configuration of security personnel
    Communications procedures
    Inner/outer perimeter	

Airfield physical security
    Entry points
    Observation points
    Remote sensors/cameras	

ADA threats
    Vulnerabilities
    Mitigation measures	

Small arms threats
    Vulnerabilities
    Mitigation measures	

Mortar threats
    Vulnerabilities
    Mitigation measures	

Dispersal plans	
Danger spaces around airfield	
Distance from airfield perimeter to aircraft	
Perimeter fencing/barriers in place	
Types of security responses	
CBRN considerations	

Appendix B

Aircraft Characteristics

The characteristics of military aircraft have a direct relationship to airfield design. Airfield design must meet the requirements of the aircraft using the airfield to ensure safe aircraft operations. The design criteria for each military airfield must be formulated individually to satisfy a specific set of operational requirements.

AIRCRAFT CHARACTERISTICS

B-1. Airfield design criteria and layout are based on specific aircraft usage in relation to battlefield location. The most demanding characteristics of those aircraft using the airfield establish the controlling criteria. Less critical types of aircraft can use these facilities; however, more critical aircraft types may only use these facilities under special limitations. Table B-1 details characteristics of selected Air Force and Army aircraft.

Table B-1. Aircraft characteristics

Aircraft Type	Wing Span (ft)	Length (ft)	Turn Radius	180 Turn Diameter	Empty WT (lbs)	Max T/O WT (lbs)
A						
A-10	57ft 6 in	53 ft 5 in			28,000	51,000
A-300	147ft 1in	177ft 4in			172,400	375,885
A-310	147ft 1in	153 ft 1in		113 ft 6 in	169,000	363,760
AC-130	132 ft 6 in	97ft 8 in	37ft	170 ft	75,745	175,000
AH-64	58 ft 3 in	58 ft 2 in			10,760	21,000
AN-12	124 ft 8 in	108 ft 3"			61,730	134,480
AN-124A	240 ft 6 in	226 ft 8 in			385,810	892,000
AN-124B	240 ft 6 in	226 ft 8 in			385,810	864,000
AN-140	80 ft 4 in	74 ft 2 in			28,240	42,218
AN-22	211ft 4 in	190 ft			251,325	551,160
AN-225	290 ft	275 ft 6 in			550,000	1,200,000
AN-26	95 ft 9 in	78 ft 1 in			33,110	52,911
AN-32	95 ft 9 in	78 ft 1 in			58,371	59,510
AN-70	144 ft 7 in	132 ft 1 in			146,000	286,600
AN-72/74	104 ft 8 in	92 ft 1 in		36 ft	41,995	76,060
AS-332	61 ft 4 in	53 ft 5 in			9,833	18,960
B						
B1	136 ft 8 in	147 ft			192,000	477,000
B2	172 ft	69 ft			150,000	376,000
B-52	185 ft	161 ft			195,000	452,000
B707300C	145 ft 9 in	152 ft 11 in		123 ft 8 in	114,800	336,600
B707300F	145 ft 9 in	152 ft 11 in		123 ft 8 in	135,500	336,600

Table B-1. Aircraft characteristics

Aircraft Type	Wing Span (ft)	Length (ft)	Turn Radius	180 Turn Diameter	Empty WT (lbs)	Max T/O WT (lbs)
B727100	108 ft	133 ft 2 in		82 ft 6 in	100,000	209,500
B727200	108 ft	133 ft 2 in		95 ft 8 in	100,000	209,500
B737600	112 ft 7 in	97 ft 9 in		60 ft 10 in	60,500	115,500
B737700	112 ft 7 in	97 ft 9 in		66 ft 5 in	60,500	115,500
B737800	112 ft 7 in	97 ft 9 in		79 ft 2 in	60,500	115,500
B737900	112 ft 7 in	97 ft 9 in		85 ft 11 in	60,500	115,500
B747100	195 ft 8 in	231 ft 10 in		102 ft (c)	375,000	750,00
B747200B	195 ft 8 in	231 ft 10 in		102 ft (c)	382,000	775,000
B747200F	195 ft 8 in	231 ft 10 in		102 ft (c)	349,000	883,000
B747400B	195 ft 8 in	231 ft 10 in		102 ft (c)	399,000	875,000
B747400F	195 ft 8 in	231 ft 10 in		102 ft (c)	399,000	875,000
B757200P	124 ft 10 in	155 ft 3 in		120 ft	128,400	220,000
B757300F	124 ft 10 in	155 ft 3 in		141 ft	114,000	250,000
B767200	156 ft 1 in	159 ft 2 in		129 ft	181,500	335,000
B767200ER	156 ft 1 in	159 ft 2 in		129 ft	180,000	351,000
B767300	156 ft 1 in	159 ft 2 in		146 ft	192,150	345,000
B767300ER	156 ft 1 in	159 ft 2 in		146 ft	205,100	407,000
B777200	199 ft 11 in	209 ft 1 in		129 ft	181,500	335,000
B777200ER	199 ft 11 in	209 ft 1 in		129 ft	180,000	351,000
B777300	199 ft 11 in	242 ft 4 in		146 ft	192,150	345,000
B777ER	199 ft 11 in	242 ft 4 in		146 ft	205,100	407,000
C						
C-12	55 ft	44 ft	19 ft 6 in	79 ft 8 in	7,800	12,500
C-130E/H	132 ft 7 in	99 ft 6 in	170 ft	85 ft	86,500	155,000
C-130J	132 ft 7 in	97 ft 9 in	169 ft 8 in	85 ft	75,475	155,000
C137	131 ft	144 ft 6 in	62 ft	210 ft	135,600	260,000
C140	54 ft 6 in	60 ft 6 in	26 ft	88 ft	21,500	40,500
C-160	106 ft 4 in	131 ft 3 in		95 ft 2 in	63,930	108,245
C-17	169 ft 10 in	174 ft		143 ft/90 ft 3 in (pt)	282,000	580,000
C-1A	100 ft 5 in	95 ft 2 in			53,571	99,206
C-2	80 ft 7 in	56 ft 10 in			36,346	54,354
C-20A	77 ft 10 in	83 ft 2 in		52 ft	41,000	69,700
C-20B-H	77 ft10 in	88 ft 4 in		52 ft	41,000	74,600
C-21	39 ft 6 in	48 ft 7 in		53 ft	10,500	18,300
C-22V	83 ft 10 in	57 ft 4 in			33,140	47,500
C-22S	83 ft 10 in	57 ft 4 in			33,140	55,000
C-23	74 ft 8 in	58 ft	37 ft 4 in	51 ft	22,000	24,600
C-27	94 ft 2 in	74 ft 6 in			34,612	61,728
C-40	112 ft 7 in	110 ft 4 in			126,000	171,000
C-5	222 ft 9 in	247 ft 10 in		150 ft (c)	380,000	769,000

Table B-1. Aircraft characteristics

Aircraft Type	Wing Span (ft)	Length (ft)	Turn Radius	180 Turn Diameter	Empty WT (lbs)	Max T/O WT (lbs)
C-5A	222 ft 9 in	247 ft 10 in		228 ft	380,000	840,000
C-9	93 ft 3 in	119 ft 3 in		72 ft 2 in	68,000	110,000
CH-46	84 ft 4 in	45 ft 8 in			23,000	50,000
CH-47	99 ft	53 ft			23,000	50,000
CH-54	88 ft 6 in	88 ft 6 in			19,233	47,000
CV/MV-22	83 ft 10 in	57 ft 4 in			33,140	47,500
D						
DC-10F	165 ft 4 in	181 ft 7 in		150 ft	243,000	580,000
DC-10CF	165 ft 4 in	181 ft 7 in		150 ft	225,000	440,000
DC-10-30F	165 ft 4 in	181 ft 7 in		150 ft	243,400	580,000
DC-10-40	165 ft 4 in	181 ft 7 in		150 ft	272,900	555,000
DC-8-61	142 ft 5 in	187 ft 5 in		115 ft	147,000	325,000
DC-8-62	142 ft 5 in	187 ft 5 in		115 ft	140,000	350,000
DC-8-63	142 ft 5 in	187 ft 5 in		115 ft	147,000	355,000
DC-8-71	142 ft 5 in	187 ft 5 in		115 ft	152,400	328,000
DC-8-73	148 ft 5 in	187 ft 5 in		115 ft	155,000	355,000
DC-9	93 ft 3 in	119 ft 3 in	54 ft	128 ft 2 in	57,200	110,000
E						
E-2	84 ft 6 in	57 ft 6 in			37,945	51,815
E-3	145 ft 8 in	152 ft 9 in	23 ft 5 in	288 ft	175,500	325,000
E-4B	195 ft 7 in	231 ft 3 in	75 ft	292 ft	482,300	800,000
E-8	145 ft 9 in	152 ft 11 in			171,000	336,000
EA-6B	53 ft	59 ft 8 in			37,630	61,500
EH-101	74 ft 9 in	64 ft 4 in			19,960	32,188
F						
F-117	43 ft 3 in	65 ft 9 in			29,500	52,500
F-15A/B	42 ft 8 in	63 ft 8 in			28,600	68,000
F-15E	42 ft 8 in	63 ft 8 in			31,700	81,000
F-16	31 ft	49 ft 3 in			18,725	37,500
F-22	44 ft 5 in	62 ft			34,000	62,000
F-35	43 ft	50 ft			24,000	50,000
FA-18A-D	37 ft 5 in	56 ft			23,050	49,225
FA-18E/F	47 ft 7 in	60 ft			30,600	66,000
H						
H-3/VH-3	72 ft 5 in	54 ft 9 in			11,770	20,883
HC-130	132 ft 7 in	98 ft 9 in	170 ft	85 ft	75,745	155,000
I						
IL-62	141 ft 9 in	174 ft 4 in			153,000	363,760
IL-76	165 ft 8 in	152 ft 10"		131 ft	196,156	418,875

Table B-1. Aircraft characteristics

Aircraft Type	Wing Span (ft)	Length (ft)	Turn Radius	180 Turn Diameter	Empty WT (lbs)	Max T/O WT (lbs)
K						
K-29	52 ft 2 in	37 ft 1 in			12,170	25,353
KC-10	165 ft 8 in	152 ft 10 in		147 ft	248,000	590,000
KC-135E	130 ft 10 in	136 ft 3 in		180 ft	122,000	300,500
KC-135R	130 ft 10 in	136 ft 3 in		180 ft	122,000	322,500
L						
L-1011	155 ft 4 in	177 ft 2 in		143 ft 3 in	248,000	466,000
M						
MC-130	132 ft 6 in	108 ft 1 in	37 ft	170 ft	83,000	172,000
MD-11	169 ft 10 in	202 ft 2 in		135 ft	256,000-294,000	630,500
MD-81/2/3/7/8-10F	165 ft 4 in	181 ft 7 in		150 ft	243,000	572,000
MD-81/2/3/7/8-10F	165 ft 4 in	181 ft 7 in		150 ft	225,150	440,000
MD-81/2/3/7/8-30F	165 ft 4 in	181 ft 7 in		150 ft	166,000	580,000
MD-81/2/3/7/8-40F	165 ft 4 in	181 ft 7 in		150 ft	166,000	272,900
MH-53E-J	98 ft	67 ft 2 in			23,628	69,750
MI-26	131 ft 4 in	117 ft 10 in			621,770	123,450
MI-8	82 ft 8 in	59 ft 9 in			15,410	24,471
MI-17	82 ft 8 in	59 ft 9 in			15,410	28,660
MQ-1C	54 ft	29 ft				3,000
MQ-5B	34.25 ft	23 ft				1,950
O						
OH-58	41 ft 3 in	41 ft			2,825	5,500
P						
P-3	99 ft 7 in	116 ft 8 in			61,490	142,000
R						
RQ-7B	14 ft	11 ft				380
RQ-8B	27.5 ft	22.9 ft				3,150
S						
S-61	64 ft 9 in	57 ft 5 in			10,700	20,500
S-92	68 ft 6 in	56 ft 2 in			16,000	28,300
U						
UH-1	57 ft 3 in	42 ft			5,055	10,510
UH-60A	64 ft 9 in	64 ft 10 in			13,648	20,250
UH-60L	64 ft 9 in	64 ft 10 in			13,648	22,000
UH-70	64 ft 10 in	64 ft 10 in			15,920	21,883
V						
VC-25	195 ft 8 in	231 ft 10 in			377,000	830,000
VC-32	124 ft 10 in	155 ft 3 in		120 ft	128,400	220,000
VC-37	93 ft 6 in	96 ft 5 in			54,500	90,500

Table B-1. Aircraft characteristics

Aircraft Type	Wing Span (ft)	Length (ft)	Turn Radius	180 Turn Diameter	Empty WT (lbs)	Max T/O WT (lbs)
W						
WC-135	130 ft 10 in	139 in 11 in			98,000	300,500

Note: All helicopter wingspans are based on blade rotating diameter. C = caster, ER = extended range, pt = point turn.

This page intentionally left blank.

Appendix C
Airfield Layout Plan

Criterion in this appendix applies to Army and Air Force airfield planning. Use of these criteria produces the right airfields in the right place at the right time. The planning and design of airfields must emphasize flight and ground safety for all types of aircraft (both permanently assigned and transient). AOB commanders will ensure that the airspace design provides required obstruction clearances and that special facilities and equipment are either constructed or installed to facilitate aircraft maintenance, ground handling, and flight operations.

PLANNING STUDIES

C-1. Prior to establishing a contingency airfield (or heliport), a study should be made to determine the conditions under which the facility will be operating. The study should include the items in the following paragraphs.

AIRCRAFT TO BE USED AT THE AIRFIELD (DESIGN AIRCRAFT)

C-2. Airfields typically are designed for a specific aircraft known as the critical or design aircraft, which is the most operationally and/or physically demanding aircraft to make substantial use of the facility. The critical or design aircraft is used to establish the dimensional requirements for safety parameters such as approach protection zones, lateral clearance for runways, taxiways and parking positions, and obstacle clearance. In many cases, the "geometric" design aircraft may not be the same aircraft as the "pavement" design aircraft.

SITE CONDITIONS

C-3. Numerous site conditions are considered when establishing a contingency airfield or heliport.

Prevailing Weather and Wind Directions

C-4. To be functional, efficient, and safe, the runway should be oriented with the prevailing winds to provide favorable wind coverage. Crosswinds exceeding 13 miles per hour should not prevail more than 13 percent of the time. Wind data, obtained from local sources, for a period of not less than five years should be used as the basis for the wind information to be shown on the airfield map (AR 210-20).

Other Considerations

C-5. Other considerations include—
- Topography.
- Vegetation.
- Existing structures.
- Soil conditions.
- Accessibility of roads and utilities.
- Capability for future expansion.

AIRFIELD LAYOUT

C-6. The layout of airfield facilities should be functional to permit operational efficiency and provide safety conditions for aircraft operations. Figure C-1 shows an example of an airfield layout intended to provide guidance to AOB planners. The following factors should be considered for functionality.

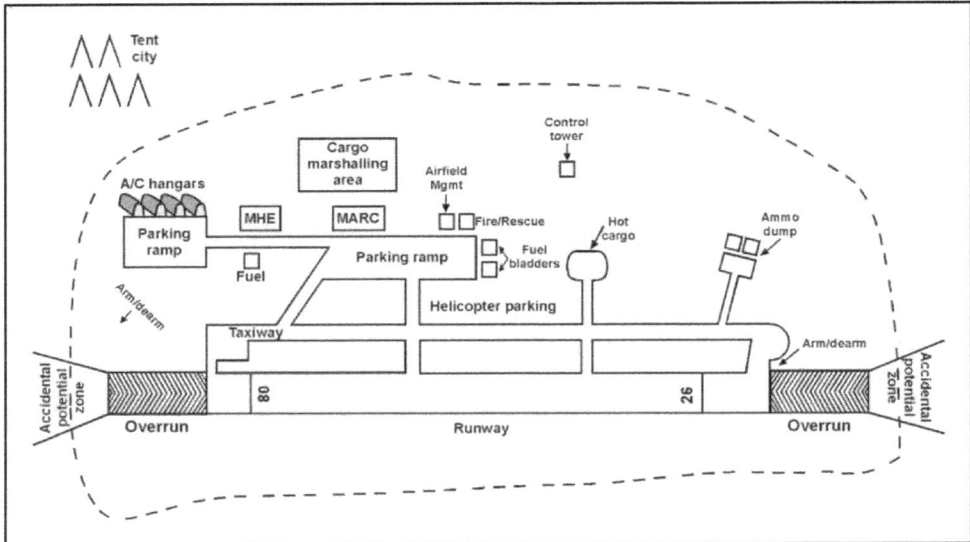

Figure C-1. Airfield layout

Taxiways

C-7. Taxiways provide for ground movement of fixed and rotary-wing aircraft. Taxiways connect airfield runways with parking and maintenance areas and provide access to hangars, docks, and various parking aprons and pads. Taxiways are designated alphabetically, avoiding the use of I, O, and X. Alphanumeric may be used when necessary (for example, A1 and B3). Runway efficiency is best accomplished by development of parallel taxiway systems with appropriate connecting laterals. At airfields with low air traffic density, such taxiways may be modified to suit local requirements.

Air Force Missions at Army Facilities

C-8. Airfield flight safety clearances applicable to Army airfields that support Air Force cargo aircraft missions will be based on an Army Class B airfield. This is coordinated between the Army and Air Force.

Required Clearances

C-9. Paved surfaces will be designed for continuous and safe aircraft operations. Pavement areas will be in compliance with airfield clearances, safety zones, and related areas as described in UFC 3-260-01.

CLASS A AND B RUNWAYS

C-10. Class A runways are primarily intended for small light aircraft. These runways do not have the potential or foreseeable requirement for development for use by high performance and large heavy aircraft. Ordinarily, these runways are less than 2,438.4 meters (8,000 feet) long and have less than 10 percent of their operations that involve aircraft in the Class B category. This is not intended to limit the number of C-130 and C-17 operations conducted on any Class A airfield.

C-11. Class B runways are primarily intended for high performance and large heavy aircraft and generally 2,438.4 meters (8,000 feet) or longer.

Dimension Criteria

C-12. Table C-1 describes requirements in detail of Class A and B runways.

Table C-1. Army Class A runway lengths

Temperature	Elevation				
	Sea Level	304.8 m (1,000 ft)	609.6 m (2,000 ft)	1524 m (5,000 ft)	1828.8 m (6,000 ft)
60 degrees F	1,615.44 m (5,300 ft)	1,676.4 m (5,500 ft)	1,767.84 m (5,800 ft)	2,042.16 m (6,700 ft)	2,164.08 m (7,100 ft)
85 degrees F	1,706.88 m (5,600 ft)	1,798.32 m (5,900 ft)	1,889.76 m (6,200 ft)	2,286 m (7,500 ft)	2,438.4 m (8,000 ft)
105 degrees F	1,798.32 m (5,900 ft)	1,889.76 m (6,200 ft)	2,042.16 m (6,700 ft)	2,468.88 m (8,100 ft)	2,682.24m (8,800 ft)

Note: The length of Army Class B runways is determined by the Air Force MAJCOM involved based on the design aircraft being used. See UFC 3-260-01 for more detailed information on runway construction and standards.

ROTARY-WING RUNWAY DIMENSIONAL CRITERIA

C-13. Table C-2 describes basic layouts for rotary-wing runways.

Table C-2. Rotary-wing runways

Item Description	Requirement	Remarks
Basic length	487.68 m (1,600 ft)	For Army and Air Force airfields increase basic length to 609.6 m (2,000 ft) when above 1219.2 m (4,000 ft) MSL.
Width	22.86 m (75 ft)	
Runway lateral clearance zone (measured perpendicularly from centerline of runway)		
VFR operations	45.72 m (150 ft)	
IFR operations	114.3 m (375 ft)	
Distance from centerline of FW runway to centerline of rotary-wing runway, helipad or landing lane		
Simultaneous VFR operations	213.36 m (700 ft)	For class B runway for Army operations.
Simultaneous VFR operations	304.8 m (1,000 ft)	For class B runway for Air Force, Navy or Marine Corps.
Nonsimultaneous operations	213.36 m (700 ft)	Distance may be reduced to 60.96m (200 ft); waiver is based on wake-turbulence and jet blast. In locating the helipad, consideration is given to hold position marking. Rotary-wing aircraft must be located on the apron side of the hold position markings (away from runway) during runway operations.
IFR using simultaneous operations	762 m (2,500 ft)	(Depart-depart) (Depart-approach)
IFR using simultaneous approaches	1310.64 m (4,300 ft)	

Table C-2. Rotary-wing runways

Distance between centerlines of rotary-wing runways, helipads or landing lanes		
VFR without intervening parallel taxiway between centerlines	213.36 m (700 ft)	
IFR using simultaneous operations	762 m (2,500 ft)	(Depart-depart) (Depart-arrival)
IFR operations using simultaneous approaches	13110.64 m (4,300 ft)	

Note: For more detailed information on rotary-wing runway design and construction, see UFC 3-260-01.

HELIPADS

C-14. Helipads allow for helicopter hovering, landing, and takeoff, except at facilities where helicopter runways are provided, and helipads are the landing and takeoff locations for helicopters. The Army and Air Force provide for three types of helipads—VFR helipad; limited use helipad; and IFR helipad. The Navy and Marine Corps provide only the standard size helipad. The helipad type depends on the following operational requirements:

- **Standard VFR helipad.** VFR design standards are used when no requirement exists or will exist in the future for an IFR helipad. Criteria for this type of helipad permit the accommodation of most helipad lighting systems.
- **Limited use helipad.** This is a VFR facility used at sites where only occasional operations are conducted. These sites may be, but are not limited to, hospitals, headquarter areas, missile sites, and established airfields or heliports where the limited-use helipad may be used to preclude mixing helicopters and FW traffic. Limited use helipads may also be used to separate light helicopter traffic (12,500 pounds or less) from medium and heavy helicopter traffic.
- **IFR helipad.** IFR design standards are used when an instrument approach capability is essential to the mission and no other instrument landing facilities, either FW or rotary-wing, are located within an acceptable commuting distance to the site.

HELIPAD LOCATION

C-15. A helipad location should be selected with regard to mission requirements, overall facility development, approach-departure surfaces, and local wind conditions.

- **Near runways.** When a helipad is to be located near fixed- and rotary-wing runways, its location should be based on type of operations, per criteria in table C-3.
- **Above ground helipads.** Construction of helipads on buildings or on any type of elevated structure above ground is not authorized for Air Force and Army. For these agencies, helipads will be constructed as a slab on grade. For Navy and Marine Corps facilities, contact the agency aviation office with safety waiver approval if deviation is required.

Parking Pads

C-16. At individual helipad sites where it is necessary to have one or more helicopters on standby, an area adjacent to the helipad, but clear of the landing approach and transitional surfaces, should be designated for standby parking.

DIMENSIONAL CRITERIA

C-17. Table C-3 presents dimensional criteria for the layout and design of helipads.

Table C-3. Rotary-wing helipads and hoverpoints

Item Description	Requirement	Remarks
Size	22.86 m x 22.86 m (75 ft x 75 ft-min)	VFR limited use helipads
	30.48 m x 30.48 m (100 ft x 100 ft)	Standard VFR and IFR helipads
Primary surface (center primary surface on helipad)	45.72 m x 45.72 m (150 ft x 150 ft-min)	Hoverpoints, limited use VFR helipads
	91.44 m x 91.44 m (300 ft x 300 ft)	Standard VFR helipads
Grade	Min 1.0%	Grade helipad in one direction
	Max 1.5%	Hoverpoints should be domed to a 6 inch height at the center.
Within primary surface area in any direction	Min 2.0% prior to channelization Max 5.0%	Exclusive of pavement and shoulders. For IFR helipads, grading requirements apply to a 300 ft x 300 ft (91.44 m x 91.44 m) area centered on the helipad.
Clear zone		
Length	121.92 m (400 ft)	Hoverpoints, VFR and standard IFR helipads, begins at the end of the primary zone.
	251.46 m (825 ft)	IFR same direction ingress/egress
Width		Corresponds to primary surface width. Center clear zone area width on extended center of the pad.
	45.72 m (150 ft)	Limited use helipads and hoverpoints
	91.44 m (300 ft)	Standard VFR helipad and VFR helipad same direction ingress/egress
	228.6 m (750 ft)	Standard IFR
Grades of clear zone (any direction)	Max 5.0%	Area to be free of obstructions. Rough grade and turf required.
Accident potential zone		
Length	243.84 m (800 ft)	Hoverpoints, VFR, and standard IFR
	121.92 m (400 ft)	IFR same direction ingress/egress
Width	45.72 m (150 ft)	Limited use VFR helipads and hover points
	91.44 m (300 ft)	Standard VFR
	228.6 m (750 ft)	Standard IFR

ROTARY-WING LANDING LANES

C-18. Contingency and combat rotary-wing operations create situations where large numbers of helicopters are parked on mass aprons at airfields or heliports. The use of landing lanes enables rapid launch and recovery operations. The efficiency of these operations will be increased when—

- Landing lanes are located in front of the parking apron.
- The locations of touchdown points are designated with numerical markings.

C-19. Table C-4 presents the dimensional criteria for the layout and design of rotary-wing landing lanes. For information on overruns, clear zones, accident potential zones, and imaginary approach surfaces for rotary-wing landing lanes, refer to UFC 3-260-01. Figure C-2 (page C-7) provides an example of a rotary-wing landing lane.

Table C-4. Rotary-wing landing lanes

Item Description	Requirement	Remarks
Length	487.68 m to 609.6 m (1,600 ft to 2,000 ft)	Based on the number of touchdown points.
Width	22.86 m (75 ft)	
Distance between		
Touchdown points	121.92 m (400 ft-min)	
Centerlines of lanes	60.96 m (200 ft)	With an operational control tower
	91.44 m (300 ft)	Without control tower
Landing lane lateral clearance zone	45.72 m (150 ft)	VFR facilities
	114.3 m (375 ft)	IFR facilities
Grades within primary surface area in any direction	2.0%	

PRIMARY SURFACE LENGTH DETERMINED BY LANDING LANE LENGTH AND FACILITY TYPE (IFR/VFR).

SERIES OF TOUCHDOWN POINTS. TREAT AS INDIVIDUAL HELIPADS.
FOR SPACING, SEE NOTE 2.

PRIMARY SURFACE WIDTH
SEE NOTE 4

SEE NOTE 5

SHOULDER

SHOULDER

75'

75'   75'   75'   75'

APPROACH-DEPARTURE
CLEARANCE SURFACE

UNPAVED
AREA

UNPAVED HOVERLANE

PARKING
SPACES

HOVERLANE

PARKING
SPACES

HOVERLANE

PARKING
SPACES

HOVERLANE

TOWLANE FOR ACCESS TO MAINTENANCE HANGARS

PAVED
AREA

NOTES

1. Width of hoverlanes and parking spaces are determined by the type of helicopter used and the clearances required.

2. The distance between touchdown points is determined by the distance between hoverlanes' centerlines and is usually not less than 400' center-to-center.

3. Size and layout of the parking apron varies with the type of helicopter used and the mission requirements.

4. Primary surface width is 300' for VFR facilities and 750' for IFR facilities.

5. Primary surface length is the landing lane length plus 225' for Air Force, Navy, and Marine Corps VFR landing lanes. For Army landing lanes and Air Force, Navy, and Marine Corps IFR landing lanes, the primary surface length is the landing lane length plus 400' or 1550', whichever is greater.

6. Minimum distance between the primary surface and the apron is determined by the transitional surface clearance to parked A/C.

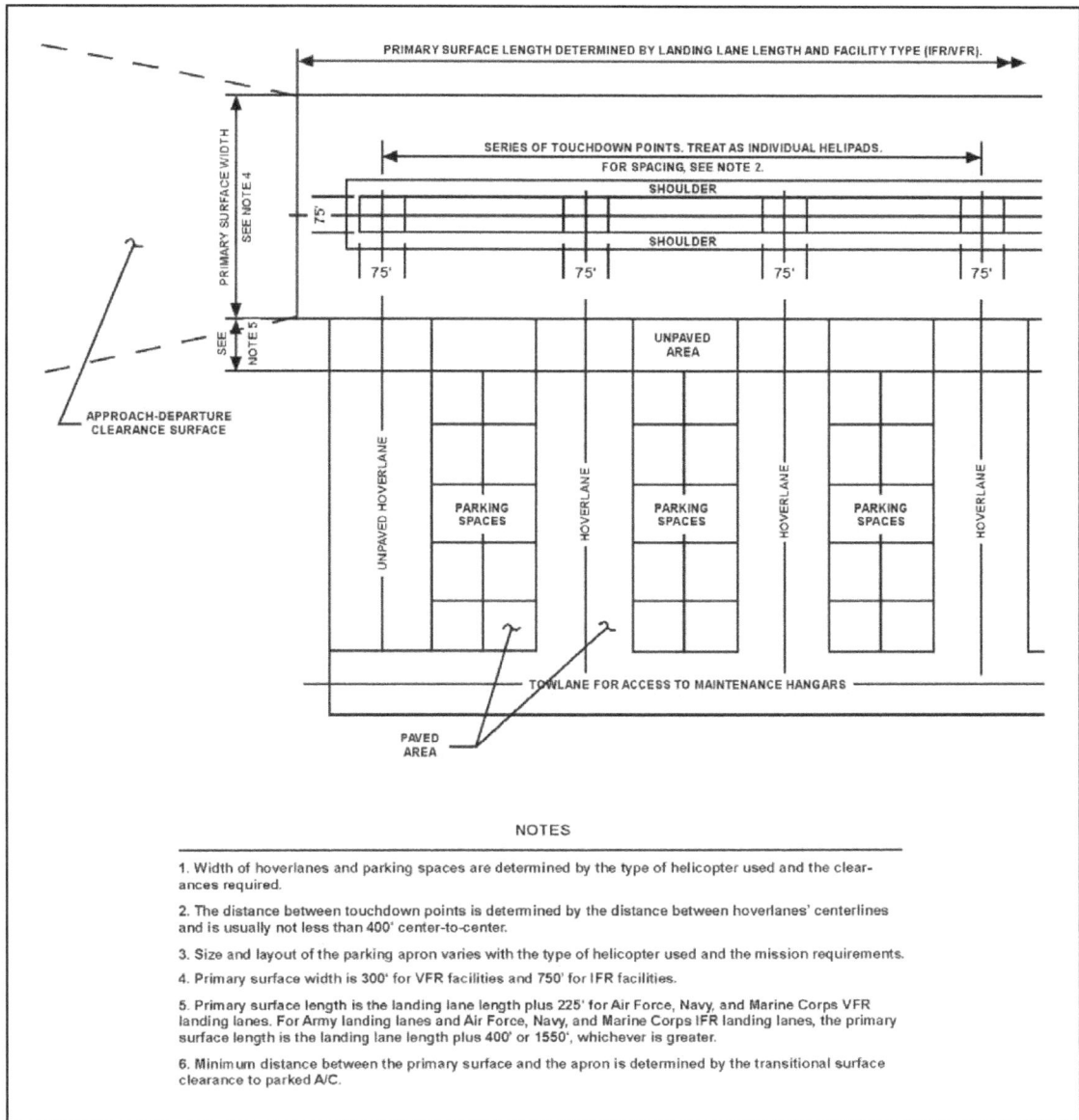

Figure C-2. Rotary-wing landing lane

FIXED-WING TAXIWAYS

C-20. Taxiway dimensions are based on the class of runway that it serves. Table C-5 presents the criteria for FW taxiway design.

Table C-5. Fixed-wing taxiways

Item Description	Class A Runway	Class B Runway	Remarks
Width	15.24 m (50 ft)	22.86 m (75 ft)	Army and Air Force airfields
Clearance from taxiway centerline to fixed or mobile obstructions	45.72 m (150 ft)	60.96 m (200 ft)	
Distance between taxiway centerline and parallel taxiway centerline	53.34 m (175 ft)	56.54 m (187.5 ft)	Army airfields
		72.39 m (237.5 ft)	Air Force airfields

ROTARY-WING TAXIWAY DIMENSIONS

C-21. Rotary-wing taxiways are either paved or unpaved. Wheel-gear configured rotary-wing aircraft require a paved surface on which to taxi. Skid-gear configured rotary-wing aircraft taxi by hovering along a paved or unpaved taxiway. Table C-6 presents the criteria for rotary-wing taxiway design including clearances, slopes and grading dimensions. Figure C-3 (page C-9) provides an example of a taxiway layout.

Table C-6. Rotary-wing taxiways

Item Description	Requirement	Remarks
Width	15.24 m (50 ft)	Army and Air Force airfields
Longitudinal grade	Max 2.0%	
Transverse grade	Min 1.0%	
	Max 1.5%	
Clearance from centerline to fixed and mobile obstacles	Min 30.48 m (100 ft)	
Grades within clear area	Max 5.0%	Clear area is area between the taxiway shoulder and taxiway clearance line.

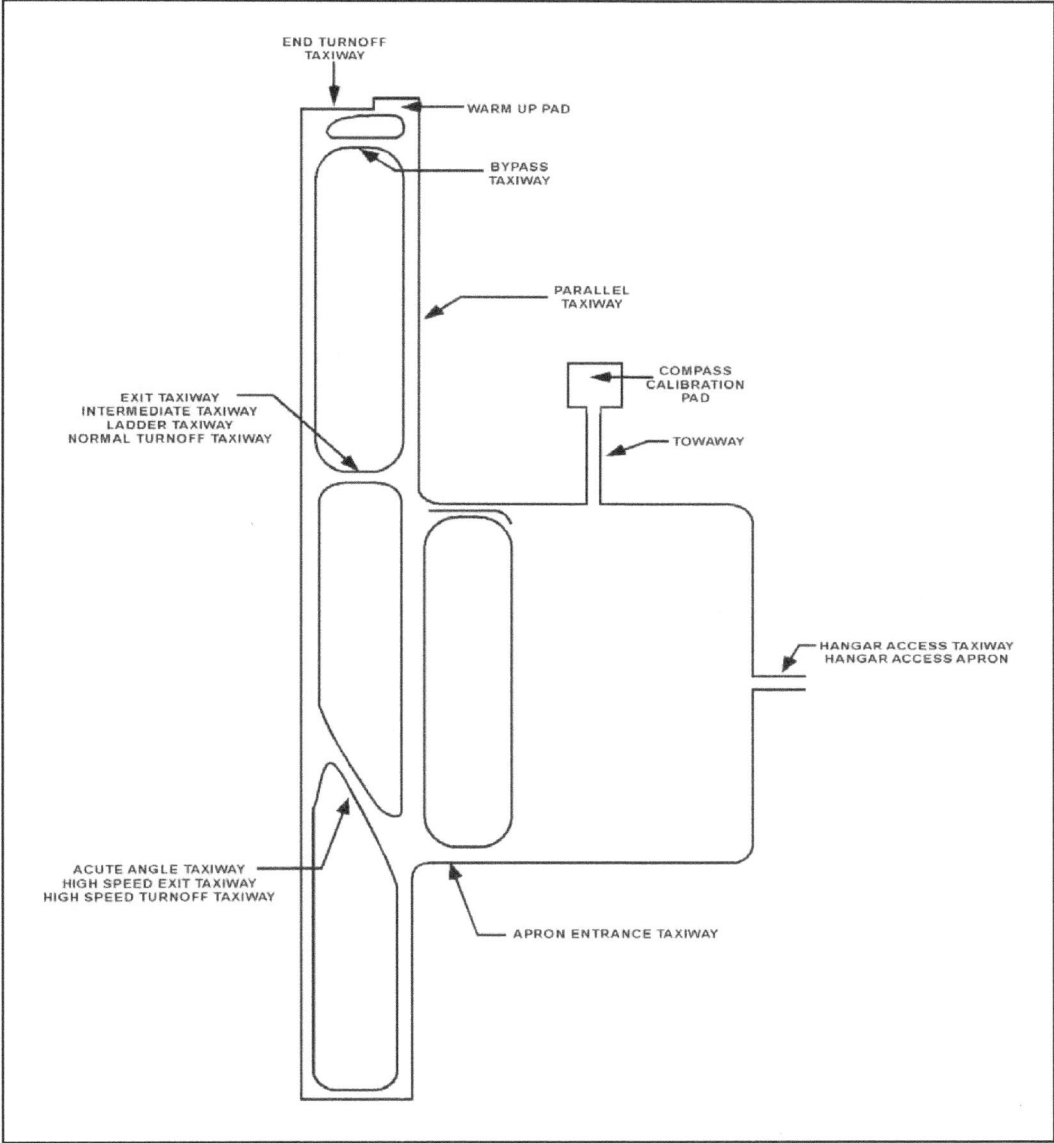

Figure C-3. Taxiway layout

This page intentionally left blank.

Appendix D

Letters and Memorandums

Each branch of airfield organization is required to maintain a file of administrative correspondence. This correspondence includes letters of agreement (LOAs), letters of procedure, operations letters, and facility memorandums.

LETTERS OF AGREEMENT

D-1. LOAs may apply to a specific facility, group of facilities, or all facilities within a designated geographical area. LOAs are prepared between the U.S. Army and other services or a host nation. They are also prepared between centers and towers, centers and terminal radar facilities, or ATC facilities located on the same or different airfields. An LOA shall be prepared to—

- Delegate areas of control jurisdiction and conditions of use.
- Define special operating conditions or specific ATC procedures.
- Define interfacility or interagency responsibilities and coordination requirements.
- Describe procedures that deviate from or are not contained in, FAA Handbook 7110.65, this manual, or other pertinent directives.

D-2. The branch responsible for developing an LOA shall—

- Confine materiel in each LOA to a single subject or purpose.
- Ensure LOA is properly prepared.
- Describe responsibilities and procedures that apply to each facility and organization involved.
- Attach charts or other visual presentations, as appropriate, to depict conditions of the agreement.
- Delegate responsibility for ATC. Describe the area responsibility that is delegated and define conditions governing use of that area. Specify and explain control, communications, and coordination procedures.
- Coordinate the LOA with the appropriate facilities, agencies, and authorities.
- Coordinate the letter with the United States Army Aeronautical Services Detachment, Europe (USAASD-E)/Eighth United States Army (EUSA)/Department of the Army Regional Representative (DARR) before an LOA with a host country is signed.
- Forward all proposed LOAs to the appropriate DARR. The DARR shall review and coordinate each LOA, then return it to the originator with comments.
- Establish effective date of the LOA at 30 days after its distribution. This gives the participants time to familiarize their personnel with the agreement and revise directives and flight charts.
- Prepare the letter in final form.
- Obtain required signatures.
- Distribute copies of the signed LOA according to the distribution stated in the letter.

D-3. A change in requirements of either party signing the agreement creates the need to rewrite or amend the letter. Revisions, attachments, or supplements to the LOA are processed as page replacements. They are coordinated the same as the original letter. Revisions are marked as follows:

- Place an asterisk to the left of each new or revised paragraph or section to signify it is new materiel.
- Identify page revisions by the revision (REV) number (for example, REV 1). Enter effective date in the lower right corner of each revised page.

D-4. To ensure timeliness and conformance to current policies and directives, the branch chief reviews all facility LOAs annually no later than the anniversary date of the original document. He also signs and dates the annual reviews. Figure D-1 shows a sample format for an FAA or a U.S. Army LOA.

__(Name)__ Air Route Traffic Control Center and FAA __(Name)__ Approach Control and __(Name)__

LETTER OF AGREEMENT

EFFECTIVE: __(Date)__

SUBJECT: Special VFR Operations Within __(Name)__ Airport Surface Area

1. PURPOSE: (List responsibilities and describe necessary coordination.)
2. CANCELLATION: (Use as required.)
3. SCOPE: (Specify areas having ATC responsibility and names and types of facilities.)
4. RESPONSIBILITIES: (Specify responsibilities.)
5. PROCEDURES:

    a. ATC-assigned airspace. (List the procedures for requesting and authorizing airspace, handling aircraft to and from airspace, and notifying ATC when the airspace is no longer required.)

    b. Transfer of control. (Specify transfer procedures.)

    c. Departures. (Specify the required advance time for filing flight plans, and outline additional items required in the flight plan. For example, list the type of departure and the control transfer points.)

    d. En route. (Include in the information that ATC is responsible for effecting separation in assigned airspace when nonparticipating aircraft are cleared to operate within that airspace.)

    e. Arrivals. (Outline handoff procedures and special instructions.)

    f. General. (Include, if appropriate, missed-approach procedures, special VFR operations, and provisions for handling movement of national-defense aircraft in emergencies.)

6. ATTACHMENTS: (List, as required, such items as a chart of ATC-assigned airspace areas and common reference or handoff points.)

Airfield Commander, __(Name)__ AAF Chief, __(Name)__ ARTCC
Chief, __(Name)__ ATC Facility Director, __(Name)__ Region
(Name and title of appropriate authority)

Figure D-1. Sample format for a Federal Aviation Administration or United States Army letter of agreement

LETTERS OF PROCEDURE

D-5. Letters of procedure (LOP) should be prepared using AR 25-50 and FAA Order JO 7610.4 as administrative guidelines. Ensure LOPs are worded so the Army maintains the greatest degree of mission flexibility within limits prescribed by law or regulation. Care must be taken to choose appropriate subject matter, terminology, and correct procedures when negotiating content.

D-6. AT&A officers must ensure LOPs are negotiated when an operational/procedural need requires cooperation or concurrence of other facilities/organizations. LOPs are prepared when it is necessary to–

- Define SUA responsibilities.
- Supplement established operational/procedural instructions.

- Define responsibilities and coordinating requirements.
- Establish or standardize operating methods.
- Describe airspace to segregate special operations.
- Specify special operating conditions or specific ATC procedures.

D-7. LOP criteria governing SUA includes at a minimum—

- Scheduling procedures and updates, to include requirement and time parameters for providing updates to the schedule.
- Activation/deactivation time and procedures.
- Authorization (signed) by the affected ATC facility manager and military representative of the originating or scheduling activity.
- Address transfer of airspace during emergency conditions. In the event of an emergency, the using agency may approve the controlling agency's request for use of SUA. The using agency, when notified by an FAA manager/supervisor of an emergency, transfers the airspace to the controlling agency as soon as safety permits. The controlling agency returns the airspace to the using agency when the emergency traffic situation is resolved.
- The using agency approves/disapproves the controlling agency's request to use SUA for situations caused by weather by assessing the immediate situation and its impact on Army and civil aircraft operations. The decision is made based on a request from an FAA supervisor and imminent/existing weather conditions (not traffic flow). Weather conditions requiring special considerations are tornadoes, hurricanes, blizzards, etc. The controlling agency returns the airspace to the using agency within 30 minutes after the weather situation is no longer a factor.

Note: The controlling agency provides using agency, on request, an AAR when SUA is transferred.

D-8. LOPs are processed per AR 95-2; the AT&A officer coordinates an LOP with the appropriate DARR prior to discussions with the FAA, during development, and when modifications are made. The DARR is provided a detailed explanation of the LOP purpose, to include a copy of the concept of operation, if applicable. If an AT&A officer is not available, the unit commander or designed representative may need to coordinate directly with the DARR.

D-9. Forward all LOPs to the DARR for review at least 45 days prior to the desired implementation date. Activities/agencies that do not have a DARR, may forward their documents directly to: USAASD-E (locations in Europe, Africa, and the Middle East), EUSA ATS Office (Korea), and Headquarters, United States Army Aeronautical Services Agency for all other areas. Include the following:

- A cover memorandum that includes any changes to existing LOP, along with background information for each change. If the LOP is new, a brief description of the operation should be outlined. The unit commander approves/signs the memorandum.
- DARR endorsement recommends approval or disapproval of the LOP, and any recommended changes.
- Leave effective date and signatures blank until all coordination is complete and all comments are considered and incorporated as required. Once this is accomplished, establish an effective date acceptable to all parties involved. This permits sufficient time for distribution and participating facilities and user groups to familiarize personnel, revise directives, flight charts, and etcetera, and complete other actions as necessary.

D-10. LOPs are reviewed at least once annually on or before the anniversary date. It is mandatory for DARRs to review LOPs per AR 95-2. Figure D-2 (page D-4) is an example of a LOP.

JOINT USE RESTRICTED AREA LETTER OF PROCEDURE

SUBJECT: Joint use letter of procedure for use of restricted areas R-OOOOA, R-OOOOB, R-OOOOC, R-OOOOD, R-OOOOE

EFFECTIVE: 25 December 2002

Per. AR 95-2, AR 385-63, FAA Order JO 7610.4, and FAA Order JO 7400.8D, this letter establishes the following procedures for the joint use of restricted areas R-OOOOA, R-OOOOB, R-OOOOC, R-OOOOD, R-OOOOE between: Jacks Air Route Traffic Control Center (controlling agency), Commander, Fort Every (using agency), Fort Every Range Control (scheduling agency), and Fort Every Army ARAC.

CANCELLATIONS: This letter of procedure cancels the (title of previous letter) Joint use of letter of procedures, same subject, dated 1 April 2001.

PROCEDURES:

1. ARAC:

    a. Inform controlling agency of activation/deactivation times for R-OOOOA, R-OOOOB, R-OOOOC, R-OOOOD, R-OOOOE.

    b. Notify controlling agency 30 minutes prior to activation of special-use airspace via landline.

    c. When notified by controlling agency manager/supervisor personnel of an emergency, Army supervisor will assess the immediate situation and its impact on Army and civil aircraft operations and make a decision to return/denial request for use of restricted area (s).

    d. When controlling agency manger/supervisor requests use of restricted airspace for a situation caused by weather, Army supervisor will make a decision to release/deny request based upon imminent/existing weather conditions (not traffic flow). Examples of weather conditions that require special considerations are tornadoes, hurricanes, blizzards, and etcetera.

2. Controlling agency:

    a. Will coordinate with the using agency for use of the designated restricted airspace when not per FAA Order 7400.8.

    b. Shall return designated airspace to the using agency within 30 minutes of request.

3. Scheduling agency:

    c. Shall coordinate schedule changes between ARAC and controlling agency.

    d. Shall forward, as soon as possible, schedule changes to the controlling agency, via dedicated or commercial line.

EXECUTED:

_____   _____
Signed   Signed

_____   _____
Title   Title

_____   _____
Date   Date

_____   _____
DARR Review By/Date:

Figure D-2. Sample format for a letter of procedure

OPERATIONS LETTERS

D-11. Operations letters apply between ATC facilities and other U.S. Army agencies or units located on the same airfield or heliport (such as ATC towers and base operations or fire station). Operations letters are prepared to—

- Supplement established operational or procedural instructions.
- Establish or standardize operating methods.
- Establish responsibilities to—
    - Operate airport equipment.
    - Provide emergency services.
    - Exchange braking action reports with airport management. (As a minimum, procedures cover prompt exchange of reports indicating runway-braking conditions have deteriorated to "poor" or "nil" or improved to "good.")
    - Report operating limitations and hazards.
    - Define responsibilities of the tower and airport management or other authority for movement and nonmovement areas.

Note: Operations letters are not written between ATC facilities; these actions require an LOA.

D-12. Appropriate subjects of operations letters between the tower and airport management/aircraft operator include—

- Airport emergency service.
- Airport lighting operation.
- Airport condition reporting.
- Vehicular traffic control on airport movement areas.

D-13. The branch responsible for developing an operations letter shall—

- Confine materiel in each letter to a single subject or purpose.
- Ensure operations letter is properly prepared.
- Describe responsibilities and procedures that apply to the facility and organization involved.
- Attach charts or other visual presentations to depict conditions or circumstances stated in the letter.
- Coordinate the letter with the airfield commander before initiating any other coordination.
- Coordinate the letter with the appropriate facilities, agencies, or authorities.
- Obtain approval of the operations letter.
- Establish an effective date that allows time for participating facilities and agencies to familiarize their personnel with the contents of the letter and complete other preimplementation actions.
- Prepare letter in final form.
- Sign letter and obtain other required signatures.
- Distribute copies of the signed letter to appropriate facilities or agencies.

D-14. All parties concerned retain a copy of the operations letter and review it annually, no later than the anniversary date of the original document. The branch chief dates and signs the annual review. Figure D-3 (page D-6) provides a sample format of a control tower or airfield operations letter.

```
Operations Letter Between __(Name)__ Airfield Operations and __(Name)__ Control Tower __(Name)__
Airfield Operations Letter No __(Name)__ Control Tower Letter No__(Name)__

SUBJECT: (Write a short statement to describe contents of the letter.)

EFFECTIVE: (Enter effective date of the letter and number of cancelled letters.)

(Write a paragraph to outline text of the letter. Give enough details to preclude a misunderstanding of
intended procedures and responsibilities and required coordination.)


____(Signature)____                    ____(Signature)____
Airfield Operations Officer            ATC Chief/ATC SR SGT/PSG/ATC
                                       Facility Chief,
                                       Tower
                                       Airfield

DISTRIBUTION: (as appropriate)
```

Figure D-3. Sample format for a control tower/airfield operations letter

D-15. A change in the requirements of any party signing the operations letter creates the need to rewrite/revise the letter. However, a change in key personnel does not require a rewrite or revision. Rewrites or revisions are processed as page replacements and coordinated the same as the original letter. Revisions are marked as follows—

- Place an asterisk to the left of each new or revised paragraph or section to signify it is new materiel.
- Identify page revisions by the REV number (for example REV 1). Enter the effective date in the lower right corner of each revised page.

FACILITY MEMORANDUMS

D-16. The branch chief issues memorandums when internal facility operations must be regulated and standardized. Facility memorandums contain instructions on administrative or operational practices and procedures within the facility. The chief may issue a memorandum as a joint document when it applies to two or more ATC facilities under his jurisdiction.

D-17. Facility memorandums follow the standard Army memorandum format and are numbered in sequence (for example, 03-1, 03-2, meaning the first/second memorandum for 2003). They are limited to one subject, operation, or procedure; enclosures and attachments may be included. Facility memorandums are reviewed for currency annually no later than the anniversary date of the original document. The branch chief dates and signs the annual review.

Appendix E

Emergency Plans and Procedures

Aviation operations involve inherently higher risk than most ground operations. Aviation accidents in combat are typically the same type experienced in peacetime. Therefore, aviation unit commanders, supervisors, and safety managers at all levels must emphasize safety and comply with policies regarding aviation safety and force protection.

EMERGENCY PLANS

E-1. Each Army airfield and aviation unit is required to publish, maintain, and test emergency plans. These plans should provide sufficient guidance to reduce the probability of personal injury and property damage on the airfield or to unit aircraft.

PERSONNEL RESPONSIBILITIES

Airfield Commander

E-2. The airfield commander—
- Coordinates the emergency plan with law enforcement personnel, rescue and firefighting personnel, medical personnel, principal airfield tenants, and other personnel who have responsibilities under the plan.
- Conducts a full-scale exercise of the emergency plan at least every three years.

Operations Officer

E-3. The airfield operations officer—
- Ensures the participation of law enforcement personnel, rescue and firefighting personnel, medical personnel, principal airfield tenants, and other personnel who have responsibilities under the plan.
- Ensures all airfield personnel having responsibilities under the plan are familiar with their assignments and properly trained.
- Rehearses and reviews the adequacy of the unit emergency plan annually.

EMERGENCY PROCEDURES

Response Instructions

E-4. The emergency plan contains instructions for responding to—
- Aircraft accidents and incidents.
- Bomb incidents, including designated parking areas for aircraft involved.
- Structural fires.
- Natural disasters.
- Radiological/biological incidents.
- Sabotage, hijack incidents, and other unlawful interference with airfield operations.
- Power failure for movement area lighting.

- Water rescue situations.
- Hazardous material spills.
- Ammunition handling procedures.

Notification Procedures

E-5. The emergency plan includes procedures for notifying appropriate personnel regarding—
- The location of the emergency.
- The number of personnel involved.
- Other information needed to carry out their responsibilities as soon as it is available.

Medical/Emergency Provisions

E-6. The emergency plan must—
- Provide access to medical services for the maximum number of persons transported by the largest aircraft the airfield can serve.
- Provide the name, location, telephone number, and emergency capability of each medical facility and the business address and telephone number of medical personnel who have agreed to provide medical services.
- Provide the name, location, and telephone number of each rescue squad, ambulance service, and government agency that has agreed to provide medical services.
- Include provisions for inventorying surface vehicles and aircraft available to transport injured and deceased persons to locations on the airfield and in the communities it serves.
- Identify hangars or other buildings available to accommodate uninjured, injured, and deceased persons.

Related Emergency Functions

E-7. The emergency plan must provide for—
- Crash alarm systems.
- Removal of disabled aircraft.
- Coordination of airfield and control tower functions relating to emergency actions.
- Marshaling, transporting, and caring for uninjured and ambulatory injured accident survivors.
- Crash site security.
- Training and equipping accident board members to deal with composite and blood-born hazards.

Water Rescue Provisions

E-8. The emergency plan should provide for the rescue of aircraft accident victims from significant bodies of water or marshlands crossed by aircraft.

Crowd Control

E-9. The emergency plan specifies the name and location of each safety or security agency that has agreed to provide assistance for crowd control in the event of an emergency on the airfield.

Disabled Aircraft Removal

E-10. The emergency plan includes the names, locations, and telephone numbers of personnel who have disabled aircraft removal responsibilities.

PREACCIDENT PLANS

E-11. Commanders will ensure—

- Crewmembers and other personnel who may have contributed to Army aircraft accident (Class A through C and selected Class D) are promptly moved by medical evacuation assets to facilities where physical examinations and blood and urine testing will be accomplished under the provisions of AR 40-8, AR 40-21, AR 40-501, AR 600-105, and DA Pam 385-40. Apparent absence of injury is not a factor in determining how or when to move personnel to medical facilities. The dynamics involved in an aircraft accident may produce injuries that are found only with a detailed medical examination. Postaccident flight evaluations will be per AR 95-1.
- The development of detailed, written, preaccident plans specifying duties, responsibilities, and immediate actions for personnel involved in accident notification procedures, search and rescue, accident investigation, and equipment recovery. The unit operations officer develops and administers the preaccident plan with technical assistance from the unit ASO.
- All operations personnel must be familiar with the preaccident plan and know what to do if an accident occurs.

E-12. The preaccident plan is coordinated with all commanders and appropriate personnel. Emergency personnel must be familiar with the crash alarm system and the pertinent provisions of AR 385-10 and DA Pam 385-90. All responsible personnel must be ready to respond to an emergency at any time. Preaccident plans will—

- Interface with airfield/installation and higher headquarters plans. Units/facilities on non-Army and non-DOD airfields ensure that plans are coordinated with appropriate local authorities to ensure compliance with applicable Army and DOD requirements.
- Focus on organized rescue of personnel, protection of property, preservation of the accident scene, and notification of appropriate personnel.
- Address both garrison and field/deployment operations.
- Address actions for both aviation and ground accidents.
- Include a crash alarm system, a crash rescue plan, and a means of notifying board members who will investigate the accident, to include the flight surgeon. AR 385-10 discusses the crash rescue plan in detail (figure E-1).
- Ensure that an air crash, search, and rescue map of the local area is provided to, and maintained by, each activity listed for the primary crash alarm systems.
- Direct that wreckage is not disturbed or moved except for purposes of rescue and/or firefighting until released by the president of the aircraft accident investigation board. DA Pam 385-40 contains guidance on the preservation of wreckage.
- Be systematically rehearsed and reviewed for adequacy quarterly (at a minimum).
- Require a daily test of the primary and secondary crash alarm systems. Figure E-1 (page E-4) provides an example of a unit aviation primary and secondary crash alarm plan.
- Ensure plans rehearsal is coordinated per AR 420-1. Frequent nontenant user flight crews will be fully knowledgeable of the host installation preaccident plan.

NATIONAL SEARCH AND RESCUE PLAN

E-13. SAR is a lifesaving service provided by the Federal agencies signatory to the National Search and Rescue Plan and agencies responsible for search and rescue within each state. Operational resources are provided by the United States Coast Guard (USCG); DOD components; Civil Air Patrol; Coast Guard auxiliary; state, county, and local law enforcement and other public safety agencies; and private volunteer organizations.

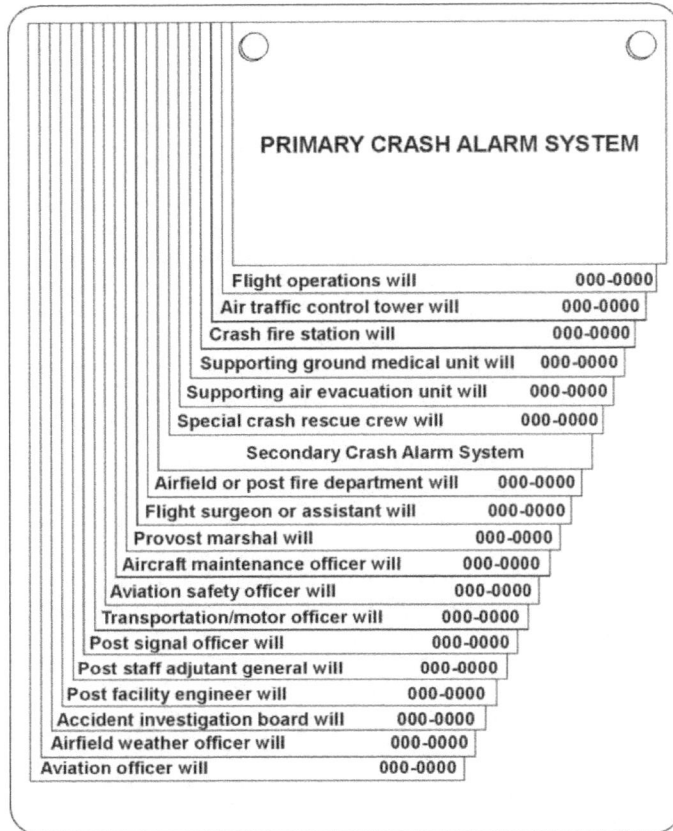

┌───┐
│   PRIMARY CRASH ALARM SYSTEM   │
├───┤
│ Flight operations will   000-0000 │
│ Air traffic control tower will   000-0000 │
│ Crash fire station will   000-0000 │
│ Supporting ground medical unit will   000-0000 │
│ Supporting air evacuation unit will   000-0000 │
│ Special crash rescue crew will   000-0000 │
├───┤
│   Secondary Crash Alarm System   │
│ Airfield or post fire department will 000-0000 │
│ Flight surgeon or assistant will   000-0000 │
│ Provost marshal will   000-0000 │
│ Aircraft maintenance officer will   000-0000 │
│ Aviation safety officer will   000-0000 │
│ Transportation/motor officer will   000-0000 │
│ Post signal officer will   000-0000 │
│ Post staff adjutant general will   000-0000 │
│ Post facility engineer will   000-0000 │
│ Accident investigation board will   000-0000 │
│ Airfield weather officer will   000-0000 │
│ Aviation officer will   000-0000 │
└───┘

Figure E-1. Sample primary and secondary crash alarm system

RESPONSIBILITIES

E-14. Overdue aircraft communications search responsibility is shared between DOD and FAA. The destination host base operations section is responsible for preliminary communication search activities, and the FAA destination tie-in FSS is responsible for all extended communication search actions.

Pilot Responsibilities

E-15. ARTCCs and FSSs alert the SAR facilities when information is received from any source that an aircraft is experiencing difficulty, overdue, or missing. A filed flight plan is the most timely and effective indicator that an aircraft is overdue. Flight plan information is invaluable to SAR forces for planning and executing search activities.

E-16. Before departing on a flight, local or otherwise, the pilot advises someone at the departure point of his destination and flight route, if it is not direct. Search efforts are often wasted and rescue is often delayed because pilots take off without informing anyone of their planned route and destination.

E-17. The life expectancy of an injured survivor decreases as much as 80 percent during the first 24 hours. The chance of survival for uninjured personnel rapidly diminishes after the first 3 days.

DESTINATION BASE OPERATIONS

E-18. If an inbound aircraft (including aircraft flying locally and round-robin) has not arrived or communications cannot be established within 30 minutes after ETA, the destination host base operations will initiate the following preliminary communications search actions:

- Contact local ATC agencies. (This action frequently resolves questions regarding IFR aircraft.)
- Initiate a ramp check.
- Check adjacent airports.

E-19. If the above procedures fail to ascertain the aircraft's whereabouts, begin the electronic communications search procedures currently in use (for example, Service B or Aeronautical Information System according to FAA Order JO 7110.10, chapter 8.)

E-20. Notify the destination tie-in FSS, by voice, of the overdue aircraft and the preliminary communications search actions taken.

RESCUE COORDINATION CENTERS

E-21. Table E-1 lists the rescue coordination centers their locations and telephone numbers.

Table E-1. Rescue coordination centers

Center	Phone	Center	Phone
USCG Rescue Centers			
Boston, Massachusetts	(617) 223-8555	Alameda, California	(510) 437-3700
Portsmouth, Virginia	(757) 398-6231	Seattle, Washington	(206) 220-7001
Miami, Florida	(305) 415-6800	Juneau, Alaska	(907) 463-2000
New Orleans, Louisiana	(504)-589-6225	Honolulu, Hawaii	(808) 541-2500
Cleveland, Ohio	(216) 902-6118	San Juan, Puerto Rico	(787) 729-6770
Air Force Rescue Coordination Centers for the 48 contiguous states			
Langley AFB, Virginia	Commercial Toll Free DSN	(757) 764-8112 (800) 851-3051 574-8112	
Alaskan Air National Guard			
Elmendorf AFB, Alaska	Commercial Toll Free DSN	(907) 428-7230 (800) 420-7230 (317) 384-6726	
Honolulu Joint USAF/USCG			
Honolulu, Hawaii	Commercial DSN	(808) 531-1112/1507 (315) 448-6665/6666	

HAZARDOUS AREA SEARCH AND RESCUE SERVICES

E-22. When lake, island, mountain, or swamp reporting services have been established and a pilot requests the service, contact is made every 10 minutes—or at designated position checkpoints—with the aircraft while it is crossing a hazardous area. If contact with the aircraft is lost for more than 15 minutes, SAR facilities are alerted.

Note: Hazardous area reporting service and chart depictions are published in the Airman's Information Manual (AIM), basic FLIPs, and local ATC publications.

SEARCH AND RESCUE PROTECTION

E-23. Military and civilian pilots are required to file a VFR flight plan with the airfield base operations or at an FAA FSS. For maximum protection, the pilot should file only to the point of first intended landing and refile for each leg to the final destination. When a lengthy flight plan is filed with several stops en route and an estimated time en route to the final destination, a mishap could occur on any leg of the flight. Unless other information is received, a search will be initiated only when the aircraft's ETA at the final destination has exceeded 30 minutes.

Note: The AIM contains more information about the emergency services available to pilots.

EMERGENCY LOCATOR TRANSMITTERS

E-24. Emergency locator transmitters (ELTs) are battery operated and emit a distinctive downward swept audio tone on 121.5 megahertz (MHz) and 243.0 MHz. When armed and subjected to crash-generated forces, they are designed to activate automatically and continuously emit these signals. ELTs will operate continuously for at least 48 hours over a wide temperature range. A properly installed and maintained emergency locator transmitter (ELT) can expedite search and rescue activities.

E-25. FAR, Part 91 authorizes the operational ground testing of ELTs during the first 5 minutes of each hour. If operational tests must be conducted outside this timeframe, coordination must be made with the base operations or control tower. Tests should be no longer than three audible sweeps.

E-26. Caution should be exercised to prevent the inadvertent activation of ELTs in the air or while ELTs are being handled on the ground. Accidental or unauthorized activation will generate an emergency signal that cannot be distinguished from an authentic signal, leading to expensive and frustrating searches. The AIM and FAA Order JO 7110.10 contain additional information on ELTs.

Glossary

SECTION I – ACRONYMS AND ABBREVIATIONS

A/DACG	arrival/departure airfield control group
AAGS	Army Air Ground System
AAR	after action review
A/C	aircraft
AC	active component; Army Command
AC2	Airspace Command and Control
ACIP	aviation career incentive pay
ACM	airspace coordinating measure
ACO	airspace control order
ACS&R	air crash, search, and rescue
ADA	air defense artillery
ADR	airfield damage repair
AFCESA	Air Force Civil Engineering Support Agency
AFCS	Army Facilities Component System
AFH	Army family housing
AFI	Air Force instruction
AFMAN	Air Force manual
AFR	Air Force regulation
AFRS	automated flight record system
AFSC	Air Force Systems Command
AFSO	airfield safety officer
AGL	above ground level
AIC	airspace information center
AIM	Airman's Information Manual
AKO	Army Knowledge Online
ALAN	aircraft landing authorization number
AM	amplitude modulation
AMC	Air Mobility Command
AMMO	ammunition
AMPS	Aviation Mission Planning System
AO	area of operations
AOB	airfield operations battalion
AOM	Airfield Operations Manual
APART	annual proficiency and readiness test
APOD	aerial port of debarkation
AQC	aircraft qualification course

AR	Army regulation
ARAC	Army radar approach control
ARIMS	Army Records Information Management System
ARNG	Army National Guard
ARTCC	air route traffic control center
ASE	aircraft survivability equipment
ASG	area support group
ASO	aviation safety officer
AT&A	Air Traffic and Airspace Command
ATC	air traffic control
ATCCS	Army Tactical Command and Control System
ATF	aviation task force
ATO	air tasking order
ATP	aircrew training program
ATS	air traffic services
avn	aviation
AWS	Air Weather Service
BAE	brigade aviation element
BASEOPS	base operations
BCOC	base cluster operations cell
BCT	brigade combat team
BDOC	base defense operations cell
BRL	building restriction line
C2	command and control
CAB	combat aviation brigade
CAFRS	Centralized Aviation Flight Records System
CALP	Civil Aircraft Landing Permit
CAS	close air support
CBRN	chemical, biological, radiological, and nuclear
CCT	combat control team
CFR	Code of Federal Regulations
COM/NAV	communication/navigational aid
COMM	communication
CONUS	continental United States
COP	common operating picture
CP	command post
CRE	contingency response element
CRG	contingency response group
CRM	crewmember
CTL	commander's task list

DA	Department of the Army
DA PAM	Department of the Army Pamphlet
DAC	Department of the Army civilian
DACG	departure airfield control group
DARR	Deparment of the Army regional representative
dB	decibel
DOD	Department of Defense
DODFMR	Department of Defense Financial Management Regulation
DOTD	Directorate of Training and Doctrine
DS	direct support
DSN	defense switched network
EED	electro-explosive device
ELT	emergency locator transmitter
ER	extended range
ETA	estimated time of arrival
ETD	estimated time of departure
EUSA	Eight United States Army
FAA	Federal Aviation Administation
FAAH	Federal Aviation Administration Handbook
FAAO	Federal Aviation Administration Order
FAR	Federal Aviation Regulation
FARP	forward arming and refueling point
FE	flight engineer
FI	flight instructor
FIX	fixed position for navigation
FLIP	flight information publication
FM	field manual; frequency modulated
FOB	forward operating base
FOD	foreign object damage
FS	front seat
FSE	fire support element
FSCM	fire support coordination measure
FSO	fire support officer
FSS	flight service station
ft	foot
FW	fixed-wing
G3	Assistant Chief of Staff, Operations and Plans
GCA	ground control approach
GP	general planning
GS	general support

HAZMAT	hazardous materials
HDIP	hazardous duty incentive pay
HF	high frequency
HN	host nation
HO	hands-on
HOTPAD	hot pad
HQ	headquarters
IE	instrument examiner
IFR	instrument flight rules
IFRF	individual flight records folder
IMCOM	Installation Management Command
in	inch
IP	instructor pilot
IPB	intelligence preparation of the battlefield
JFC	joint force commander
JP	joint publication
kg	kilogram
LA	engineer firefighting headquarters team
LAN	local area network
LB	engineer firefighting firetruck team
lb	pound
LC	engineer firefighting water truck team
LNO	liasion officer
LOA	letters of agreement
LOC	line of communication
LOP	letter of procedure
LOS	line of sight
LZ	landing zone
m	meter
MACI	military adaptation of commercial items
MCS	Maneuver Control System
MDMP	military decisionmaking process
ME	maintenance evaluator
MEDEVAC	medical evacuation
METT-TC	mission, enemy, terrain and weather, troops and support available, time available and civil considerations
MEVA	mission-essential or vulnerable area
MHz	megahertz
MIL-HDBK	military handbook
MMC	materiel management center
MMLS	mobile microwave landing system

MOA	military operations area
MOS	military occupational specialty
MP	maintenance pilot
MSA	missed approach
MSL	mean sea level
MTOE	modified table of organization and equipment
MTR	miltary training route
MX	maintenance
NAS	National Airspace System
NATO	North American Treaty Organization
NAVAID	navigational aid
NAVFAC	naval facility
NCO	noncommissioned officer
NCOIC	noncommissioned officer in charge
NCRM	noncrewmember
NFPA	National Fire Protection Association
NG	night goggles
NGB	National Guard Bureau
NGO	nongovernmental organization
NOE	nap-of-the-earth
NOTAM	notice to airman
NS	night system
NSRS	National Spatial Reference System
N.T.S.	not to scale
NV	night vision
NVD	night vision device
NVG	night vision goggles
NVS	night vision system
OCONUS	outside the continental United States
O&I	operations and intelligence
OHR	operational hazard report
OIC	officer in charge
OL	operations letter
OPCON	operational control
OPS	operations
OPSEC	operations security
ORB	officer records brief
PC	pilot-in-command
PCN	pavement classification number
PCS	permanent change of station

PM	provost marshal
PMCS	preventive maintenance checks and services
POL	petroleum, oils, and lubricants
PPR	prior permission required
pt	point turn
Q-D	quantity-distance
QRF	quick reaction force
RAD	radius
RASA	ready ammunition supply area
REV	revision
RFO	request for orders
ROC	rear operations center
RON	remain overnight
RW	rotary wing
RWY	runway
S-1	personnel staff officer
S-2	intelligence staff officer
S-3	operations staff officer
S-4	logistics staff officer
SA	situational awareness
SAA	senior airfield authority
SAR	search and rescue
SATCOM	satellite communications
SFL	sequenced flashing lights
SI	standardization instructor
SIAP	special instrument approach procedure
SO	safety officer
SOP	standard operating procedure
SP	standardization pilot
SPINS	special instructions
SPOD	sea port of debarkation
SSN	Social Security number
STANAG	Standardization Agreement
STP	soldier training publication
SU	situational understanding
SUA	special-use airspace
TAC	Theater Aviation Command
TACAN	tactical air navigation
TAC	tactical
TAC CP	tactical command post

TACOPS	tactical operations
TACT	tactical aviation control team
TAGS	Theater Air Ground System
TAIS	Tactical Airspace Integration System
TAOG	theater airfield operations group
TB	training brochure
TC	training circular
TD	Transmitter distributor
TDA	table of distribution and allowances
TERP	terminal instrument procedure
TFR	temporary flight restriction
TM	technical manual
TMD	theater missile defense
TO	theater of operations
TOE	table of organization and equipment
TOFDC	total operational flying duty credit
TR	terrain
TSC	Theater Sustainment Command
TWY	taxiway
TYP	typical
UAS	unmanned aircraft system
UFC	unified facilities criteria
UHF	ultra high frequency
USAACE	United States Army Aviation Center of Excellence
USAASD-E	United States Army Aeronautical Services Detachment, Europe
USAF	United States Air Force
USAR	United States Army Reserve
USCG	United States Coast Guard
UT	unit trainer
UTC	universal time coordinated
UXO	unexploded ordinance
VASI/PAPI	visual approach slope indicator/precision approach path indicator
VFR	visual flight rules
VHF	very high frequency
VIP	very important person
WETM	weather team
wt	weight
XP	experimental test pilot

SECTION II – TERMS

channelization

    To direct or guide along a desired course.

ponding

    The accumulation of standing water around the runway area.

spalling

    The flaking, chipping, or fragments of the runway

References

SOURCES USED
These are the sources quoted or paraphrased in this publication.

ARMY PUBLICATIONS
AR 25-50, *Preparing and Managing Correspondence*, 3 June 2002.

AR 37-104-4, *Military Pay and Allowances Policy*, 8 June 2005.

AR 40-8, *Temporary Flying Restrictions due to Exogenous Factors effecting Aircrew Efficiency*, 16 May 2007.

AR 40-21, *Medical Aspects of Army Aircraft Accident Investigation*, 23 November 1976.

AR 40-501, *Standards of Medical Fitness*, 14 December 2007.

AR 95-1, *Flight Regulations*, 3 February 2006.

AR 95-2, *Airspace, Airfields/Heliports, Flight Activities, Air Traffic Control, and Navigational Aids*, 10 April 2007.

AR 95-10, *Department of Defense Notice to Airman (NOTAM) System*, 1 August 2004.

AR 95-11, *Military Flight Data Telecommunications System*, 26 August 1994.

AR 95-23, *Unmanned Aircraft System Flight Regulations*, 7 August 2006.

AR 95-27, *Operational Procedures for Aircraft Carrying Hazardous Materials*, 11 November 1994.

AR 115-10, *Weather Support for the U.S. Army*, 30 June 1996.

AR 200-1, *Environmental Protection and Enhancement*, 13 December 2007.

AR 210-20, *Real Property Master Planning for Army Installations*, 16 May 2005.

AR 215-1, *Military Morale, Welfare, and Recreation Programs and Nonappropriated Fund Instrumentalities*, 31 July 2007.

AR 385-10, *The Army Safety Program*, 23 August 2007.

AR 385-63, *Range Safety*, 19 May 2003.

AR 420-1, *Army Facilities Management*, 12 February 2008.

AR 570-4, *Manpower Management*, 8 February 2006.

AR 600-8-22, *Military Awards*, 11 December 2006.

AR 600-105, *Aviation Service of Rated Army Officers*, 15 December 1994.

AR 600-106, *Flying Status for Nonrated Army Aviation Personnel*, 8 December 1998.

AR 25-400-2,ARIMS, *Army Records Information Management System (ARIMS)*, 2 October 2007.

DA PAM 25-51, *The Army Privacy Program-System of Records Notices and Exemption Rules*, 30 April 1999.

DA PAM 385-40, *Army Accident Investigation and Reporting*, 1 November 1994.

DA Pam 385-90, *Army Aviation Accident Prevention Program*, 28 August 2007.

DA PAM 738-751, *Functional Users Manual for the Army Maintenance Management System-Aviation (TAMMS-A)*, 15 March 1999.

FM 3-04.120, *Air Traffic Services Operations*, 16 February 2007.

FM 3-04.301, *Aeromedical Training for Flight Personnel*, 29 September 2000

FM 3-04.303, *Air Traffic Services Facility Operations, Training, Maintenance, and Standardization*, 3 December 2003.

FM 3-52.2, *Multi-Service Tactics, Techniques and Procedures for the Theater Air Ground System*, 10 April 2007.

FM 4-01.011, *Unit Movement Operations*, 31 October 2002.

FM 5-430-00-2, *Planning and Design of Roads, Airfields, and Heliports in the Theater of Operations-Airfield and Heliport Design Volume II*, 29 September 1994.

FM 10-1, *Quartermaster Principles*, 11 August 1994.

FM 10-67-1, *Concepts and Equipment of Petroleum Operations*, 2 April 1998.

FM 21-60, *Visual Signals*, 30 September 1987.

FM 100-10-1, *Theater Distribution*, 1 October 1999.

FMI 3-04.155, *Army Unmanned Aircraft System Operations*, 4 April 2006.

STP 1-93P1-SM-TG, *Soldier's Manual and Trainer's Guide, for MOS 93P, Aviation Operations Specialist Skill Level l*, 1 October 2002.

STP 1-93P24-SM-TG, *Soldier's Manual and Trainer's Guide, MOS 93P, Aviation Operations Specialist Skill Levels 2/3/4*, 1 October 2002.

TB 5-4200-200-10, *Hand Portable Fire Extinguishers Approved for Army Users*, 30 September 1991.

TC 1-210, *Aircrew Training Program Commander's Guide to Individual, Crew, and Collective Training*, 20 June 2006.

TC 1-400, *Brigade Aviation Element Handbook*, 27 April 2006.

TC 1-600, *Unmanned Aircraft Systems Commander's Guide and Aircrew Training Manual*, 23 August 2007.

TC 5-340, *Airbase Damage Repair (Pavement Repair)*, 27 December 1988.

TM 1-1500-204-23-1, *Aviation Unit Maintenance (AVUM) and Aviation Intermediate Maintenance Manual (AVIM) for General Aircraft Maintenance (General Maintenance and Practices), Volume 1*, 31 July 1992.

TM 1-1500-204-23-2, *Aviation Unit Maintenance and Aviation (AVUM) Intermediate Maintenance Manual (AVIM) for General Aircraft Maintenance (Pneudraulics Maintenance and Practices), Volume 2*, 31 July 1992.

TM 5-811-3, *Electrical Design: Lightning and Static Electricity Protection*, 29 March 1985.

TM 38-250, *Preparing Hazardous Materials for Military Air Shipment*, 15 April 2007.

TM 95-225, *United States Standard Flight Inspection Manual*, 1 May 1963.

AIR FORCE PUBLICATIONS

Air Force Handbook (AFH) 32-1084, *Facility Requirements*, 1 September 1996.

Air Force Instruction (AFI) 13-213, *Airfield Management*, 29 January 2008.

AFI 32-1065, *Grounding Systems*, 1 October 1998.

AFI 32-1044, *Visual Air Navigation Systems*, 4 March 1994.

Air Force Manual (AFMAN) 88-9, *Electrical Design Lighting and Static Electricity Protection*, 29 March 1985.

AFMAN 91-201, *Explosives Safety Standards*, 18 October 2001.

Air Force Technical Order (TO) 00-105E-9, *Aerospace Emergency Rescue and Mishap Response Information (Emergency Services)*, 1 May 2007.

OTHER PUBLICATIONS

Department of Defense (DOD) Standard 6055.9, *DOD Ammunition and Explosives Safety Standards*, 29 February 2008.

Federal Aviation Association (FAA) Advisory Circular 70/7460-1, *Obstruction Marking and Lighting*, 1 February 2007.

FAA Advisory Circular 150/5340-1J, *Standards for Airport Markings*, 29 April 2005.

FAA Advisory Circular 150/5340-26A, *Maintenance of Airport Visual Aid Facilities,* 4 April 2005.

FAA Order JO 7110.65S, *Air Traffic Control,* 14 February 2008.

FAA Order JO 7110.10T, *Flight Services,* 14 February 2008.

FAA Order JO 7350.8D, *Location Identifiers,* 5 June 2008.

FAA Order JO 7400.8P, *Special-Use Airspace,* 16 February 2008.

FAA Order JO 7610.4, *Special Operations,* 14 February 2008.

FAA Order (FAAO) 8240.52, *Aeronautical Data Management,* 1 October 2006.

MIL-STD-3007, Unified Facilities Criteria and Unified Facilities Guide Specifications. 13 December 2006. (http://dodssp.daps.dla.mil/)

National Fire Protection Agency (NFPA) Standard 10, *National Fire Prevention Agency Standard for Portable Fire Extinguishers,* 9 July 2007.

NFPA 780, *National Fire Prevention Agency Standard for Installation of Lightning Protection Systems,* 2008 Edition.

NOTE: All NFPA Publications can be located at:
http:\\www.nfpa.org\aboutthecodes\list_of_codes_and_standards.asp

---

STANAG 3117 FS (Edition 8), *Standard NATO Agreement Aircraft Marshalling Signals,* 11 June 1999.

UFC 2-000-05N, *Facility Planning Criteria for Navy and Marine Shore Installations,* 31 January 2005.

UFC 3-260-01, *Airfield and Heliport Planning and Design,* 19 May 2006.

UFC 3-260-05A, *Marking of Army Airfield Heliport Operational and Maintenance Facilities,* 16 January 2004.

UFC 3-535-01, *Visual Air Navigation Facilities,* 17 November 2005.

DOCUMENTS NEEDED

These documents must be available to the intended users of this publication. DA forms are available on the APD website (www.apd.army.mil). DOD forms are available on the OSD website (www.dtic.mil/whs/directives/infomgt/forms/formsprogram.htm).

DA Form 201A, *Field Personnel Divider.*

DA Form 759, *Individual Flight Record and Flight Certificate-Army*

DA Form 759-1, *Individual Flight Record and Flight Certificate-Army Aircraft Closeout Summary*

DA Form 759-2, *Individual Flight Record and Flight Certificate-Army Flying Hours Worksheet*

DA Form 759-3, *Individual Flight Record and Flight Certificate-Army, Flight Record and Flight Pay Worksheet*

DA Form 1059, *Service School Academic Evaluation Report*

DA Form 1594, *Daily Staff Journal or Duty Officer's Log*

DA Form 2028, *Recommended Changes to Publications and Blank Forms*

DA Form 2408-12, *Army Aviator's Flight Record*

DA Form 2696, *Operational Hazard Report*

DA Form 3513, *Individual Flight Records Folder, United States Army*

DA Form 4186, *Medical Recommendation for Flying Duty*

DA Form 4730, *Certificate for Performance of Hazardous Duty*

DA Form 5484, *Mission Schedule/Brief*

DA Form 7120-R, *Commander's Task List (LRA)*

DD Form 175, *Military Flight Plan*

DD Form 175-1, *Flight Weather Briefing*

DD Form 365-4, *Weight and Balance Clearance Form F-Transport/Tactical*

DD Form 1801, *DOD International Flight Plan*

DD Form 1898, *Fuel Sale Slip.*

FAA Form 8240-22, *Facility Data Sheet*

READINGS RECOMMENDED

FM 1-02, *Operational Terms and Graphics*, 21 September 2004.

FM 3-01.11, *Air Defense Artillery Reference Handbook*, 23 October 2007.

FM 3-01.48, *Divisional Air and Missile Defense Sentinel Platoon Operations*, 12 December 2003.

FM 3-04.104, *Tactics, Techniques, and Procedures for Forward Arming and Refueling Point*, 3 August 2006.

FM 3-19.1, *Military Police Operations*, 22 March 2001.

FM 3-52, *Army Airspace Command and Control in a Combat Zone*, 1 August 2002.

FM 4-93.4, *Theater Support Command*, 15 April 2003.

FM 5-430-00-1, *Planning and Design of Roads, Airfields, and Heliports in the Theater of Operations-Road Design*, 26 August 1994.

FM 6-20-30, *Tactics, Techniques, and Procedures for Fire Support for Corps and Division Operations*, 18 October 1989.

TC 1-611, *Small Unmanned Aircraft System Aircrew Training Manual*, 2 August 2006.

TM 95-226, *United States Standard for Terminal Instrument Procedures (TERPS)*, 1 July 1976.

FAA Advisory Circular 150/5340-26A, *Maintenance of Airport Visual Aid Facilities*, 4 April 2005.

Air Force TO 00-25-172, *Ground Servicing of Aircraft and Static Grounding/Bonding (ATOS)*, 15 July 2002.

CFR Part 91,Part 91, Title 14, Code of Federal Regulations (14CFR91--PART 91), *Code of Federal Regulations General Operating and Flight Rules*, 1 January 2001.

DOD Financial Management Regulation (FMR) 7000.14R, *Financial Management Regulation*, 2 September 2007. (http://www.defenselink.mil/comptroller/fmr/)

JP 3-10, *Joint Doctrine for Security Operations in Theater*, 1 August 2006.

JP 3-17, *Joint Doctrine and Joint Tactics, Techniques, and Procedures for Air Mobility Operations*, 14 August 2002.

WEBSITES RECOMMENDED

Reimer Digital Library http://www.train.army.mil: Used to access military publications

Defense Technical Information Center http://www.dtic.mil.

Joint Electronic Library http://www.dtic.mil/doctrine.

Army Aviation Association of America (AAAA) Homepage http://www.quad-a.org.

Active FM–Army Doctrine and Training ePublications. http://www.army.mil/usapa/doctrine

Air War College http://www.au.af.mil: References, online and off.

AKO/Army Homepage http://www.army.mil: Used by military personnel and authorized civilians to access e-mail, publications, current events, other military organizations, & special project groups.

Army Publishing Directorate http://www.apd.army.mil.

Directorate Home Page Association of the United: States Army http://www.ausa.org.

Center for Army Lessons http://www.call.army.mil/: Used to gather & provide Learned Public Web information on lessons learned Page during military operations. Information is available for download. Provisions are established for special requests.

Defend America–United States Defense Dept War on Terror 07-13200400-Edition 3 http://www.defenselink.mil

Fort Rucker–The Home http://www-rucker.army.mil: Provides data about Fort Rucker, Army aviation, units & directorates, current events, & points of contact.

Military.com. http://www.military.com.

TRADOC Homepage http://www.tradoc.army.mil.

Army Warrant Officer Career Center: http://usawocc.army.mil/.

This page intentionally left blank.

Index

www.ingramcontent.com/pod-product-compliance
Lightning Source LLC
LaVergne TN
LVHW081323060426

835511LV00011B/1823